TEACHER EDUCATION FOR 21ST CENTURY

By

Dr. Naraginti Amareswaran

Deptt. of Education
Sri Venkateswara University
Tirupati
Andhra Pradesh
(India)

DPH

DISCOVERY PUBLISHING HOUSE PVT. LTD.
NEW DELHI-110 002

Published by:
Tilak Wasan
DISCOVERY PUBLISHING HOUSE PVT. LTD.
4831/24, Ansari Road, Prahlad Street
Darya Ganj, New Delhi-110002 (India)
Phone: +91-11-23279245, 43764432
Fax: +91-11-23253475
E-mail: parul.wasan@gmail.com
info@discoverypublishinggroup.com
web: www.discoverypublishinggroup.com

***First Edition:* 2011**
ISBN: 978-81-8356-727-5

Teacher Education for 21st Century

Preface

The development of any nation depends mainly on the standards of its educational institutions. Education is the most powerful and effective instrument for inducing radical changes in the behaviour of students. Education is the process through which an individual is developed into individuality and a person into a personality. Education should be individualised and personalised to the utmost and should constitute preparation for self-learning.

Education, according to Indian tradition, is not merely a means to earn a living, nor is it only a nursery of thought or a school for citizenship. It is an initiation into the life of spirit, a training of human soul in pursuit of truth and the practice of virtue. Aristotle, however, held that education exists exclusively to develop man's intellect in a world of reality, which men can know and understand.

Man has created education, yet it has become indispensable in his life; for man seeks education for betterment of his life, both inward and outward, and even for survival. It is no wonder, therefore that the U.N.O., in its Universal Declaration of Human Rights, proclaims: "Everyone has the right to education" (Article 26). Not only is this, 'educability' now considered as one of the capacities which distinguish man from other species. Man is educable, whereas other animals and birds etc., are not, although some of them can be trained to do certain things. Hirst and Peters rightly state: "We distinguish now between 'training' and 'education', whereas previously people did not. We would not now naturally speak of educating animals and we would never speak in this way of plants. But we do speak of training animals and of training roses and other sort of plants.

Man can, not only create objects, machines, institutions and ideas, but also can envision a life which he can be or become if he wills. To elaborate a little more-man imagines the concept of a chair or a machine with some particular form, qualities or functions and builds it with a degree of perfection, approaching that of the concept, depending on his ability. Similarly man can envision a life with certain qualities: truthfulness, love, tolerance, peace etc., and can become the being he envisions. To explain in the words of Maslow, "being" is "that which the person is" and "becoming", "that which the person could be", Gordon W. Allport can be aptly quoted in this connection. He writes: "If the prejudiced style of life can be learned and certainly it is not innate—then surely the tentative style or in Gandhi's term, 'equi-minded outlook' can also be acquired".

Thus man can envision lives with different styles, virtues, states etc., and can become like those. Creativity of this kind, envisioning a life and devising ways for becoming the envisioned personality can very well be termed as "creativity in the field of being and becoming".

In ancient India, the highest conception of education was: Sâ Vidyâ Yâ Vimuktaye-Learning or education is that which liberates or makes one liberated. Although other aims were there, certainly there had been a stress on 'to-be'—to be a liberated person (jivanmukta) and to be completely free in ultimate sense. In modern age, quite for a long time education has been conceived as that which helps to achieve—mostly outward things. But it seems, there is a revival of the interest in a kind of education that helps 'to be'— kind of person. The emphasis on 'to be'—to be a 'lifelong learner' and to be a 'complete man' by the International Commission on the Development of Education, and naming of their report as 'Learning to Be', symoblises such an interest.

Education encompasses both the teaching and learning of knowledge, proper conduct, and technical competency. It thus focuses on the cultivation of skills, trades or professions, as well as mental, moral and aesthetic development.

The present book is aimed to identify the importance of education in the human life. The main aim of the present book is to find out the impact of education on different fields. The book was touched all the field like Health, Poverty, Assessment, Violence, Illiteracy, Alcoholism, Medicine, Education, Teacher Education, Higher Education, Special Education, Professional Education, Female Education, Adult Education, Values, Ethics, Management, Culture, Research, Privatisation, Globalisation, Technology, Transportation, Schools, Colleges, Banks and Organisations. The present book is more useful not only for students but also for teachers.

Contents

1. A Study of Education in India and Asia-Pacific 1
Dr. Naraginti Amareswaran
2. Adult Education — An Instrument of Poverty Alleviation 14
Dr. K. Sudha Rani, Dr. R.B. Sathya Vathi and Dr. Naraginti Amareswaran
3. Assessment and Accreditation of Schools 22
Dr. B. Ramachandra Reddy and Dr. Naraginti Amareswaran
4. Curricular Changes in Teacher Education 28
Dr. Naraginti Amareswaran
5. Educating Children with Learning Difficulty Dyslexia 39
Dr. Naraginti Amareswaran
6. Educational School Psychology in the Pursuit of Human Well-being 56
Dr. Naraginti Amareswaran
7. Female Education in India—Community Participation 53
Dr. K. Radhika and Dr. Naraginti Amareswaran
8. Forms of Domestic Violence and Development of Women Through Education 65
Dr. C. Manchala, Dr. Naraginti Amareswaran and Dr.B. Ramachandra Reddy
9. Impact of Education on Domestic Violence and Development of Women Through Education 74
Dr. Naraginti Amareswaran, Dr. B. Ramachandra Reddy and Dr. C. Manchala

10. Impact of Education on Ethno-Medicine and Health Care Practices Among the Tribal People of India 84

Dr. Naraginti Amareswaran

11. Impact of Globalisation on Teacher Education 92

Dr. K. Radhika and Dr. Naraginti Amareswaran

12. Importance of Values in Teacher Education 100

Dr. Naraginti Amareswaran

13. Inculcation of Ethics through Education and Globalisation Effects on Ethics 110

Dr. Naraginti Amareswaran,
Dr. B. Ramachandra Reddy and Dr. C. Manchala

14. Inculcation of Human Values Through Education..... 119

Dr. Naraginti Amareswaran, Dr. C. Manchala and
Dr. B. Ramachandra Reddy

15. Inculcation of Organisational Ethics in Management Students Through Education 131

Dr. Naraginti Amareswaran, Dr. B. Ramachandra
Reddy & Dr. C. Manchala

16. Pioneering Institutions in Adult Education — AICMED, AMS, IAEA, LITERACY HOUSE, RDT, SEVAMANDIR 138

Dr. K. Sudha Rani and Dr. Naraginti Amareswaran

17. Poverty, Education and Health in India

Dr.Naraginti Amareswaran, N. Koteeswari and
Dr. K. Sudha Rani

18. Poverty, Illiteracy and Alcoholism in India and Solutions Through Education 166

Dr. B. Ramachandra Reddy, Dr. Naraginti
Amareswaran and Dr. C. Manchala

19. Preservation of Indian Values and Culture through Education 173

Dr. Naraginti Amareswaran & N. Koteeswari

20. Preservation of Medicinal Plants by Tribes Through Education in India 183

Dr. Naraginti Amareswaran

21. Privatisation of Professional Education 193
Dr. B. Ramachandra Reddy, Dr. C. Manchal and Dr. Naraginti Amareswaran

22. Research in Teacher Education 200
Dr. B. Ramachandra Reddy, Dr. Naraginti Amareswaran

23. Role of Commercial Banks and Education in the Development of Weaker Sections in India 211
Dr. Naraginti Amareswaran, N. Koteeswarai and Dr. B. Ramachandra Reddy

24. Role of Higher Educational Institutions in Promotion of Rural Human Resources 230
Dr. Naraginti Amareswaran and Dr. C. Manchala

25. Role of Information Technology in Teacher Education 234
Dr. Naraginti Amareswaran and Dr. B. Ramachandra Reddy

26. Role of NCTE, NCERT, CIET, SCERT for the Cause of Teacher Education.................................. 244
Dr. B. Ramachandra Reddy, Dr. C. Manchala & Dr. Naraginti Amareswaran

27. Role of Teachers in Building Modern India 255
Dr. Naraginti Amareswaran

28. Some Reflections on Public Transportation for Disabled Persons in Academic Institution 261
Dr. B. Ramachandra Reddy, Dr. Naraginti Amareswaran & Dr. C. Manchala

29. Strategies to Create Awareness on Domestic 273
Violence Through Educational Institutions
Dr. B. Ramachandra Reddy, Dr. C. Manchala and Dr. Naraginti Amareswaran

30. Values in Teacher Education................................ 281
Dr. Naraginti Amareswaran

Index 291

List of Contributors

1. Dr. B. Ramachandra Reddy, Retired Professor, Dept. of Education, S.V. University, Tirupati, Andhra Pradesh, India.
2. Dr. C. Manchala, School Assistant, Z.P.H. School, M.R. Palli, Tirupati Rural, Tirupati, Andhpradesh, India.
3. Dr. K. Radhika, Assitant Professor, Dept. of Economics, S.V. University, Tirupati, Andhpradesh, India.
4. Dr. K. Sudha Rani, Associate Professor, Dept. of Adult & Continuing Education, S.V. University, Tirupathi, Andhpradesh, India.
5. Dr. Naraginti Amareswaran, Researcher, Dept. of Education, S.V. University, Tirupati, Andhpradesh, India.
6. Dr. R. B. Sathya Vathi, Assistant Professor, Dept. of Audlt & Continuing Education, S.V. University, Tirupathi, Andhpradesh, India.
7. N. Koteeswari, Research Scholar, Dept. of Economic, S.V. University, Tirupati, Andhpradesh, India.

CHAPTER 1

A Study of Education in India and Asia-Pacific

—Dr. Naraginti Amareswaran

> *Education means an all round drawing out of the best in child and man—body, mind and spirit... .*
>
> *—Mahatma Gandhi*

Introduction

The development of any nation depends mainly on the standards of its educational institutions. Education is the most powerful and effective instrument for inducing radical changes in the behaviour of students. Education is a powerful instrument of national development—social, economic and cultural. Today's children are tomorrow's citizens. So, it is necessary to take care about children. Now we are living in the scientific, modern and technological world. The teacher occupies pivotal position in the system of education. Teaching has been one of the oldest and most respected professions in the world.

Importance of Education

Education is the process of instruction aimed at the all round development of boys and girls. Education dispels ignorance. It is the only wealth that cannot be robbed. Learning includes the moral values and the improvement of character and the methods to increase the strength of mind.

History of Education in India

The history of education in India is very rich and interesting. One can trace the ancient India education to the 3rd century BC. Research shows that in the ancient days, sages and scholars imparted education orally, but after the development of letters, it took the form of writing. Palm leaves and barks of trees were used for education, and this in turn helped spread the written literature. Temples and community centers often took the role of schools. When Buddhism spread in India, education became available to everyone and this led to the establishment of some world famous educational institutions Nalanda, Vikramshila and Takshashila. These educational institutes in fact arose from the monasteries. History has taken special care to give Nalanda University, which flourished from the fifth to 13th century AD, full credit for its excellence. This university had around 10,000 resident students and teachers on its roll at one time. These students included Chinese, Sri Lankan, Korean and other international scholars.

It was in the 11th century that the Muslims established elementary and secondary schools. This led to the forming of few universities too at cities like Delhi, Lucknow and Allahabad. Medieval period saw excellent interaction between Indian and Islamic traditions in all fields of knowledge like theology, religion, philosophy, fine arts, painting, architecture, mathematics, medicine and astronomy.

Later, when the British arrived in India, English education came into being with the help of the European missionaries. Since then, Western education has made steady advances in the country. With hundreds of universities and thousands of colleges affiliated to them, in fact scores of colleges in every discipline, India has positioned itself comfortably as a country that provides quality higher education to its people in specific and to the world in general.

Stages of Education

India and China are big brothers in Asia-Pacific countries. 1/3 of total population of world is living in these two countries. Both are developing countries. Socio-economic, cultural and political impacts of these two countries are very much on other countries in these regions. It is very important to study about these two countries.

India: There are broadly four stages of school education in India, namely primary, upper primary, secondary and higher secondary (or high school). Overall, schooling lasts 12 years, following the "10+2 pattern". However, there are considerable differences between the various states in terms of the organisational patterns within these first 10 years of schooling. The government is committed to ensuring universal elementary education (primary and upper primary) education for all children aged 6-14 years of age. The general educational system in India was 10+2+3+2 for science and arts courses, 10+20+4 or 5 for engineering and medicine including school education.

China: The People's Republic of China has a nation-wide system of public education, which includes primary schools, middle schools (lower and upper), and universities. Nine years of education is technically compulsory for all Chinese students. Education in China is the help of the Ministry of Education. The education system provides free primary education for six years (some provinces may have 5 years for primary school but 4 years for middle school), starting at the age of seven or six, followed by six years of secondary education for ages 12 to 18. At this level, there are three years of middle school and three years of high school. The general school educational system in China was 6+3+3 or 5+4+3.

Total Literacy: Total literacy rates of India and China

Country	Primary School		Middle School		High School		Colleges/ Universities	
	Age	Class	Age	Class	Age	Class	Age	Class
India	6-10	I-V	11-12	VI-VII	13-15	VIII-X	16-	XI-Ph.D
China	6/7-12	I-VI	13-15	VII-IX	16-18	X-XII	18-	...Ph.D

Literacy Rate by Sex in India and China

Year	India			China		
	Literacy Rate (%)					
	Persons	Males	Female		Males	Females
1951	18.33	27.16	8.86		-	-
1961	28.30	40.40	15.35		-	-
1971	34.45	45.96	21.97		-	-
1981(1980)	43.57	56.38	29.76	62.35	78.6	52.7
1991(1981)	52.21	64.13	39.29	77.55	87.0	68.1
2001(2000)	64.84	75.26	53.67	84.8	92.3	77.3
2000/01 2010	67.30 (2005)	77.00 (2005)	57.00 (2005)	90.85	95.9 (2010)	85.8 (2010)

China and India: The adult literacy rates of China and India are given below.

Country	Adult Literacy Rate (%)	Youth Literacy Rate (%)
China	90.9	98.9
India	60.3	71.3

Adult literacy rate is for the age group 15 years and above. Youth literacy rate is for the age group 15-24 years. The youth literacy rate for India relates to 2001.

Educational Institutions

India: Overall, according to the latest Government Survey undertaken by NUEPA (DISE, 2005-06), there are 11,24,033 schools. Overall, the percentage enrollment of pre-primary classes to total enrollment (primary) is 11.22% (DISE, 2005-06). In 1950-51, only 3.1 million students had enrolled for primary education. In 1997-98, this figure was 39.5 million. The number of primary and upper-primary schools was 0.223 million in 1950-51. This figure was 0.775 million in 1996-97. In 2006-07, an estimated 93% of children in the age group of 6-14 were enrolled in school. The Government of India aims to increase this to 100% by the end of the decade. To achieve this, the Government launched Sarva Shiksha Abhiyan.

Higher education in India has evolved in distinct and divergent streams with each stream monitored by an apex body, indirectly controlled by the Ministry of Human Resource Development and funded by the state governments. Most universities are administered by the States, however, there are 18 important universities called Central Universities, which are maintained by the Union Government. The increased funding of the central universities gives them an advantage over state competitors.

Indian higher education has been developing steadily. The Indian Institutes of Technology were placed 50th in the world and Second in the field of Engineering (next only to MIT) by Times Higher World University Rankings There are several thousands colleges (affiliated to different universities) that provide undergraduate science, agriculture, commerce and humanities courses in India. Amongst these, the best also offer post graduate courses while some also offer facilities for research and PhD studies.

Technical Education has grown rapidly in recent years. With recent capacity additions, it now appears that the nation has the capability to graduate over 5,00,000 engineers (with 4-yr undergraduate degrees) annually, and there is also a corresponding increase in the graduation of computer sciences (roughly 50,000 with post-graduate degree). In addition, the nation graduates over 1.2 million scientists. Furthermore, each year, the nation is enrolling at least 3,50,000 in its engineering diploma programmes (with plans to increase this by about 50,000). Thus, India's annual enrollment of scientists, engineers and technicians now exceeds 2 million.

China: The United Nations Development Programme reported that in 2003 China had 116,390 kindergartens with 613,000 teachers and 20 million students. At that time, there were 425,846 primary schools with 5.7 million teachers and 116.8 million students. General secondary education had 79,490 institutions, 4.5 million teachers, and 85.8 million students. There also were 3,065 specialised secondary schools with 199,000 teachers and 5 million students. Among these specialised institutions were 6,843 agricultural and vocational schools with 289,000 teachers and 5.2 million students and 1551 special schools with 30,000 teachers and 365,000 students.

In 2003 China supported 1552 institutions of higher learning (colleges and universities) and their 725,000 professors and 11 million students (see List of universities in the People's Republic of China). While there has been intense competition for admission to China's colleges and universities among college entrants, Tsinghua and Beijing universities are amongst more than 100 other key universities that have been the most sought after. **Tsinghua** is a top university in Mainland China.

Literacy Facts And Figures in Asia and Pacific

1. Distribution of Global Adult Illiterate Population (15 and over) by Region, 2000-2004 (Total Number of Adult Illiterate Population: 781 millions)

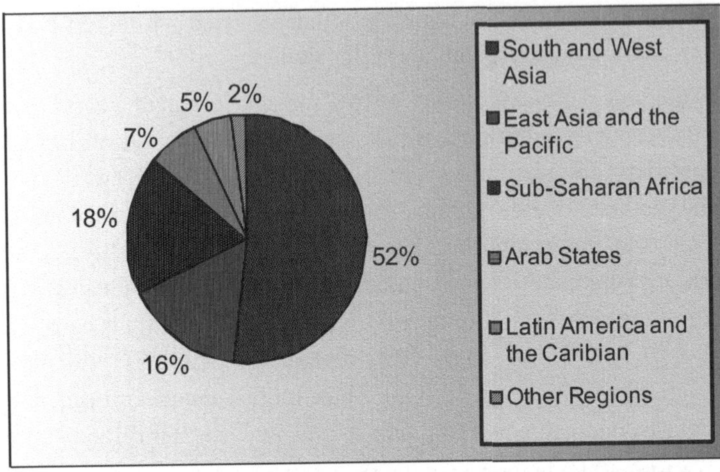

Fig. 1.1. Global Adult Illiterate Population (15 and over) by Region

The fig. 1.1 shows that, in 2000-04; 52% of illiterates are in South and West Asia. 18% in Sub-Saharan Africa, 16% in East Asia and the Pacific, 7% in Arab States, 5% in Latin America and the Caribian and 2% of illiterates are in other regions. "More than two-thirds of the world's adult illiterates live in Asia and the Pacific Region." Political and cultural impacts are very much on literacy.

2. Distribution of Global Adult Illiterate Population (15 and over) by Gender, 2000-2004 (Total Number of Adult Illiterate Population: 781 millions)

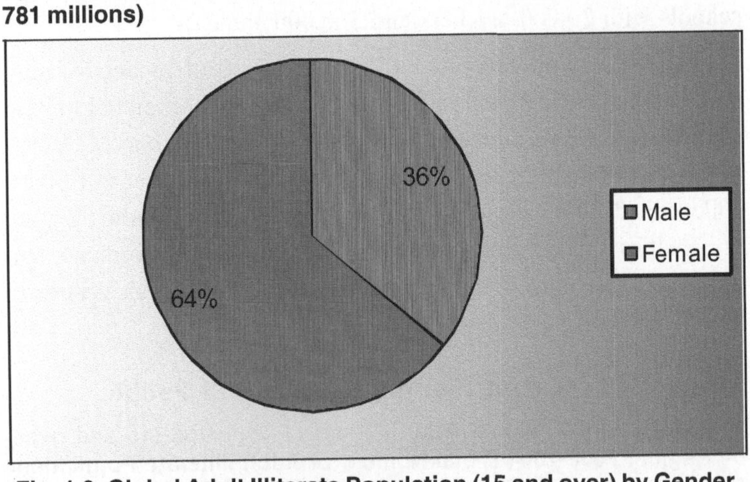

Fig. 1.2. Global Adult Illiterate Population (15 and over) by Gender.

The fig. 1.2 shows that, in 2000-04 female illiterates (64%) are more when compared to male illiterates (36%). i.e., "Women continue to constitute the majority of the illiterate." It shows the negligence of women literacy.

3. Number of Adult Illiterate Population (15 and over) by Region and Gender, 2000-2004

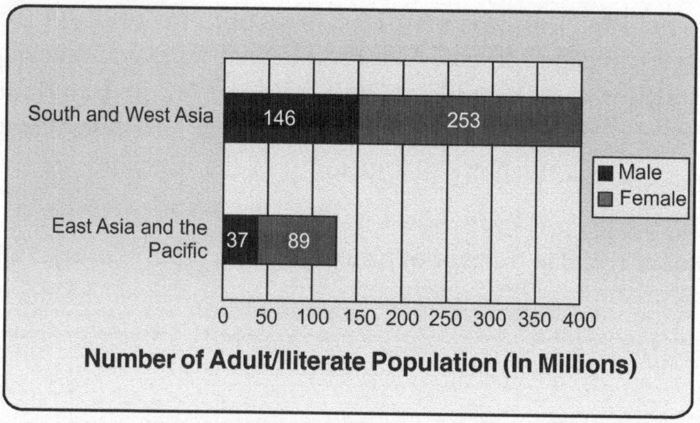

Fig. 1.3. Adult Illiterate Population (15 and over) by Region and Gender

4. Distribution of Adult Illiterate population (15 and over) by country, 2000-2004

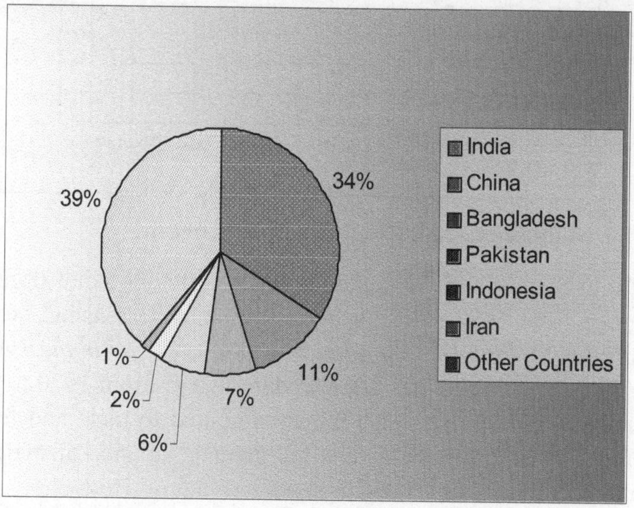

Fig. 1.4. Adult Illiterate Population (15 and over) by country.

The Fig. 1.3 shows that, in 2000-04 there are 146 million male illiterates and 253 million female illiterates in South and West Asia and 37 million male and 89 million female illiterates in East Asia and the Pacific. 52% of illiterates are in South and West Asia (2000-04) and 16% in East Asia and the Pacific. East Asia and Pacific is better when compared to South and West Asia.(fig-1).

The Fig. 1.4 gives full information in 2000-04 about illiterate population of some Asia-Pacific countries and other countries. 34% illiterates in India, 11% in China, 7% in Bangladesh, 6% in Pakistan, 2% in Indonesia, 1% in Iran and 39% illiterates are in other countries. It shows that majority of the illiterates are live in India.

5. Global Trend in Number of Adult Illiterates (15 and over), 1970 to 2015

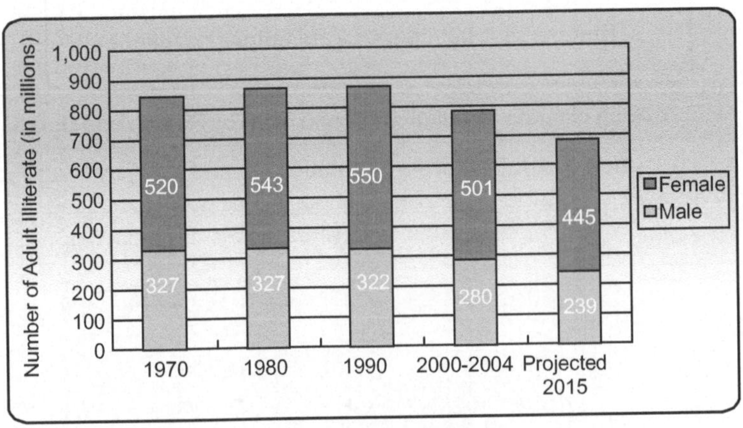

Fig. 1.5. Number of Adult illiterates (15 and over).

From the Fig. 1.5 we conclude that in 2000-04 adult illiterates increased from 1970 to 1990, from 1990 it is decreasing. i.e."*The overall number of adult illiterates began to decrease in the 1990s.*" Male and female illiterates are also decreasing. From 1970 to 1980 the male literacy is constant. When compared to male and female illiterates males are best. It tells the greater variance of male and female illiterates.

6. Adult Literacy Rates (15 and over) by gender in Asia-Pacific Countries, 2000-2004

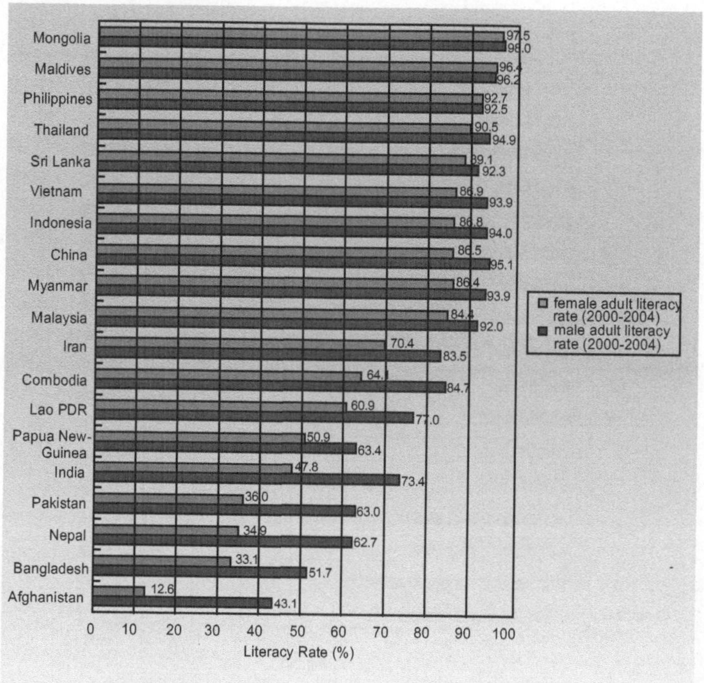

Fig. 1.6. Adult Literacy rates (15 and over) by gender in Asia-Pacific Countries.

From the Fig. 1.6 we note that, in 2000-04 Afghanistan literacy rate is very low (female-12.6% and male-43.1%) and Mangolia Adult literacy rate is very high (female-97.5% and male-98%) when compared to other Asia-Pacific countries. In India male and female Adult literacy rates are 73.4 and 47.8 respectively. *"The gap between female and male literacy rate is greater in countries where overall adult literacy rate is lower."*

From the Fig. 1.7 we conclude that Nepal's Adult literacy rate tripled from 16.4% in 1970 to 48.6% in 2000-2004. It is a rapid increase when compared to other Asia-Pacific countries. The Adult literacy rate of India in 1970 is 33.1% and 61% in 2000-04. Only Mongolia crossed 90% literacy at 1970. "Since 1970, literacy rates have increased, but at a different pace."

7. Adult Literacy Rates (15 and over) in Asia-Pacific countries, 1970-2000-04

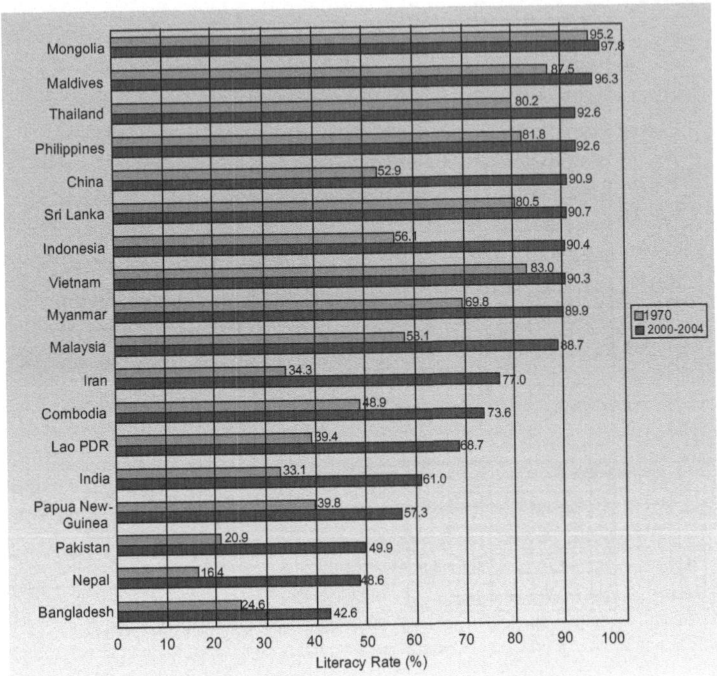

Fig. 1.7. Adult Literacy rates in Asia-Pacific countries.

Note: Ranked by total adult literacy rate in 2000-2004.

Public Education Expenditure

	India		China	
	Year		Year	
Annual budget for non-formal education	1995	Rs. 2.3 billions (US$ 293 millions)	....	...
Public expenditure on education as percentage of GNP (%)	1995	3.5	1995	2.3
% share of nonformal education in total education budget	...	...	...	...

Indian Prime Minister Dr. Manmohan Singh declared that his government was allotted 4% of GND for Public Education Expenditure in the 11th Five Year Plan during the period 2007-2011.

The Main Points Related to Education in the Present Year Budget of India

- Education at the center of the social sector reforms
- Rs. 34,400 crores to be allocated for education
- Rs. 13,100 crores to be allocated for Sarva Shiksha Abhiyaan
- Rs. 8,000 crores allocated for Mid-day Meal Programme
- 6,000 model high schools to come up
- 16 central universities to be established
- 3 IITs to be set up in Bihar, Rajasthan and Andhra Pradesh
- Rs. 85 crores allocated for the development of a knowledge society

Education Around the World

Studies reveal that United States of America is the only country investing the maximum in matters related to education. It has been ascertained that public education budget of United States of America, if taken into account equals the public education budget of the following nations, if combined together.

- Central Asia
- Caribbean and Latin America
- Arab Regions
- Eastern as well as Central Europe
- Sub Saharan Africa
- West and South Asia

Suggestions

The following suggestions are necessary to increase literacy rate and quality of education in the low literacy countries.

- Frame very effective and strong educational policies.

- Student-Teacher ratio should be 20:1.
- Arrange good infrastructure for schools and colleges.
- Student-Student; Teacher-Teacher; cultural exchange programme should be continued in every year.
- Organisation of regional seminars, conferences and workshops on the eve of education.
- Minimise corruption in the field of education.
- Give high-quality education for trainee teachers.
- Use Science and Technology from the school stage.
- Introduce computer education at primary level.
- Adult and continuing education should be strengthening.
- Give autonomous status for monitoring bodies of education.
- Raise the amount of public education expenditure.
- Conduct regularly; in-service programmes for all teachers.
- Continue mid-day meals programme for all schools up to X class.
- Give free and compulsory education for all children up to X class and for girls up to Degree.
- Minimise political influence in the field of education.
- Take care in the framing of curriculum. i.e., it should be effective and easy to understand.
- Establish some higher educational institutions both in rural and urban areas.
- Give equal importance for science and arts subjects.
- Conduct educational tours, field work in the systematic manner.
- Give importance for student centered learning and activity based learning.
- Introduce Yoga, Meditation and Value Education at school level.
- Conduct sports and games regularly.
- Give proper importance for cultural programmes in the curriculum.

Conclusion

Through education it is easy to motivate all types of people in the society. Now we are facing so many problems like terrorism, poverty, high-population and illiteracy. By inculcating values in the students; we can change the future generation. It is the suitable time to remember the thoughts of Sri Sathya Sai Baba...

> *"If human values take root in the educational system, the emerging individuals will have the following attributes:*
>
> *They will want peace and justice in a world that acknowledges the rule of law and in which no nation or individual need live in fear;*
>
> *Freedom and self reliance to be available to all;*
>
> *The dignity and work of every person to be recognised and safeguarded;*
>
> *All people to be given an opportunity to achieve their best in life; and*
>
> *They will seek equality before the law and the equality of opportunity for all".*

REFERENCES

1. 2nd to 7th Educational Survey of India.
2. Carol Chapnick, Mukhopadhyay, Susan Seymour; '*Women, Education, Family Structure in India*' (1994), published by West View Press.
3. Gopal Ji Malaviya in "*Indian and Chinese Foreign Policies in Perspective*", edited by Surjit Man Singh, 1998, Radiant Publishers, New Delhi.
4. Literacy Mission of India, New Delhi.
5. National Council of Education Research and Training, New Delhi.
6. Times Higher Education Supplement- 2006, London.
7. UNDP report on education-2003.
8. www.accu.or.jp./litdbase/policy/index.htm

CHAPTER 2

Adult Education—An Instrument of Poverty Alleviation

—*Dr. K. Sudha Rani*
—*Dr. R.B. Sathya Vathi*
—*Dr. Naraginti Amareswaran*

Poverty can be defined as a social phenomenon in which a section of the society is unable to fulfil even its basic necessities of life. Poverty in India still remains unabated. The country has hardly been able to establish her identity free from the age old impression 'India is a poor country'. Despite decades long effort, most of our population are still struggling below poverty line. The Gandhiji's dream to provide each and every Indian poor an access to basic needs of life is yet to be materialised. Although the Planning Commission of India has added qualitative parameters to the concept of basic needs, in terms of minimum food, clothing and shelter, our country has failed to provide the same to its citizens.

Poverty Scenario in India

Millions of people in India are unable to meet these basic standards, and according to government estimates, in 2007 there were nearly 220.1 million people living below the poverty line.

Nearly 21.1% of the entire rural population and 15% of the urban population of India exists in this difficult physical and financial predicament. The following chart presents the poverty situation:

The division of resources, as well as wealth, is very uneven in India — this disparity creates different poverty ratios for different states. For instance, states such as Delhi and Punjab have very low poverty ratios. On the other hand, 40-50% of the populations in Bihar and Orissa live below the poverty line.

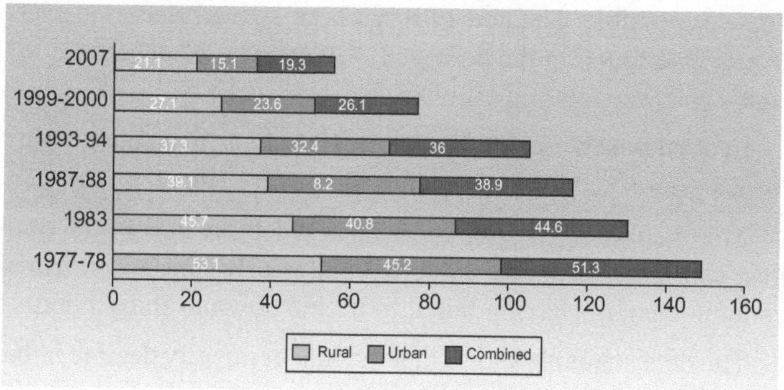

Source: World Development Indicators Database, April, 2002

Poverty in India—Fresh Figures

Despite sustained high GDP growth in India, latest estimates of global poverty by World Bank suggest that India has more people living below US$ 2 than even sub-Saharan Africa. These new figures should compel political leaders and policymakers to devise fresh strategies to reduce poverty.

None other than the World Bank (WB) has busted the hype about India's post-liberalisation success. According to the Bank's new estimates not only is India home to roughly one-third of all the poor in the world, it has a higher proportion of its population living on less than $2 a day than even sub-Saharan Africa.

Compared with India's 828 million people, or 75.6% of the population living below US$ 2 a day, sub-Saharan Africa, considered the world's poorest region, ranks better with 72.2% of its population — about 551 million people — below the US$ 2 a day level.

India has 456 million people, or around 42% of its population living below the new international poverty line of $ 1.25 a day. The number of Indian poor constitutes 33% of the global poor – pegged at 1.4 billion people.

New Estimates

The new estimates are based on recently re-calculated purchasing power parity (PPP) exchange rates that make comparisons across countries possible. The new PPP has been arrived at as "the average poverty line found in the poorest 10-20 countries," according to the Bank's briefing note.

In other words, nearly five out of 10 Indians live below what the world's poorest countries consider the poverty line.

These sobering figures have emerged from the World Bank's latest estimates on global poverty, and clearly hint at the fruits of economic benefits having failed to trickle down to India's poor.

The data available shows that the rate of poverty decline in India was faster between 1981 and 1990 than between 1990 and 2005. The poverty rate — those below $ 1.25 per day — for India declined from 59.8% in 1981 to 51.3% by 1990, or 8.5 percentage points over nine years. Between 1990 and 2005 it declined to 41.6%, which is a drop of 9.7 percentage points over 15 years, clearly a much slower rate of decline.

Provisions

Right from the independence our Government started a number of poverty eradication programmes. Swarnajayanti Gram Swarojagar Yojana (SGSY), Drought Prone Area Programme (DPAP), Tribal Area Development Programme (TADP), High Yield Variety Programme (HYVP), Minimum Needs Programme (MNP), Training of rural Youth for Self-Employment (TRYSEM) etc. Though some of the above programmes recorded appreciable progress in some areas, by and large all programmes and their approaches were selective, sporadic, sectorial in nature and suffered from several defects.

However there is no denying the fact that our progress is very slow and most corresponding adequately to the extent of our need. Although there is a lot of provision for the poverty stricken masses of our country the former always fails to reach the latter properly. This may be attributed to the procedural and attitudinal rigidities in government machinery, corrupt practices, and lack of proportionate distribution on the part of clients, misuse of government benefits by the clients etc.

It can hardly be said that the government is not doing enough for the poor. There is no doubt in the fact that a lot of need based schemes are in progress for the eradication of poverty and the uplift of the poor. However our achievement is still insignificant. The reasons are two dimensional. On the one hand governmental schemes are not properly reaching the poor. On the other hand the latter are not able to receive the benefits due to their ignorance or lack of awareness. Thus there is a wide gap between need and supply which in turn allows poverty to prevail as poverty with a little variation from time to time.

Creation of awareness, dissemination of information on government programmes, vocational training and increase the income of the labour may be measures that would help to bridge the gap between the need and supply. This can be achieved through certain specified levels of educational preparation among the masses. Adult education is such a type of education which provides the instruments for liberation form ignorance and important input for human development as the quality of human factors determine the quality of development.

Concept and Chronology of Adult Education in India

Adult Education is a package of educational programmes for adults out side the formal educational system aiming at providing more information and better knowledge and skills for improving their life style and also their earning capacity. Adult education helps the adults to become aware of themselves and their society to come to some understanding about the problems which they face and to encourage them to select their own task. Knowledge and skills is then the secondary part of adult education to make available the knowledge and skill they need to tackle the problems which they face and to encourage them to select their own task. Knowledge and skills is then the secondary part of adult education to make available the knowledge and skills they need to tackle the problems. This understanding will come slowly. Action — integral to the acquisition of knowledge and skills will be true encouragement to act in some way or another — thus the adult education has been a major tool and important input for human resource development.

S.No.	Approaches	Cycles/Periods	Key concepts	Programmes
1.	Traditional	First cycle (1882-1947)	Basic Literacy	Night Schools
2.	Life-oriented	Second cycle (1949-1966)	Civic Literacy	Social Education
3.	Work-oriented	Third cycle (1967-1977)	Functional Literacy	Farmers Functional Literacy Programme and Shramik Vidyapeeths
4.	Social Change	Fourth cycle (1978 to till date)	Developmental Literacy	NAEP, MPFL, TLC, CEP.

It is possible to discern a pattern and certain cyclical trends in the history of Indian Adult Education. Broadly, there are four cycles which represent the four major approaches and concepts of adult education in India. While the traditional approach to literacy adopted the view that learning the traditional approach to literacy adopted the view that learning to read and write had an innate goodness in itself. Manifested during the face of social education, the life-oriented approaches continue even today. It goes beyond the acquisition of knowledge and the emphasis is on the application of learning to daily living. The work-oriented approach dominated during the phase of functional literacy. Based on Paulo-Freire's philosophy conscientisation, the social change approach made its debut during the phase of NAEP and is continues even to day.

Thus recognising the role of literacy of education in all-round development of the individual and nation as a whole, the Government of India has launched the above programmes and continuously improved in terms of its quality based on the experiences and research findings. To create a learning society by providing for life-long leaning opportunities which may result in the release of creative energies of the people, the National Literacy Mission has been implementing the Continuing Education Programme by establishing Continuing Education Centres and organizing the programmes which are multifarious, for reaching and essential for the upliftment of quality of life.

Role of Adult Education in Poverty Alleviation

Poverty alleviating programmes in the country are the first level of response to overcome the problem of poverty. The second level response consists of meeting the needs of the people through supplementing and complementing the large formal educational system through non-formal and open learning systems of education. Adult education is a type of non-formal education in this direction has an important role in this regard. Some of its important dimensions are discussed in the context of the objective of poverty alleviation.

Increasing Effectiveness of Development Programmes

It is widely recognised that the successful implementation of any developmental programme needs the participation of its target group at various stages of the programme implementation starting from planning to evaluation. Due to their ignorance the people does not come forward to receive the assistance that are offered to them. The access to information is so limited that they do not know about the programme designed to promote their development. Information window is one of the important activities of CECs, provides information about various development schemes formulated by the Government, new agricultural practices, legal rights etc. will ensure that their benefits actually reach the target groups.

Promotion of Employment

Education of the right type increases quality of labour and inculcates a sense of self-confidence among the recipients. Therefore, a right kind of education to remove the mass unemployment and disguised unemployment which are principal causes of mass poverty must be developed. The relevance of functional and vocational training to benefit the lower income groups is much greater in under developed countries where there is marked shortage of labour skills, the adult education should, there cater for these needs through Income Generating Programmes in continuing education centres in simple trades and occupations leading to greater employment opportunities and self-employment avenues.

Strengthening of Communication Channels

If the rural and urban poor are insufficiently linked with the modern sectors through effective communication system, the benefits of the industrial growth are unlikely to trickle down for a long time to come, the problem of ensuring access to education for lower income groups is important for reaching the economic development to lower strata of the economy thus strengthening the process of development. The adult education programme with its bias in favour of the poor and the disadvantaged instrument providing educational opportunities through equivalency programmes in continuing education centres.

Awareness Generation

The process of Economic Development makes growing demands on human resources and in a democratic set-up it calls for social values and attitudes where in education enters as an important factor. The adult education facilitates and contributes to economic development not only by skilled manpower for specific tasks of development, but, by creating the requisite attitudes and personality traits among the masses leading to a proper climate for development through the quality of Life Improvement Programmes in Continuing Education Centres.

Mobilisation and Co-ordination of the Resources

Non-Government Organisations, Government Development Departments, Universities, Youth Clubs and such other agencies have been able to organise local specific programmes, according to the felt needs of the society. They help in providing infrastructure, motivating people, grass-root level planning etc. The Preraks in the CECs will make the efforts to mobilise money and material resources from these agencies to help the community.

Co-ordination is always seen inadequate in the functioning of various government and NGO's, universities, functionaries and in the implementation of various schemes and programmes. Continuing Education Centres build proper co-ordination among the government, NGOs, the community to concentrate in this aspect for maintaining the momentum.

Motivation of the Learners

The Individual Interest Promotion Programmes organising in the CECs aims to provide opportunity for individuals to participate in and learn about their chosen social, cultural, spiritual, health, physical and artistic interests motivate these programmes will promote self-reliance, learners to attend the C.E.Cs personal development and self-actualisation interests help in the quality of human resources of the society.

To sum up Information and communication technologies today have divided people globally into two groups based on knowledge irrespective of gender, caste and region. While a small section of people in every society are ensuring developing technology, they are also the main beneficiaries of this advancement. Government and Non-Government efforts in civilised societies are directed towards ensuring that the pace of development is accelerated and the benefits accrue to large numbers in society. Adult education in the 21st century will cover education in this direction. The intellectuals, academics, the media, the men and women should show concern to arouse social conscience of mankind to build a new social order free from diseases, hatred, fear and apathy. Slogans like 'Education for all', 'Science for All' and 'Food for All' should be converted into reality.

REFERENCES

1. 'One World South Asia News', 12th December 2008.
2. 'Poverty in India: A New Dimension', Meri News, 4th November 2008.
3. The Times of India, 11 September 2008.
4. World Development Indicators database, April 2002
5. World Development Indicators database, April 2002.
6. World Bank Report 2002.

CHAPTER 3

Assessment and Accreditation of Schools

—Dr. B. Ramachandra Reddy
—Dr. Naraginti Amareswaran

"Excellence of institutions of education is a function of many aspects; self evaluation and self-improvement are important. If a council sets up a mechanism, which will encourage self-assessment in institutions and also assessment and accreditation, the quality process, participation, achievement etc, will be constantly monitored and improved" — *The National Policy on Education (NPE)—1986 and Programme of Action (POA)—1992.*

Assessment and Accreditation of institutions of education has recognised as the quality ensuring mechanism all over the world. It has become necessary and relevant to our country as we have developed the world's second largest system of education rather rapidly during last 50 years. On the recommendations of the Programme of Action (1992) on the National Policy on Education (1986), the UGC has established the National Assessment and Accreditation Council (NAAC) in 1994 with its head quarters at Bangalore for assessing and grading the institutions of Higher Education. Though the assessment is voluntary, the UGC has already indicated that its plan based developmental support will be related to the out come of assessment and accreditation.

NAAC's process of assessment and accreditation is neither an inspection to ensure minimum standards nor an exercise of faultfinding. In the Value Judgement continuum the process of assessment is towards the holistic, systematic, data-based, transparent and shared experience for institutional improvement. It is an exercise based on mutual trust.

Assessment refers to the scientific process of obtaining all round information about an institution's progress and achievement, *i.e.*, what and how well the institution has performed during and at the end of a period and assigning a value or grade to the performance. Assessment of the educational institution is a complex procedure that is found to be hotly debated.

Various individuals and organizations define accreditation in different ways. Accreditation, as defined in the Encyclopedia of Education is "a process of quality control and assurance in higher education, whereby, as a result of assessment or inspection or both, an institution or its programmes are recognised as meeting minimum standards". According to Zook and Haggerty (1993), "accreditation is the recognition to an education institution, by some agency or organisation, which sets up standards or requirements that must be complied with, in order to secure approval". Accreditation as commonly understood is a mechanism, which provides quality assurance that the aims and objectives of the institution are known to be honestly available, and that the institution has demonstrated capabilities to ensure continued effectiveness of the educational programmes, over the period.

Accreditation is nothing but institutional evaluation and quality certification. Institutional assessment is a planned and organised inquiry by institutional personnel itself into the total working and effectiveness of institutional establishment and operations. This process assesses the institutions (university) in terms of efficiency and effectiveness to realize institutional goals. If planned properly and carried out systematically, institutional assessment study would lead to institutional reformation besides improving public image (reputation) of the institution. The institutional assessment and accreditation studies require honesty, flexibility, open mindedness and commitment to quality and effectiveness among the top decision making authorities and higher officers.

Institutional accreditation today is closely linked to institution's continuing efforts to assess its effectiveness and to ensure the fullest possible realisation of its mission and goals. It does not require similarity of aims, uniformity of processes, or comparability among institutions. Rather, it indicates that in the judgement of responsible members of the academic community, an institution's goals are soundly conceived and appropriate, that its educational programmes have been intelligently planned and are competently conducted, and that institution is accomplishing the majority of its goals substantially and has the resources to continue doing so for the foreseeable future.

Institutional accreditation embraces all educational endeavours conducted by an institution regardless of its complexity. Specialised or programmatic accreditation deals with schools, departments, programmes or other segments of institution. To prepare for such evaluations, the process of institutional self-study was introduced. Its guiding principles include broad constituent involvement, candour and a willingness to take an honestly critical look at all aspects of the institution. A twelve-month to twenty four-month period of self-study precipitates a report that serves to inform visiting team of professional peers and the accrediting agency of the nature and purpose of the institution and to convey the institution's own assessment of its effectiveness. With continual refinement and adaption, self-study and periodical evaluation are now essential features of all institutional and most specialised accrediting.

In India, there is NAAC for assessing and accrediting institutions of higher education. At present there is no such assessing and accrediting body for schools. Again schools are following different types of syllabuses, time-table, programmes, examination patterns etc. There are different types of schools namely; pre-primary, primary, upper-primary, secondary, higher secondary special etc. The school pupils' population in India is in crores. Schools are run under different managements. Rural, semi urban, urban etc schools are available, with different mission and clientele. Well equipped and ill equipped schools are available. Management and funding wise some are governmental and others are private, and some others are in-between. Their size, in terms of pupils' strength, is also quite variable from a couple of hundreds to thousands. Hence assuring quality of all these institutions is a necessity in the interest of public.

The concept of assessment and accreditation is new to our country. When the concept is new and the school education system is so complex, there is a natural reluctance or apprehension about anything new. Reluctance is for trying to experiment themselves and apprehensions are due to their feeling of their own inadequacies and the fear of being rated low in comparison to others. Besides, accepting the concept of quality audit through assessment is expensive in terms of time, money and efforts.

Professional accreditation of institutions is generally seen by academics and others concerned with education, as a desirable provision rather than a requirement like affiliation of colleges by universities or recognition of schools by state Governments concerned or other bodies. Accredited status of an institution or programme is a mark of good standards, a stamp of quality, a certificate of dependability, trustworthiness, and credibility, an expression of responsibility even accountability, a matter of reputation or prestige for the institution of accreditation.

The future of accreditation hinges more directly on the integrity of educational institutions and on the responsibility of their leaders. The benefits of accreditation are: (i) fostering of their education through development of criteria and guidelines for assessing institutional effectiveness; (ii) assuring the academic community, the general public, the professions, and other agencies that an institution or programme has clearly defined and appropriate educational objectives, has established conditions to facilitate their achievement, appears in fact to be achieving them substantially, and is so organised staffed and supported that it can be expected to continue doing so; (iii) in providing counsel and assistance to established and developing institutions; and (iv) in protecting institutions from encroachments that might jeopardise their educational effectiveness or academic freedom.

Assessment and accreditation provides a professional approach to look into the working of the institutions, and helps to meaningfully pursue and achieve the constitutional and legal mandates. Keeping in mind the noble constitutional and legal requirements, there is great need to assess and accredit the quality of the various aspects of the schools. The following aspects of the schools may be considered for assessment and accreditation.

1. The school's mission and objectives in cognitive, affective and psychomotor domains.
2. Curricular and co-curricular activities.
3. Instructional strategies and practices.
4. Leadership and school organisation
5. School resources for learning.
6. Community resources for learning
7. Assessment, feedback and counselling mechanism.
8. Infrastructural and instructional facilities available in school.
9. Staff qualifications, in-service training programmes.
10. Action research, innovation, creative arts, consultancy and extension.
11. Student support and progression.
12. Organisation and Management.
13. Development of text books and instructional materials.
14. School administration and supervision.
15. Functioning of the teaching staff, non-teaching staff.
16. Curriculum development and review.
17. Examination and evaluation system.
18. Maintenance of records and registers.
19. Developmental plans.
20. Generation and management of financial resources.
21. Parents and community participation.
22. Interaction with other institutions.
23. Networking and collaboration with other agencies.
24. Interaction with alumni.

Rating scales and norms may be developed on the above aspects of the school. Scales and norms already developed may be reviewed. Then only assessment and accreditation of schools is possible.

REFERENCES

1. Bolashetty, S.S. (2001): "*A Study on Assessment and Accreditation of Universities*"; unpublished Ph.D. Thesis, P.G. Dept. of Education, Gulbarga University, Gulbarga.
2. Zook, G.F. and Haggerty, M.E.(1993); "*The Evaluation of Higher Institutions*", Vol.1, Principles of Accrediting Higher Institutions, University of Chicago Press, Chicago.

CHAPTER 4

Curricular Changes in Teacher Education

—Dr. Naraginti Amareswaran

India is a developing country. We have thousand years of tradition and Culture. Different types of people are living in India. In olden days the educational institutions were called as 'Ashramam' and teacher was called as 'Guru'. Guru is a respectable person in the society after mother and father. According to our Vedas Guru is a third God. In olden days they were given importance for shravana, dhyana and asana. All types of information are there in Vedas. Yoga is a greatest gift of India to the world. Yoga has its origin in the Vedas, texts that were heard by ancient sages in their state of meditation, and hence are known as srutis. The great sage Vyasa organised the Vedas in a systematic manner. Hence he is known as Veda Vyasa.

Now we are living in the technological world. Vast changes are occurring in day to day life of human being. The effect of Television, Telephone, Radio, Computer, Internet and Mobile is very much in our daily life. Even today also teacher is a role model for the students in the society. Teaching profession is a respectable job in the society. But there are enormous changes occurred in the system of education.

Western culture is increased. Because of globalisation we see everything in the form of commercial. But it is not good. Teacher is a nation builder. The development of any country depends upon its educational system. Any type of development is possible through education.The concept of curriculum can be perceived as a connective link between teacher and student, organized in such a way to achieve goals previously set by the teacher, the learning organisation or by the curriculum specialists.

Curriculum is a means to the education. While education is learning, curriculum signifies situations for learning. While education deals with 'how' and 'when', Curriculum deals with 'what' education is a product, curriculum is the plan.

Teacher Education

Teacher education is an integral component of the educational system. It is intimately connected with society and is conditioned by the ethos, culture and character of a nation. The constitutional goals, the directive principles of the state policy, the socio-economic problems and the growth of knowledge, the emerging expectations and the changes operating in education, etc. call for an appropriate response from a futuristic education system and provide the perspective within which teacher education programmes need to be viewed.

When India attained freedom, the then existing educational system was accepted as such because it was thought that an abrupt departure from the same would be disturbing and destabilising. Thus a predisposition to retain the system acquired preponderance and all that was envisaged by way of changes was its rearrangement. Consequently, education including teacher education largely remained isolated from the needs and aspirations of the people. During the last five decades certain efforts have been made to indigenise the system. The gaps, however, are still wide and visible. The imperatives for building the bridges may be as follows:

- To build a national system of teacher education based on India's cultural ethos, its unity and diversity synchronising with change and continuity.
- To facilitate the realisation of the constitutional goals and emergence of the new social order.
- To prepare professionally competent teachers to perform their roles effectively as per needs of the society.

- To upgrade the standard of teacher education, enhance the professional and social status of teachers and develop amongst them a sense of commitment.

Scenario of Teacher Education

The need for improved levels of educational participation for overall progress is well recognised. The key role of educational institutions in realising it is reflected in a variety of initiatives taken to transform the nature and function of education — both formal as well as non-formal. Universal accessibility to quality education is considered essential for development. This has necessitated improvement in the system of teacher education so as to prepare quality teachers.

Various Commissions and Committees, Sarvepalli Radhakrishnan Commission (1948), Secondary Education Commission (1953), Kothari Commission (1964-66) etc., are appointed by the Central and the State Governments in recent decades have invariably emphasised the need for quality teacher education suited to the needs of the educational system. The Secondary Education Commission (1953) observed that a major factor responsible for the educational reconstruction at the secondary stage is teachers' professional training. The Education Commission (1964-66) stressed that 'in a world based on science and technology it is education that determines the level of prosperity, welfare and security of the people' and that 'a sound programme of professional education of teachers is essential for the qualitative improvement of education.'

India has a large system of education. There are nearly 5.98 lakh Primary Schools, 1.76 lakh Elementary Schools and 98 thousand High / Higher Secondary Schools in the country, about 1300 teacher education institutions for elementary teachers and nearly 700 colleges of education / university departments preparing teachers for secondary and higher secondary schools. Out of about 4.52 million teachers in the country nearly 3 million are teaching at the primary/ elementary level. A sizeable number of them are untrained or under-trained. In certain regions, like the North-East, there are even under-qualified teachers. As far as in-service education is concerned the situation is not very encouraging. It is estimated that on an average

40% of the teachers are provided in-service teacher education once over a period of five years. Regarding non-formal education, though a number of models are in vogue in various states in the country, much more needs to be done to prepare teachers and other functionaries for the system.

The National Council for Teacher Education (NCTE) as a non-statutory body (1973-1993) took several steps as regards quality improvement in teacher education. Its major contribution was to prepare Teacher Education Curriculum Framework in 1978. Consequently, teacher education curricula witnessed changes in teacher preparation programmes in various universities and boards in the country. A similar effort was made in 1988.

During the last decade, new thrusts have been posed due to rapid changes in the educational, political, social and economic contexts at the national and international levels. Curriculum reconstruction has also become imperative in the light of some perceptible gaps in teacher education. Teacher education by and large, is conventional in its nature and purpose. The integration of theory and practice and consequent curricular response to the requirements of the school system still remains inadequate. Teachers are prepared in competencies and skills which do not necessarily equip them for becoming professionally effective. Their familiarity with latest educational developments remains insufficient. Organised and stipulatory learning experiences whenever available, rarely contribute to enhancing teachers' capacities for self-directed life long learning. The system still prepares teachers who do not necessarily become professionally competent and committed at the completion of initial teacher preparation programmes. A large number of teacher training institutions do not practice what they preach. Several of the skills acquired and methodologies learnt are seldom.

Definitions of Curriculum, from Oliva (1997)

Curriculum is:

- That which is taught in schools
- A set of subjects
- Content

- A programme of studies
- A set of materials
- A sequence of courses
- A set of performance objectives
- A course of study
- Is everything that goes on within the school, including extra-class activities, guidance, and interpersonal relationships
- Everything that is planned by school personnel
- A series of experiences undergone by learners in a school.
- That which an individual learner experiences as a result of schooling

Flexibility of the Curriculum

In India there are large number of communities living in the hilly area, the plateau area, the dessert area, plain area and costal area all having their own peculiar individuality, environment customs and needs. There fore, the same curriculum can't be forced upon all, irrespective of their needs and environment. It must differ from locality to locality and from society to society.

"The destiny of India now being shaped in her class rooms". In the world based on science and technology it is education that determines the level of prosperity, security and welfare of the people (Education Commission 1964-66).

Different types of Curricula

There are eleven types of curricula

1. Overt, explicit, or written curriculum
2. Societal curriculum
3. The hidden or covert curriculum
4. The null curriculum
5. Phantom curriculum
6. Concomitant curriculum
7. Rhetorical curriculum

8. Curriculum-in-use
9. Received curriculum
10. The internal curriculum
11. The electronic curriculum

Teacher Education Curriculum at Different Stages — NCTE

Teacher Education at the Pre-Primary Stage

Objectives

- Enabling student teachers to inculcate among children a desire to know their immediate natural environment, to love and respect it;
- Preparing student teachers to use local resources and local contexts.

Curriculum Content and Transaction

Teacher education curriculum at this stage need to develop awareness about literacy programmes, community dynamics, national and local customs, fairs and festivals and community mode of social living. It may also develop awareness of forces affecting environment including pollution, appreciation of places of historical and cultural significance and special educational features and developmental tasks contained in policies and programmes.

Teacher Education at the Primary Stage

Objectives

- Developing among student teachers skills for teaching integrated environmental studies, integrated social sciences and integrated science and technology;
- Enabling student teachers to inculcate among children a desire to know their immediate natural environment, to love and respect it;

IMPLICATIONS FOR PRE-SERVICE TEACHER EDUCATION

Curriculum Content and Transaction

It is necessary that student teachers be sensitised to the need for reducing curriculum load, organise appropriate learning experiences which are joyful in nature and related to immediate environment of the learner and help them develop and imbibe desirable values.

Teacher education programmes at this stage shall have to provide subject based orientation. Teaching and learning of mathematics would be woven around the environment of the learners so that environmental concerns are properly integrated. The activities would focus on local culture and environment using the local specific contexts and resources. Student teachers shall have to be provided with experiences to help children develop socio-emotional and cultural aspects. A realistic awareness and perspective of the phenomena occurring in the environment will have to be linked with social or scientific events. This may be accomplished by emphasising observation, classification, comparison and drawing of inferences, conducted within and outside the classroom.

Teacher Education at the Secondary Stage and Higher Secondary Stage

Objectives

- Developing among student teachers awareness and sensitivity towards environment concern and promoting skills for meeting environmental challenges.

IMPLICATIONS FOR PRE-SERVICE TEACHER EDUCATION

Academic Stream

In addition, concerns like ecological imbalances, environmental degradation also have to be studied in their socio-cultural-economic context.

Addressing Special Educational Needs of Learners

EDUCATION OF THE GIFTED AND TALENTED: MAJOR THRUSTS

Objectives

- Enabling student teachers to develop among the gifted and talented students social responsibility and commitment to the society and the environment

IN-SERVICE EDUCATION OF TEACHERS

Objectives

- Enabling teachers to be sensitive to gender and environment-related issues

Need of Curriculum Changes in Teacher Education

India has thousand years of tradition and culture. Educational institutions were called as Ashramam and teacher was called as Guru. A tremendous change was occurred in our daily life. Due to globalisation now the educational system is affected totally. Now the educational institutions give importance for technical education. Teacher is a national builder. He has a capacity to change the society. By knowing the importance of technology, communication skills, National Council of Teacher Education (NCTE) introduced a separate subject on technology known as 'Educational Technology' at both B.Ed and M.Ed levels. Computer Education, Communicative English, Personality Development are also introduced at B.Ed. level. Now we are facing so many problems like terrorism, poverty and high-population. We want such type of curriculum which improves peace, non-violence, positive attitude and values in the society. By inculcating these things in teacher education curriculum, we will get positive change in the society. Our National Education Policy (1986) and other Education Committees and Commissions were also given importance for quality teacher education. But it is our duty that to follow such type of curriculum. By conducting national seminars, workshops and conferences it is important to collect eminent scholars attitude towards importance of curricular change in the present scenario. There are many recommendations about curriculum change, but they are not in practice.

Guidelines/Suggestions

- The present curriculum format of teacher education at different levels, pre-primary, elementary and secondary education is generally based, apart from others on Foundation Courses, which includes philosophical, sociological and psychological perspectives of education. The intention is that the teacher must have a conceptual understanding of the field of education, its significant concerns which are relevant for political, social and cultural development of the nation so that the teacher is just not responsible only for performing "knick knacks" of the task of teaching but is also imbued with the perspectives of creating individuals who can apply their minds to the diverse situations that obtain in the field of education. It is the Foundation Courses which provide a lot of scope for being recast to lay focus on discussion on the issues listed in the preceding chapters. Apart from others, it can re-look at the existing curriculum and divide it into appropriate cluster of topics which include the core elements of the NPE and the Constitutional concerns related to non-discrimination. Other areas of equal relevance for development of the ideas are the internship in teaching and working with the community.
- The type of exercises for developing the values related to non-discrimination as given in the chapters on sex/gender, caste/ tribe, disability, etc. could become the central themes of co-curricular and extra-curricular activities of the teacher education institutions. It is not the intention to repeat the listing of those activities here in this chapter; a reference can be made to these activities in the appropriate chapters in which they have been listed.
- It could also be helpful to plan orientation programme on teacher education on this theme. The seminars could familiarise the teacher educators with strategies for operationalising the

teaching-learning dimensions relevant to the theme. An effective way to institutionalize the concept is to incorporate it in the elementary and secondary pre-service teacher education curriculum. This could be supplemented by a suitable co-curricular programme which should aim at offsetting some of the shortcomings in the curricular approach especially in terms of attitude and value development.

- What is needed is a vigorous advocacy with state educational agencies, teacher education institutions and university departments of education for conscious inclusion of such components in the curricula.
- In order to overcome the disadvantage of fragmented treatment of the theme, it is suggested that an independent comprehensive unit comprising familiarisation with the Constitution of India and its concerns as impinge on education should be incorporated in the elementary and secondary teacher education courses.
- In India, evaluation system influences the educational process especially the quality of classroom teaching significantly, and as such a separate unit of educational imperatives of Constitution will ensure due importance and weightage to the theme in the classroom teaching.
- A great deal depends on the ingenuity and dedication of teachers and teacher educators in achieving anything substantial through education. If the concerns are handled with sincerity and purpose, they could definitely bring about the desired transformation in the educational system through teacher education.

Conclusion

Today we are in a technological world where things are happening fast. Parents and teachers would like to be getting results fast. India has kept pace in science and technology with forward nations but we have shown slower pace in our value system even when we have a strong heritage of human values.

An overview of the context and concerns as discussed earlier, teacher's profile and general and specific objectives would define the boundaries of a curriculum framework. The perceived characteristics of the envisaged curriculum framework would include the following:

- Reflects the Indian heritage, acts as an instrument in the realisation of national goals and fulfills aspirations of people
- Responds to the latest developments in the field of education
- Establishes integration of theory and practice of education
- Provides multiple educational experiences to teachers
- Enables teachers to experiment with new ideas
- Ensures inseparability of pre-service and in-service education of teachers
- Sets achievable goals for various stages of teacher education

According to Swami Vivekananda, Teacher gives knowledge and bright future to his students. He always trying to help students and encourages good habits not only in the students but also in the society. Teacher is a backbone for country's development. The influence of teacher is more in the student life. Any type of social development depends upon its educational system. So it is very important to give prime priority for Teacher Education Curriculum. It is very important to give place to science and technology in Teacher Education Curriculum. Then surely India will become powerful and rich country in the world.

REFERENCES

1. Saxena N.R., Mishra B.K., Mohanthy R.K. 'Teacher Education', Surya Publications, Near Govt. Inter College, Meerut, First Edition, 1998.
2. http://www.ncte-in.org/
3. http://www.aponline.gov.in/
4. http://www.ncert.nic.in/

CHAPTER 5

Educating Children with Learning Difficulty Dyslexia

–Dr. Naraginti Amareswaran

Introduction

If we are to teach real peace in this world,
and if we are to carry on a real war against war,
we shall have to begin with the ***children****.*

...M.K.Gandhi

If hope and salvation are to come,
they can only come from the ***children****,*
for the ***children*** *are the makers of men*

...Maria Montessori

We know 'Today's children are tomorrow's citizens'. It is necessary to take care about children. Education is the solution for all types of problems. Through education we can solve all types of problems in the society. Education gives strength, power, character, courage and knowledge. So, it is necessary to give education for all in the world without considering castes, religions and regions.

- Specific Learning Disabilities
- Reading Disability
- Writing Disability
- Non-verbal Learning Disability
- Disorders of Speaking and Learning
- Auditory processing Disorder

Dyslexia

Dyslexia is a learning disability that manifests primarily as a difficulty with written language, particularly with reading and spelling. It is separate and distinct from reading difficulties resulting from other causes, such as a non-neurological deficiency with vision or hearing, or from poor or inadequate reading instruction.

Evidence suggests that dyslexia results from differences in how the brain processes written and/or verbal language. Although dyslexia is the result of a neurological difference, it is not an intellectual disability. Dyslexia occurs at all levels of intelligence; sub-average, average, above average, and highly gifted.

According to the findings of a University of Hong Kong study, dyslexia affects different structural parts of children's brains depending on the language they read. The study focused on comparing children that were raised reading English and children raised reading Chinese. Using MRI technology researchers found that the children reading English used a different part of the brain then those reading Chinese. Researchers were surprised by this discovery and hope that the findings will help lead them to any neurobiological cause for dyslexia. The word *dyslexia* comes from the Greek words dys and lexis. People with dyslexia are called *dyslexic* or *dyslectic*.

Causes of Dyslexia

Dyslexia has not been generally recognised as a learning difficulty until the last decade or two. *John Bradford* presents an overview of the latest research on its causes, and suggests further reading.

Dyslexia is brought about either though inherited traits (developmental dyslexia) or by early ear infections such as 'glue ear', which cause hearing loss (acquired dyslexia). Its cause has not been fully established, but the effect is to create lifelong neurological anomalies in the brain. These anomalies bring about varying degrees of difficulty in learning when using words, and sometimes symbols.

Symptoms of Dyslexia

Children or students who are dyslexic have phonological difficulties, that is, they find it difficult to sort out the sounds within words. This means that they have problems with reading, writing and spelling.

The majority of dyslexic children have difficulty with text, memory and the sequencing processes of basic mathematics.

At what age does it become a problem?

Children are either born with dyslexia, or they acquire the difficulty during early childhood through hearing loss, but it is when they begin to learn using words and sometimes other symbols at school that it becomes a noticeable problem.

What level of intelligence does it affect?

Dyslexia can occur in children and students of all abilities, and dyslexic people are frequently of average or above average ability. It is found in all socio-economic groups and in every country in the world. If no help is given, it often results in low self-esteem.

Can Dyslexia be Cured?

Each dyslexic person's difficulties are different and vary from slight to very severe disruption of the learning process. There is no total cure, but skilled specialist teaching of phonics, sequencing and techniques to raise the person's self-esteem can alleviate the effects of dyslexia.

The neurological differences also give some dyslexic people visual, spatial, physical co-ordination and lateral thinking abilities that enable them to be successful in a wide range of careers. One famous architect's practice gives preference to employing people who are dyslexic because of their strong spatial awareness and lateral thinking abilities.

How many people are affected by dyslexia?

It is estimated that between 4% and 7% of the population are dyslexic.

Are boys affected more than girls?

Roughly equal numbers of boys and girls are affected.

Does dyslexia affect a child's self-esteem?

As literacy skills are so strongly emphasized during the schooling process, dyslexic children experience a great deal of failure which can easily lower their self-esteem and make them feel that they must be stupid.

This is why it is important for dyslexic children to receive as much praise, credits, certificates, gold stars, etc. as the other children. To complete a piece of written work in class is twice as hard as for a non-dyslexic child.

It is also important for a dyslexic child to have art, crafts, physical education and sports during their week in school, as these are the only areas in which they may excel and experience a feeling of satisfaction in learning.

Having to learn a foreign language — like French — is a virtual impossibility for a dyslexic child, and a sure route to failure: schools need to be flexible and take account of this.

Limited Career Prospects

Given proper support, dyslexic students are perfectly able to go on to achieve degrees at university and pursue successful careers. Many dyslexic people find success and fulfillment in:

- Creative areas;
- In areas which allow them to use their physical co-ordination skills; and
- In areas that allow them to use their ability to empathize with others.

How can a parent help their dyslexic child?

The most important thing you can do is to build up the damaged confidence and self-esteem of your child. Make sure s/he knows s/he is loved for himself, and that this love is not dependent on how well s/he does at school.

- Make it clear that the child's difficulties are not his fault. Be very encouraging and find things he is good at.
- Praise him for effort — remember how hard he has to try to achieve success in reading, writing and math/s.
- Help with homework from school, or from any special needs lessons.

- Help him to be organised.
- Encourage areas in which he can experience success, such as creative areas and activities such as sports, which involve physical co-ordination.
- Encourage hobbies, interests and out of school activities.

Treatment and Intervention

Poor academic achievement can be addressed with a variety of interventions. Although the underlying processing difficulty is usually considered to be a lifelong disorder, academic skills themselves can be improved with targeted interventions. Some (adjustments, equipment and assistants) are designed to accommodate or help compensate for the disabilities while others (specialised instruction) are intended to make improvements in the weak areas. Practice is a particularly important component in developing competence, regardless of the starting point. Children who start out with a weakness in a basic skill, such as reading, may miss out on the necessary practice because of the need to catch up with their chronological age peers. Thus a small weakness can snowball into a larger problem.

INTERVENTIONS INCLUDE

Mastery Model

- Learners work at their own level of mastery.
- Practice
- Gain fundamental skills before moving onto the next level.

Note: this approach is most likely to be used with adult learners or outside the mainstream school system.

Direct Instruction

- Highly structured, intensive instruction
- Emphasises carefully planned lessons for small learning increments
- Scripted lesson plans
- Rapid-paced interaction between teacher and students

- Correcting mistakes immediately
- Achievement-based grouping
- Frequent progress assessments

Classroom Adjustments

- Special seating assignments
- Alternative or modified assignments
- Modified testing procedures

Special Equipment

- Electronic spellers and dictionaries
- World processors
- Talking calculators
- Books on tape

Classroom Assistants

- Note-takers
- Readers
- Proof Readers

Special Education

- Prescribed hours in a special class
- Placement in a special class
- Enrollment in a special school for learning disabled students

Sternberg has argued that early remediation can greatly reduce the number of children meeting diagnostic criteria for learning disabilities. He has also suggested that the focus on learning disabilities and the provision of accommodations in school fails to acknowledge that people have a range of strength and weaknesses, and places undue emphasis on academic success by insisting that people should receive additional support in this arena but not in music or sports.

Conclusion

Some critics of the concept of learning disabilities and of special education take the position that every child has a different learning style and pace and that each child is unique, not only capable of learning but also capable of succeeding. These critics assert that applying the medical model of problem solving to individual children who are pupils in the school system, and labelling these children as disabled, systematically prevents the improvement of the current educational system.

REFERENCES

1. Aaron, P.G. (1995). "*Differential Diagnosis of Reading Disabilities.*" School Psychology Review 24(3): 345-60.
2. Bandian, N.A. (1999) *Reading Disability Defined as a Discrepancy Between Listening and Reading Comprehension: A Longitudinal Study of Stability, Gender Differences, and Prevalence*. Journal of Learning Disabilities, 32 (2) 138-148.
3. Marcia A. Barnes; Fletcher, Jack; Fuches, Lynn. *Learning Disabilities: From Identification to Intervention*. New York: The Guilford Press.
4. Patil L. Harrison; Flanagan, Dawn P. (2005). *Contemporary Intellectual Assessment: Theories, Tests, and Issues*. New York: Guildford Press.
5. Sternberg, R.J., and Grigorenko, E.L. (1999). *Our Labelled Children: What Every Parent and Teacher Needs to Know About Learning Disabilities*. Reading, M.A. Perseus Publishing Group.

CHAPTER 6

Educational School Psychology in the Pursuit of Human Well-being

–Dr. Naraginti Amareswaran

Introduction

Now we are living in the technological modern world. With the help of science and technology we have developed in all fields. India is a developing country. We have lot of human resources after China. But the literacy rate is very low when compared to other developed and developing countries in the world. India is a rich country, but Indians are poor. With the help of science and technology and by utilising all sources in the proper way it is possible to India to become a developed country in the world. In the modern world people living with high tension. The student in schools and colleges are also living with high tension because of heavy competitions. It is necessary to introduce psychology as a general subject in all the classes both at school and college levels. Yoga and meditation is also necessary for each and every one in the world.

Definition of Education

- *Education is the learning of human souls to what is best, and making what is best out of them?* – ***John Ruskin***
- *Education is a weapon, whose effect depends on who holds it is his hands and at whom it is aimed.* – ***Joseph Stalin***

The word *education* is derived from the *Latin educare,* meaning *"to raise", "to bring up", "to train", "to rear"*. Education means the gradual process of acquiring knowledge. Education is a preparation for life. Education is also defined as the profession of teaching (especially at a school or college or university).

Importance of Education

India is a union comprised of twenty eight states and seven Territories. The Constitution provides directives regarding the development of education throughout the country. The areas in which the respective central and state governments have domain have been identified in the Constitution as the *central* list, *state* list and *concurrent* list. Until the late 1970s, school education had been on the *state* list, which meant that states had the final say in the management of their respective school systems. However, in 1976, education was transferred to the *concurrent* list through a constitutional amendment, the objective being to promote meaningful educational partnerships between the central and state governments. Today, the central government establishes broad education policies for school curricula development and management practices. These serve as guidelines for the states.

Generally, at the start of a very young age, children learn to develop and use their mental, moral and physical powers, which they acquire through various types of education. Education is commonly referred to as the process of learning and obtaining knowledge at school, in a form of formal education. However, the process of education does not only start when a child first attends school. Education begins at home. One does not only acquire knowledge from a teacher; one can learn and receive knowledge from a parent, family member and even an acquaintance. In almost all societies, attending school and receiving an education is extremely vital and necessary if one wants to achieve success.

Educational Psychology

Educational psychology is the study of how humans learn in educational settings, the effectiveness of educational interventions, the psychology of teaching, and the social psychology of schools as organisations. Although the terms "educational psychology" and "school psychology" are often used interchangeably, researchers and theorists are likely to be identified as educational psychologists, whereas practitioners in schools or school-related settings are identified as school psychologists. Educational psychology is concerned with the processes of educational attainment among the general population and sub-populations such as gifted children and those subject to specific disabilities.

Educational psychology can in part be understood through its relationship with other disciplines. It is informed primarily by psychology, bearing a relationship to that discipline analogous to the relationship between medicine and biology. Educational psychology in turn informs a wide range of specialities within educational studies, including instructional design, educational technology, curriculum development, organisational learning, special education and classroom management. Educational psychology both draws from and contributes to cognitive science and the learning sciences. In universities, departments of educational psychology are usually housed within faculties of education, possibly accounting for the lack of representation of educational psychology content in introductory psychology textbooks.

USES OF EDUCATIONAL PSYCHOLOGY

For finding Individual differences and Disabilities

Each person has an individual profile of characteristics, abilities and challenges that result from learning and development. These manifest as individual differences in intelligence, creativity, cognitive style, motivation, and the capacity to process information, communicate, and relate to others. The most prevalent disabilities found among school age children are attention-deficit hyperactivity disorder (ADHD), learning disability, dyslexia, and speech disorder. Less common disabilities include mental retardation, hearing impairment, cerebral palsy, epilepsy, and blindness.

Although theories of intelligence have been discussed by philosophers since Plato, intelligence testing is an invention of educational psychology, and is coincident with the development of that discipline. Continuing debates about the nature of intelligence revolve on whether intelligence can be characterised by a single, scalar factor (Spearman's general intelligence), multiple factors (as in Sternberg's triarchic theory of intelligence and Gardner's theory of multiple intelligences), or whether it can be measured at all. In practice, standardised instruments such as the Stanford-Binet IQ test and the WISC are widely used in economically developed countries to identify children in need of individualized educational treatment. Children classified as gifted are often provided with accelerated or enriched programmes. Children with identified deficits may be provided with enhanced education in specific skills such as phonological awareness.

For Social, Moral and Cognitive Development

To understand the characteristics of learners in childhood, adolescence, adulthood, and old age, educational psychology develops and applies theories of human development. Often cast as stages through which people pass as they mature, developmental theories describe changes in mental abilities (cognition), social roles, moral reasoning, and beliefs about the nature of knowledge.

For example, educational psychologists have researched the instructional applicability of Jean Piaget's theory of development, according to which children mature through four stages of cognitive capability. Piaget hypothesised that children are not capable of abstract logical thought until they are older than about 11 years, and therefore younger children need to be taught using concrete objects and examples. Researchers have found that transitions, such as from concrete to abstract logical thought, do not occur at the same time in all domains. A child may be able to think abstractly about mathematics, but remain limited to concrete thought when reasoning about human relationships. Perhaps Piaget's most enduring contribution is his insight that people actively construct their understanding through a self-regulatory process.

Piaget proposed a developmental theory of moral reasoning in which children progress from a naive understanding of morality based on behaviour and outcomes to a more advanced understanding based on intentions. Piaget's views of moral development were elaborated by Kohlberg into a stage theory of moral development. There is evidence that the moral reasoning described in stage theories is not sufficient to account for moral behavior. For example, other factors such as modelling (as described by the social cognitive theory of morality) are required to explain bullying.

Developmental theories are sometimes presented not as shifts between qualitatively different stages, but as gradual increments on separate dimensions. Development of epistemological beliefs (beliefs about knowledge) have been described in terms of gradual changes in people's belief in: certainty and permanence of knowledge, fixedness of ability, and credibility of authorities such as teachers and experts. People develop more sophisticated beliefs about knowledge as they gain in education and maturity.

Psychology and Teacher

Teacher is a national builder. He has a power to change the world through education. According to our Indians teacher is a third god. Teacher plays a prominet role in the development of society. Educational Psychology is a main subject in teacher education at D.Ed., B.Ed., and M.Ed. levels. It is necessary for each and every teacher to know about psychology. Because it is necessary to know the behaviour of the students in the class. Teacher has different roles like father, advisor, councellor, administrator and well wisher. The future of any country is in the hands of teachers. So it is necessary to give importance for teacher education. So our government introduced psychology subject in teacher education curriculum.

After undergoing the course, the student teacher

1. Explains psychology and its relationship with Education.
2. Classifies different branches of psychology and explains their significance.
3. Explains the importance of heredity and environment and its influences in educational process.
4. Explains the different aspects of the development of the child.
5. Explains the growth and human beings and their behaviour.
6. Describes the individual aspects of the development of the child.
7. Explains the primary needs of the children.
8. Explains the secondary needs of the children.
9. Explains the theories of learning and the factors influencing learning.

10. Explains the concept of socialisation.
11. Explains the different types of learning.
12. Understands the concept of motivation and the steps to be taken to motivate the children.
13. Explains attention and its uses.
14. Develops skill of observation, listening, responding and understanding.
15. Describes memory, remembering and forgetting and identifies conditions of good memory.
16. Describes the effects of different methods used for learning process.
17. Explains thinking process and its uses-perception, conception, apperception for different ages.
18. Explains the role of creativity and its development.
19. Explains the meaning of intelligence and understands the changing concept of intelligence.
20. Enhances personality development of pupils.
21. Describes the mental hygiene and mental health.
22. Understands exceptional children and their significance.
23. Practices guidance and counselking for school pupils.

Conclusion

Educational psychology is an application of the principles of psychology for effective learning and modification of behaviour on desirable dimensions. Knowledge of educational psychology makes a teacher effective in motivating the pupils in their learning. In short it is an inseparable part of strategy in education. Education gives knowledge, wealth and health. Education is a solution for all types of problems in the society. Through education only it is possible overall development of a person in the society. Through education it is easy to know about behaviour of the students and persons in the society with the help of psychology. So it is necessary to study psychology all persons in the society in the modern world. Educational Psychology helps the overall development of the student.

REFERENCES

1. *Educational Psychology A Cognitive View* by Asubel, D.P.
2. *Element of Educational Psychology* by Bhatia, H.R.
3. *Educational Psychology* by Cole, E.C. and Bruce, W.F.
4. *Psychology Applied to Teaching* by Bichler, R.F.

CHAPTER 7

Female Education in India–Community Participation

–Dr. K. Radhika
–Dr. Naraginti Amareswaran

Introduction

The development of any nation depends on its' standards of educational institutions. Education is the most important instrument for human resource development. Education of girls therefore, occupies top priority amongst various measures taken to improve the status of the girl child. Efforts have been made over the four and half decades of planned development to enroll more girls in schools to continue their education as long as possible. The National Policy on Education (NPE) envisages that education would be used as a strategy for achieving a basic change in the status of women. High priority has been accorded to primary school education in the various five years plans to fulfill the requirements under Article 45 of the constitution for universals, free and compulsory elementary education upto the age of 14 years. Recognising the need for a literate population and provision of elementary education as a crucial input for nation building, the government's stand was reiterated in the NPE and the Programme of Action 1992, to work towards provision of education of satisfactory quality to all children upto 14 years. Sarva Shiksha Abhiyan (Education for all) is a wonderful programme in the development of elementary education in India.

The government has resolved to make the right to free and compulsory elementary education a Fundamental Right and to enforce it through suitable statutory measures. Universalisation of Elementary Education (UEE) has been accepted as a national goal since 1950. In order to achieve the goal, concerted efforts have been made and as a result, the elementary education system in India has become one of the largest in the world. Universal access, universal retention and universal achievement are the broad parameters to achieve UEE.

Female Literacy in India

We got independence on 1947. After completing sixty years of independent also we can't reach 60 per cent of female literacy. It indicates that some more encouragement and importance are necessary towards female literacy programmes.

Table 7.1. Literacy Rates (% Age), 1951 to 2004-05

Census year	Persons	Males	Females	Male-Female gap in literacy rate
1951	18.33	27.16	8.86	18.30
1961	28.30	40.40	15.35	25.05
1971	34.45	45.96	21.97	23.98
1981	43.57	56.38	29.76	26.62
1991	52.21	64.13	39.29	24.84
2001	64.84	75.26	53.67	21.59
2004-05*	67.84	77.00	57.00	20.00

*NSS 61st Round Survey Report No. 517, 2004-05, p. 24.

Literacy rate of female was 8.86 per cent in 1951 where as male literacy rate was 27.16 per cent in the same year. The rate of literacy gap between male and female was 18.30 per cent. After fifty years the literacy rate of female was 53.67 whereas male literacy rate was 75.26 per cent. The rate of literacy gap between male and female was 21.59 per cent. The rate of literacy gap was increased from 18.30 in 1951 to 21.59 in 2001, *i.e.*, 3.29 per cent of literacy gap was increased in the last fifty years. But in the case of female literacy rate, it was increased and increasing year by year.

Enrolment of Female Students (I-XII)

The enrolment of female students from Class I to Class XII was showed in the table 7.2.

Table 7.2. Enrolment by Stages of School Education all Categories of Students 1950-51 to 2005-06

(Figures in million)

Year	Primary(I –V)			Middle/Upper Primary(VI-VIII)			Sec./Sr. Sec./Inter/ Pre-Degree(IX-XII)		
	Boys	Girls	Total	Boys	Girls	Total	Boys	Girls	Total
1950-51	13.8	5.4	**19.2**	2.6	0.5	**3.1**	1.3	0.2	**1.5**
1955-56	17.1	7.5	**24.6**	3.8	1.0	**4.8**	2.2	0.4	**2.6**
1960-61	23.6	11.4	**35.0**	5.1	1.6	**6.7**	2.7	0.7	**3.4**
1965-66	32.2	18.3	**50.5**	7.7	2.8	**10.5**	4.4	1.3	**5.7**
1970-71	35.7	21.3	**57.0**	9.4	3.9	**13.3**	5.7	1.9	**7.6**
1975-76	40.6	25.0	**65.6**	11.0	5.0	**16.0**	6.5	2.4	**8.9**
1980-81	45.3	28.5	**73.8**	13.9	6.8	**20.7**	7.6	3.4	**11.0**
1985-86	52.2	35.2	**87.4**	17.7	9.6	**27.1**	11.5	5.0	**16.5**
1990-91	57.0	40.4	**97.4**	21.5	12.5	**34.0**	12.8	6.3	**19.1**
1991-92	58.6	42.3	**100.9**	22.0	13.6	**35.6**	13.5	6.9	**20.4**
1992-93	57.9	41.7	**99.6**	21.2	12.9	**34.1**	13.6	6.9	**20.5**
1993-94	55.1	41.9	**97.0**	20.6	13.5	**34.1**	13.2	7.5	**20.7**
1994-95	60.0	45.1	**105.1**	22.1	14.3	**36.4**	14.2	7.9	**22.1**
1995-96	60.9	46.2	**107.1**	22.7	14.8	**37.5**	14.6	8.3	**22.9**
1996-97	61.4	46.8	**108.2**	22.9	15.2	**38.1**	15.3	8.7	**24.0**
1997-98	62.3	48.0	**110.3**	23.6	15.9	**39.5**	13.1	9.3	**25.4**
1998-99	62.7	49.0	**111.7**	23.9	16.5	**40.4**	16.6	10.1	**26.7**
1999-00	63.6	50.0	**113.6**	24.3	17.0	**41.3**	17.2	10.8	**28.0**
2000-01	64.0	49.8	**113.8**	25.3	17.5	**42.8**	19.9	10.7	**27.6**
2001-02	63.6	50.3	**113.9**	26.1	18.7	**44.8**	18.4	12.1	**30.5**
2002-03	65.1	57.3	**122.4**	26.3	20.6	**46.9**	19.5	13.7	**33.2**
2003-04	68.4	59.9	**128.3**	27.3	21.5	**48.7**	20.6	14.4	**35.0**
2004-05	69.7	61.1	**130.8**	28.5	22.7	**51.2**	21.7	15.4	**37.1**
2005-06	70.5	61.6	**132.1**	28.9	23.3	**52.2**	22.3	16.1	**38.4**

Source: Time Series of India—2007

In the year 1950-51 the enrolment of female student at primary level (class I-V) was 5.4 million; at middle and upper primary level (class VI-VIII) was 0.5 million and at secondary/senior secondary/ intermediate/pre-degree level was 0.2 million. From the above table we conclude that the enrolment of female students was increased year by year except 1992-93. In the year 2005-06 the female enrolment was 61.6 million at primary level (I-V); 23.3 million at middle and upper primary level and 16.1 million at secondary/senior secondary/ intermediate/pre-degree level. It is necessary to take actions to increase enrolments of female students at middle and upper primary and intermediate levels.

Percentage of Girls' Enrolment to Total Enrolment

The percentage of girls' enrolment to total enrolment was given in the table-7.3. The rate of girls' enrolment was increased year by year expect some years (2000-01, 2003-04, 2004-05 and 2005-06 at primary level; 1991-92, 2003-04, 2004-05 and 2005-06 at higher education) at all four levels.

Table 7.3. Percentage of Girls' Enrolment to Total Enrolment by Stages (1950-51 to 2005-06)

YEAR	Primary I-V	Upper Primary VI-VIII	Sec./Sr.Sec/ Intermediate (IX-XII)	Hr. Education (Degree & above level)
1950-51	28.10	16.10	13.30	10.00
1955-56	30.50	20.00	15.40	14.60
1960-61	32.60	23.90	20.50	16.00
1965-66	36.20	26.70	22.00	20.40
1970-71	37.40	29.30	25.00	20.00
1975-76	38.10	31.30	26.90	23.20
1980-81	38.60	32.90	29.60	26.37
1985-86	40.30	35.60	30.30	33.00
1990-91	41.50	36.70	32.90	33.30
1991-92	41.90	38.20	33.80	32.30
1992-93	42.60	38.80	33.90	33.20

(cont...)

YEAR	Primary I-V	Upper Primary VI-VIII	Sec./Sr.Sec/ Intermediate (IX-XII)	Hr. Education (Degree & above level)
1993-94	42.70	39.10	34.30	33.50
1994-95	42.90	39.30	35.90	34.00
1995-96	43.10	39.50	36.10	36.00
1996-97	43.20	39.90	36.40	36.70
1997-98	43.50	40.30	36.50	37.50
1998-99	43.90	40.80	37.80	38.80
1999-00	44.02	41.09	38.70	38.70
2000-01	43.70	40.90	38.60	39.40
2001-02	44.10	41.80	39.50	39.90
2002-03	46.80	43.90	41.30	40.10
2003-04	46.70	44.00	41.10	39.70
2004-05	46.70	44.40	41.50	38.90
2005-06	46.60	44.70	42.00	38.30

Source: Time Series of India—2007.

Drop-out Rates of Female Students

The drop-out rate of female students was showed in the table-7.4. In the year 1960-61 the drop-out rate of girls at primary (I-V) was 70.90 per cent, it was decreased to 21.77 per cent in the year 2005-06. The drop-out rate at elementary level (I-VIII) was decreased from 85.00 per cent in 1960-61 to 48.98 per cent in the year 2005-06. In the case of secondary level (I-X); the drop-out rate was decreased from 76.90 per cent in the year 1990-91 to 63.56 per cent in the year 2005-06. From the table 7.4 (*see on next page*) it is clear that drop-out rate was high at higher classes.

Why Female Education is Important?

The primary education enrolment rates of girls have a positive impact on economic well-being of women, their families and society in the long run. Since the mother carries the main burden of looking after the health of her child, how well she does this task depends on the knowledge and confidence that she gains from education. Higher levels of schooling for girls increase children's chances of getting immunized and are therefore increase their chances of survival.

Table 7.4. Drop-out Rates of All Categories of Students (1960-61 to 2005-06)

Year	Primary (I –V)			Elementary (I-VIII)			Secondary (I-X)		
	Boys	Girls	Total	Boys	Girls	Total	Boys	Girls	Total
1960-61	61.70	70.90	**66.30**	75.00	85.00	**80.00**	N.A	N.A	N.A
1970-71	64.50	70.90	**67.70**	74.60	83.40	**79.00**	N.A	N.A	N.A
1980-81	56.20	62.50	**59.35**	68.00	79.40	**73.70**	N.A	N.A	N.A
1990-91	40.10	46.00	**43.05**	59.10	65.10	**62.10**	67.50	76.90	**72.20**
1992-93	43.80	46.70	**45.25**	58.20	65.20	**61.70**	70.00	77.30	**73.65**
1995-96	41.40	43.00	**42.20**	56.60	61.70	**59.15**	66.70	73.70	**70.20**
1996-97	39.70	40.90	**40.30**	54.30	59.50	**56.90**	67.30	73.70	**70.05**
1997-98	37.50	41.50	**39.50**	53.80	59.30	**56.55**	66.60	73.00	**69.80**
1998-99	40.90	42.30	**41.75**	54.20	59.20	**56.70**	64.50	69.80	**67.15**
1999-00	39.80	41.00	**40.40**	53.30	57.70	**55.50**	64.90	69.90	**67.40**
2000-01	39.70	41.90	**40.80**	50.30	57.70	**54.00**	66.40	71.50	**68.95**
2001-02	38.40	39.90	**39.15**	52.90	56.90	**54.90**	64.20	68.60	**66.40**
2002-03	35.85	33.72	**34.78**	52.28	53.45	**52.86**	60.72	64.97	**62.84**
2003-04	33.74	28.57	**31.15**	51.85	52.92	**52.38**	60.98	64.92	**62.95**
2004-05	31.81	25.42	**28.61**	50.49	51.28	**50.88**	60.41	63.88	**62.14**
2005-06	28.71	21.77	**25.24**	48.67	48.98	**48.82**	60.10	63.56	**61.83**

Source: Time Series of India—2007.

Female literacy rate correlates with lower fertility and infant mortality rates. The mother's education appears to reduce the negative effects of poor community sanitation and hygiene. Educated women generally marry late and likely to practice family planning and have smaller families. Education empowers women, it increases women's status in the community and leads to greater input into family and community decision-making. Perhaps more importantly, education provides girls with a basic knowledge of their rights as individuals and citizens. Having knowledge and decision-making power can place women on a more equal footing with their male counterparts. Education also provides people with knowledge and skill especially in the areas of health, nutrition, water and sanitation, and the environment. Girl's education is a necessary condition to ensure that development efforts will be sustained. Therefore girls education is necessary for overall development of any country.

Participation

Participation means that people are closely involved in the economic, social, cultural and political processes that affect their lives People may, in some cases, have complete and direct control over these processes—in other cases, the control may be partial or indirect. The important thing is that people have constant access to decision-making and power. Participation in this sense is an essential element of human development.

Community Participation

Community participation in public affairs goes back to the beginning of human society and the concept has taken new significance as societies have grown in size and complexity. In literature its origin can be traced to Aristotle. According to Aristotle, participation was essential to development. According to him, the best state was one where there was broad participation with no class domination. The need for participation of people in different areas has been the central theme of many scholars. Detokeville, J.S. Mill, Robert Owen, Rousseall Bentham and Karl Marx were great advocates of participation of the citizen. The literature on development shows that followers of various. Approaches *i.e.,* structural-functional approach, comparative history approach, social process approach, political approach etc. all emphasised the significance of people's participation in the development process. Community participation is an integral part of area development planning.

The involvement of the people in the planning process becomes necessary so that the plan is more responsive to the local needs, reflects more accurately the local perceptions and produces a sense of ownership and responsibility. Such community participation is of particular relevance for mobilizing community resources in which participation is viewed as a facilitator or a desired plan output, to sort any differences in the planning and implementation stages, to speed up the process of implementation, and to complement and supplement the efforts of the government in the development process. Achieving successful public participation in local level development is no easy task. It is being realised now that unless people are involved in the process of development, no real improvement will take place. Therefore there is a need for an effective local level institution to energise and involve the public in managing and controlling their resources. The local leaders of the community, teachers, students, people's representatives, beneficiaries' groups, non-governmental organisations, farmers' groups, self help groups, users groups, research institutions etc., need to be actively involved in the various stages of the planning. People's participation in the developmental schemes can be assured if the programmes are based on the felt needs of the people.

Community Participation in Education

The District Primary Education (DPED) is another thrust area in primary education. The DPED is distinct from conventional project as it takes a holistic view of elementary education, emphasises decentralised management, community mobilisation and undertakes district and population specific planning. It emphasises on building an integrated and locally relevant curriculum. A number of other externally assisted projects such as— Uttar Pradesh Basic Education Programme, Bihar Education Project, Shiksha Karmi and Lok-Jambish Project in Rajasthan, Mahila Samakhya Project. Mahila Samakhya Programme is a direct outcome of the commitment to affirmative action in support of women's education mandated in the National Policy on Education.

Women Sangh as have taken an active lead in the area of girl child education. In U.P. Centres called Udan Khatolas, Hindola or

Buransh cater to children who have dropped out, never gone to school and to pre-schoolers. In Karnataka, some Sanghas are running Balwadis with no financial assistance from Mahila Samakhya except the initial setting up and training to the workers. These Sanghas are playing active role in enrolling children into primary schools. The Bal Mitra Kendras for girls have been started in Andhra Pradesh to cater to the needs of girls. An important feature of these kendras is the focus on establishing and creating a sense of partnership and ownership in this activity among the Sangha women, parents play important role in selection of teachers, monitoring the centres and contribution to teacher's fees. At present, 590 voluntary agencies are running 38,900 centres in the country, under experimental and innovative programmes, new strategies on a pilot basis for micro-planning survey training, material development, education for the disabled and working children health education, running of non-formal education are taken up. In addition, NGOs are running District Resource Units for providing resource support to the programme. The Bal Bhavan Society of India through its Bal Bhavan Kendras helps the children to explore their inner potential by giving opportunities for expression of ideas through various mediums. Article 243G (11th Schedule) of the constitution provides necessary power and functions to Panchyati Raj Institutions to plan and implement schemes for socio-economic development including primary and secondary school education.

The Central Advisory Board of Education (CABE) Committee has proposed a broad framework for education management in the light of 73rd Constitution amendment. A crucial feature of the framework is the provision for a village level panchayat standing committee in case of single panchayat and a village education committee in the case of group of panchayat. The Constitution of the committee was specified : the number of members had to be not less than seven and not more than 15 apart from the chairman or panchayat member and the headmaster of the primary school, a representative of the Schedule Castes and Tribes, a parent and an Anganwadi worker were to be included. The committee was expected to have the power to check attendance registers and report on among the other things, regularity of students, teacher's attendance and school functioning. While such measures to involve people's institutions in the education process are welcome steps there is need to revitalise these committees.

Strategies for Participation

Participation must begin at the lowest level. There must be real opportunities for participative decision-making and community should be involved from the earliest planning to the implementation, monitoring and evaluation.

- A separate educational scheme should be formulated by giving priority for parents of female children.
- A mechanism should be evolved to involve representatives of panchayati raj institutions, voluntary agencies, youth club, mahila mandals and other local level institutions to prepare micro planning at the village, block and district level. Special emphasis should be given to elicit women's participation.
- A village education committee should be formed with the involvement of elected representatives of panchayats and other local level people's institutions. The school teacher should facilities the meeting. The discussion outcome should be recorded by the teacher.
- An education register should be maintained and updated based on the household survey.
- Monitoring and evaluation are essential to provide feedback in order to identify the problems and constraints in implementation. Community participation is essential not only to know how many but who benefits from education. If help to determine which need and whose needs are met. It is increasingly gaining ground that the best monitoring system is one in which beneficiaries do some checking themselves.
- People's perceptions about a number of issues related to school education management example — time, holiday curriculum etc. should receive due consideration.
- Teacher, Pupil and People (TPP) meetings should be arranged regularly.

- The community inputs along with school inputs should be identified properly and responsibilities should be fixed.
- The people's institutions like Youth club, mahila mandals and local NGO's should be effectively involved along with Anganwadi Workers of the area at various stages.
- Vidya committees should be appointed in each and every village for proper utilisation of funds and to minimize drop-outs.
- Women elected representatives should made responsible for ensuring full enrolment of girls in the village.

Action Needed to Improve Female Education

To increase enrolment of female students the following actions are necessary.

- Ancillary facilities like drinking water, urinals and lavatories should be provided in schools.
- Awareness programme should be conducted to parents of female students.
- Community and rural people's institutions should be mobilised to create a positive climate for girls' education among rural people.
- Drop-out rate is higher amongst girls, still higher among rural girls and highest among tribal girls. Therefore special efforts may be made by the community and people's institutions to check the problems of drop-outs.
- Efforts should be made to sensitise the education structure and innovative projects with region culture specific issues should be developed.
- Importance of education should be explained to parents.
- Mass media should be utilised for projecting positive image of girl child and gender sensitisation campaign for community should be initiated. The school teacher should also be oriented towards gender issues.
- Mid-day meals, books, uniform etc., should be more available for all female students especially in rural areas.

- Plan of action should be created at village level for the success of government programmes.
- Scholarship, bicycles should be given to improve women enrolment.
- Support facilities should be provided to parents to enable girls to continue schooling.
- The role of non-governmental organisations should be increased for better enrolment and continuation of female education.
- Vidya committees should be taken responsible for ensuring enrolment and attendance of girls should be attempted.

REFERENCES

1. Ali, Aruana Assaf, (1975) 'The Necessity for Education Parassar', Vol. 2 No. 4, pp. 10-14.
2. Bhatt B.D. and Sharma S.R. 1980 Women's Education and Social Development, Kaushika Publication Delhi.
3. Census of India—2001.
4. Chattopadhyay, Kamla Devi (1929) The Awakening of Indian Women's, Calcutta.
5. India— Ministry of Community Development and Co-operation.
6. Leela Kumari (1984) Development of Women's Education in Uttar Pardesh Since 1950 to 2000.
7. National Action Plan-India, Ministry of Human Resource Development, Government of India, New Delhi.
8. NSS 61st Round Survey Report No. 517, 2004-05, p. 24.
9. Pandey Balagi (1985) Women Education Social Scientist .Oct – Nov. Volume 13, pp. 11-19.
10. Ramchandra P. and Others (1963) Women's and Education, Tata institute of Social Development.
11. Rao S.S. (1975) The Changing Indian Women's Yojana Vol XIX No. 6,158 September pp. 12-15.
12. Women's Role in Community Development, Delhi Pub (1961).

CHAPTER 8

Forms of Domestic Violence and Development of Women through Education

—Dr. C. Manchala
—Dr. Naraginti Amareswaran
—Dr. B. Ramachandra Reddy

Introduction

However much a mother may love her children, it is all but impossible for her to provide high-quality child care if she herself is poor and oppressed, illiterate and uninformed, analmic and unhealthy, has five or six other children, lives in a slum or shanty, has neither clean water nor safe sanitation, and if she is without the necessary support either from health services, or from her society, or from the father of her children.

—Vulimiri Ramalingaswami, "The Asian Enigma"

Women constitute almost half of the population in the world. But the hegemonic masculine ideology made them suffer a lot as they were denied equal opportunities in different parts of the world. The rise of feminist ideas has, however, led to the tremendous improvement of women's condition through-out the world in recent times. Access to education has been one of the most pressing demands of these women's rights movements. Women's education in India has also been a major preoccupation of both the government and civil society as educated women can play a very important role in the development of the country.

1. India has world's largest number of professionally qualified women.
2. India has largest population of working women in the world.
3. India has more number of doctors, surgeons, scientists, professors than the US.

What is Domestic Violence?

Domestic violence is controlling behaviour and includes all kinds of physical, sexual, economic, psychological and emotional abuse within all kinds of intimate relationships. The perpetrators of domestic violence or abuse are usually men and the victims or survivors are usually women and children that they know. It includes:

- Punching and slapping
- Kicking and hair pulling
- Biting and pinching
- Pushing and shoving
- Being forced to have sex
- Being beaten or cut with other objects
- Disrespect, neglect and emotional blackmail
- Verbal abuse and swearing
- Being prevented from going out or seeing people – being isolated

Forms of Domestic Violence

The following are the forms of Domestic Violence:

1. Physical Abuse
2. Sexual Abuse
3. Psychological Abuse
4. Emotional Abuse
5. Financial Abuse

1. Physical Abuse : Physical abuse is the most visible form of abuse and most likely (with sexual abuse) to give rise to criminal charges. Injuries include black eyes, cut lips, bruising, fractures, deafness, blindness, internal bleeding, missing teeth, persistent ill health, miscarriages, and injuries to a foetus and death. Injury sites are often concealed by clothing or hair. It can include slaps, shoves, pushing, being thrown across the room or down the stairs, kicking, stamping, strangulation, burns and scalds, being attacked with weapons such as knives, household objects, firearms etc internally as well as externally.

2. Sexual Abuse : Sexual Abuse in an abusive relationship is another form of violence, control and degradation. It includes rape, sexual assaults (including with implements),enforced prostitution, enforced sexual practices including being forced to watch or engage in pornography.

3. Psychological Abuse : Psychological abuse examples include "Jeckyll and Hyde" behaviour, preventing contact with friends and families, constant belittling and humiliating things being said, claims that children will be removed if anyone is told of abuse, controlling behaviours, deliberately enforcing dependency, constant statements that the victim is mentally ill etc.

4. Emotional Abuse : Emotional abuse is an attack on victims' personality and well being and is often described as worse than physical violence. It may be referred to as "mind-games". It frequently amounts to the abuser assuming a tight and unhealthy control of all members of the family, which may become increasingly isolated in the community.

Examples include threats of violence to all members of family, constant criticism of the victim saying she is ugly, ignorant or worthless, using the children as ammunition, family life and mood being dictated by abuser (abuser-centric) continual questioning, humiliation in public, playing on community and cultural fears, threats to have the children removed, threats to kill or have deported, threat that the abuser will commit suicide, threats and actual violence to family pets etc.

5. Financial Abuse : Financial Abuse is essentially the deprivation of and / or the control of money whether earned or benefits.

An abuser may refuse to pay bills or prevent the victim from having any control over the family finances. The abuser may steal money belonging to the victim or children. Essential services such as gas and electricity may be cut off. The mother may be forced to support the children solely on what she can earn without assistance or child benefit if this is claimed by the abuser. An abuser may deliberately spend money on him or sell the woman's possessions and family furniture.

Crime against Women in India

1. One crime against women every three minutes
2. One rape every 29 minutes
3. One dowry death case every 77 minutes
4. One case of cruelty by husband and relatives every nine minutes
5. Once suicide every 4 hours

Source: National Crime Records Bureau

The Main Problems of Indian Women

- **Malnutrition :** India has exceptionally high rates of child malnutrition, because tradition in India requires that women eat last and least throughout their lives, even when pregnant and lactating. Malnourished women give birth to malnourished children, perpetuating the cycle.
- **Poor Health :** Females receive less health care than males. Many women die in childbirth of easily prevented complications. Working conditions and environmental pollution further impairs women's health.
- **Lack of Education :** Families are far less likely to educate girls than boys, and far more likely to pull them out of school, either to help out at home or from fear of violence.
- **Overwork :** Women work longer hours and their work is more arduous than men's, yet their work is unrecognised. Men report that "women, like children, eat and do nothing." Technological progress in agriculture has had a negative impact on women.
- **Unskilled :** In women's primary employment sector — agriculture — extension services overlook women.
- **Mistreatment :** In recent years, there has been an alarming rise in atrocities against women in India, in terms of rapes, assaults and dowry-related murders. Fear of violence

suppresses the aspirations of all women. Female infanticide and sex-selective abortions are additional forms of violence that reflect the devaluing of females in Indian society.

- **Powerlessness :** While women are guaranteed equality under the constitution, legal protection has little effect in the face of prevailing patriarchal traditions. Women lack power to decide who they will marry, and are often married off as children. Legal loopholes are used to deny women inheritance rights.

India has a long history of activism for women's welfare and rights, which has increasingly focussed on women's economic rights. A range of government programmes have been launched to increase economic opportunity for women, although there appear to be no existing programmes to address the cultural and traditional discrimination against women that leads to her abject conditions.

Government Role to Minimise Domestic Violence in India

Overall, a crime against women is committed every three minutes in India, according to India's National Crime Records Bureau. Despite the scale of the problem, there had been no specific legislation to deal with actual abuse or the threat of abuse at home. Domestic violence, under the new law, includes "actual abuse or the threat of abuse whether physical, sexual, emotional or economic," a statement from the federal ministry of women and child development said.

"We have been trying for long to protect women from domestic violence. In India alone, around 70% of women are victim of these violent acts in one or the other form," junior minister for women and child development Renuka Chowdhury told the Press Trust of India news agency. They say a bill alone will not help in preventing domestic abuse; what is needed is a change in mind sets.

In January 1992, the National Commission for Women (NCW), was set up as a statutory body under the National Commission for Women Act, 1990 (Act No. 20 of 1990 of Govt.of India) to review the constitutional and legal safeguards for women; recommend remedial legislative measures, facilitate redressal of grievances and advise the Government on all policy matters affecting women.

There are so many government and non-government organisations are working for the benefits of women. Both Central and State governments are continuing so many programmes for the development of women in the country.

Development of Women through Education

You can tell the condition of a nation by looking at the status of its women.

—Jawaharlal Nehru

Female Literacy in India

According to last census held in 2001, the percentage of female literacy in the country is 54.16%. The literacy rate in the country has increased from 18.33% in 1951 to 65.38% as per 2001 census. The female literacy rate has also increased from 8.86% in 1951 to 54.16%. It is noticed that the female literacy rate during the period 1991-2001 increased by 14.87% whereas male literacy rate rose by 11.72%. Hence the female literacy rate actually increased by 3.15% more compared to male literacy rate.

Factors Responsible for Poor Female Literacy Rate

Historically, a variety of factors have been found to be responsible for poor female literate rate, *viz.*

- Gender based inequality
- Social discrimination and economic exploitation
- Occupation of girl child in domestic chores
- Low enrolment of girls in schools
- Low retention rate and high drop-out rate

The Main Strategies Adopted by the Government for Increasing Female Literacy in the Country Include:

- National Literacy Mission for imparting functional literacy
- Universalisation for Elementary Education
- Non-formal Education

History of Women's Education in India: Although in the Vedic period women had access to education in India, they had gradually lost this right. However, in the British period there was revival of interest in women's education in India. During this period, various socio-religious movements led by eminent persons like Raja Ram Mohan Roy, Iswar Chandra Vidyasagar emphasised on women's education in India. Mahatma Jyotiba Phule, Periyar and Baba Saheb Ambedkar were leaders of the lower castes in India who took various initiatives to make education available to the women of India. However women's education got a fillip after the country got independence in 1947 and the government has taken various measures to provide education to all Indian women. As a result women's literacy rate has grown over the three decades and the growth of female literacy has in fact been higher than that of male literacy rate. While in 1971 only 22% of Indian women were literate, by the end of 2001 54.16% female were literate. The growth of female literacy rate is 14.87% as compared to 11.72% of that of male literacy rate.

Importance of Women's Education in India: Women's education in India plays a very important role in the overall development of the country. It not only helps in the development of half of the human resources, but in improving the quality of life at home and outside. Educated women not only tend to promote education of their girl children, but also can provide better guidance to all their children. Moreover educated women can also help in the reduction of infant mortality rate and growth of the population.

Obstacles: Gender discrimination still persists in India and lot more needs to be done in the field of women's education in India. The gap in the male-female literacy rate is just a simple indicator. While the male literary rate is more than 75% according to the 2001 census, the female literacy rate is just 54.16%. Prevailing prejudices, low enrollment of girl child in the schools, engagements of girl children in domestic works and high drop out rate are major obstacles in the path of making all Indian women educated.

According to the Women and Child Development study, 45 per cent of Indian women are slapped, kicked or beaten by their husbands. India also had the highest rate of violence during pregnancy. Of the women reporting violence, 50 per cent were kicked, beaten or hit when pregnant. About 74.8 per cent of the women who reported violence have attempted to commit suicide. It shows the importance of education. Educated woman has more strength and power to face the challenges when compared to uneducated woman.

Kumud Sharma of the Centre for Women's Development Studies in New Delhi traced the correlation between education and domestic violence to patriarchal attitudes. "Educated women are aware of their rights," she said. "They are no longer willing to follow commands blindly. When they ask questions, it causes conflicts, which, in turn, leads to violence. In many Indian states, working women are asked to hand over their paycheck to the husband and have no control over their finances. So, if they stop doing so or start asserting their right, there is bound to be friction."

It is necessary to establish some more colleges and universities in India. The number of Residential Schools for SC/ST and BC's is not sufficient today. So, increase the number of these schools in the both rural and urban areas. Today's children are tomorrow's citizens. Take care about future generation. Then only India will become developed country in the future.

Conclusion

Now we are living in the modern and technological world. Women are also entering in all the fields like men for doing job. Educated women have better opportunity compared to uneducated women in the society. They are facing so many problems in the society. With the help of education and law and order it is easy to escape from those problems. So it is necessary to educate all types of women in the society. Education gives strength, wealth, health and power to the individual.

According to Swami Vivekandanda:

"We want that education by which character is formed, strength of mind increased and intellect is expanded, and by which one can stand on one's own feet".

The plight of women in medialval India and at the starting of modern India can be summed up in the words of great poet Rabindranath Tagore:

"O Lord! Why has you not given woman the right to conquer her destiny?
Why does she have to wait head bowed,
By the roadside, Waiting with tired patience,
Hoping for a miracle in the morrow?"

REFERENCES

1. *Census of India*, (2001), Government of India, New Delhi.
2. *Child and Women Development Report*, (2006), Ministry of Women and Child Development, Government of India, New Delhi.
3. *National Crime Records Bureau*, (2007), Government of India, New Delhi.
4. *National Family Health Survey*, (2006), Government of India, New Delhi.
5. *National Institute of Child Health and Human Development.* (2001). The National Reading Panel: Reports of the Subgroups.
6. *UNESCO Institute for Statistics: Literacy Rates, Youth (15-24) and Adult (15+)*, by Region and Gender (September 2006 Assessment).

CHAPTER 9

Impact of Education on Domestic Violence and Development of Women Through Education

–Dr. Naraginti Amareswaran
–Dr. B. Ramachandra Reddy
–Dr. C. Manchala

Introduction

You can tell the condition of a nation by looking at the status of its women. ***—Jawaharlal Nehru***

Literary education is of no value, if it is not able to build up a sound character. ***—Mahatma Gandhi***

Education has been regarded as the most significant instrument for changing women's subjugated position in the society. It not only develops the personality and rationality of individuals, but qualifies them to fulfill certain economic, political and cultural functions and thereby improves their socio-economic status. One of the direct expectations from educational development in a society is the reduction in the inequality among individuals and that is why Education was included as the basic right of every human being in the Universal Declaration of Human Rights. The constitution of UNESCO also directs its efforts to achieve 'The ideal of equality of educational opportunity without regard to race, sex or any distinction, economic or social'.

Domestic Violence (sometimes referred to as domestic abuse or spousal abuse) occurs when a family member, partner or ex-partner attempts to physically or psychologically dominate another. Domestic violence often refers to violence between spouses, or spousal abuse but can also include cohabitants and non-married intimate partners. Domestic violence occurs in all cultures; people of all races, ethnicities, religions, sexes and classes can be perpetrators of domestic violence.

Domestic violence is perpetrated by both men and women, occurring in both same-sex and opposite-sex relationships.

What Is Domestic Violence?

Domestic violence is controlling behaviour and includes all kinds of physical, sexual and emotional abuse within all kinds of intimate relationships. The perpetrators of domestic violence or abuse are usually men and the victims or survivors are usually women and children that they know. It includes:

- Punching and slapping
- Kicking and hair pulling
- Biting and pinching
- Pushing and shoving
- Being forced to have sex
- Being beaten or cut with other objects
- Disrespect, neglect and emotional blackmail
- Verbal abuse and swearing
- Being prevented from going out or seeing people – being isolated
- Lying, harassment and putting pressure on you through threats

1:4 women experience domestic violence at some point in their lives and 1:10 will be experiencing domestic violence today

Women Violence in Different States of India

Over 37 per cent married women in the country were victims of physical or sexual abuse by their husbands with Bihar topping the list. Women in Himachal Pradesh faced less violence at home compared to other states in the country. The latest National Family Health Survey-III found that 37.2 per cent women had experienced violence and cited lack of education as the key reason behind their woes. "Women with no education were much more likely than other women to have suffered spousal violence. However, spousal abuse also extends to women who have secondary or higher secondary level education, with 16 per cent reporting abuse," the survey said.

The survey showed that countrywide more women face violence in rural areas (40.2) as compared to those in the urban areas (30.4).

In Bihar, women in urban areas fared worse than those in rural areas. While 62.2 per cent underwent the trauma in urban areas, it was 58.5 per cent women in villages.

It is followed by Rajasthan (46.3) Madhya Pradesh (45.8), Tripura (44.1), Manipur (43.9), Uttar Pradesh (42.4), Tamil Nadu (41.9), West Bengal (40.3) and Arunachal Pradesh (38.8).

Among the metros, the fairer sex was better off in Delhi (16.3) and Mumbai (19.5) recorded relatively low percentage as compared to Chennai (40.6) and Kolkata (26.7).

Nearly, 17 per cent women in Goa have experienced violence, with 17.2 women in rural areas at the receiving end as compared to 16.4 per cent women in urban areas.

In Chhattisgarh, a total of 30 per cent women suffered at the hands of their husbands, while in Jharkhand, the figure was 37 per cent. About 40.8 per cent women in Jharkhand villages found the going tough as compared to 24.6 per cent in the urban areas.

In the hill state of Uttarakhand, nearly 28 per cent women experienced violence, with those in villages (29.8) fared worse than their urban counterparts (22.8). After Himachal Pradesh, women fared relatively better in Jammu and Kashmir (12.6), Meghalaya (13.1), Nagaland (15.4), Sikkim (16.5) and Kerala (16.4).

Other states where women find themselves vulnerable are Assam (39.6), Arunachal Pradesh (38.8), Orissa (38.5), Maharashtra (30.7), Andhra Pradesh (35.2), Haryana (27.3), Gujarat (27.6) Punjab (25.4), Mizoram (22.5) and Karnataka (20).

Crime against Women in India

- One crime against women every three minutes
- One rape every 29 minutes
- One dowry death case every 77 minutes
- One case of cruelty by husband and relatives every nine minutes
- Once suicide every 240 minutes

Source: National Crime Records Bureau

Child Violence

Children are the nation's assets. A happy child will make his/her home and the country happy. The future of any country depends upon the right upbringing of its children, for which a congenial environment and adequate opportunities for wholesome development are essential.

According to UNICEF's "The State of the World's Children," report for 2006, one-third of the world's children lack adequate shelter, 31% lack basic sanitation and 21% have no access to clean, potable water. Illness, malnutrition, and premature death are common when children lack the most basic protection.

A government commissioned survey has found that more than 53 per cent of children in India are subjected to sexual abuse, but most don't report the assaults to anyone.

The survey, released last April and which covered different forms of child abuse physical, sexual and emotional as well as female child neglect, found that two out of every three children have been physically abused.

Parents and relatives, persons known to the child or in a position of trust and responsibility were mostly found to be the perpetrators of child sexual abuse in the country. According to the women and child development ministry-sponsored report, which assumes greater significance in the backdrop of the Nithari killings that brought into focus the issue of children's safety, those in the age group of 5-12 years reported higher levels of abuse.

While releasing the survey, *Women and Child Development Minister Renuka Chowdhury* said, "Child abuse is shrouded in secrecy and there is a conspiracy of silence around the entire subject. The ministry is working on a new law for protection of children's rights by clearly specifying offences against children and stiffening punishments."

The survey carried out across 13 states and with a sample size of 12,447, revealed that 53.22 per cent of children reported having faced one or more forms of sexual abuse, with Andhra Pradesh, Bihar, Assam and Delhi reporting the highest percentage of such incidents. In 50 per cent of child abuse cases, the abusers were known to the child or were in a position of trust and responsibility and most children did not report the matter to anyone.

The survey, sponsored by WCD ministry and carried out by the NGO Prayas in association with UNICEF and Save the Children, found that more than 50 per cent children were subjected to one or the other form of physical abuse and more boys than girls were abused physically. The first-ever survey on child abuse in the country disclosed that nearly 65 per cent of school children reported facing corporal punishment beatings by teachers mostly in government schools.

Of children physically abused in families, in 88.6 per cent of the cases, it was the parents who were the perpetrators. More than 50 per cent had been sexually abused in ways that ranged from severe such as rape or fondling to milder forms of molestation that included forcible kissing.

The study also interviewed 2,324 young adults between the ages of 18 and 24, almost half of whom reported being physically or sexually abused as children. When it comes to emotional abuse, every second child was subjected to emotional assault and in 83 per cent of the cases, parents were the abusers.

Children living with domestic violence may:

- Express behavioural problems
- Be more likely to truant or have difficulties at school
- Turn to alcohol or drugs
- Self-harm or attempt suicide

According to the *NSPCC* (National Society for the Prevention of Cruelty to Children) of Children living with domestic violence:

- 100% are emotionally abused
- 48% are psychologically abused
- 26% are physically abused
- 13% are accidentally injured
- 7% are sexually abused

Recent figures from the International Labour Organisation (ILO) show that:

- Globally, 1 in 6 children work.
- 218 million children aged 5—17 are involved in child labour world-wide.
- 126 million children work in hazardous conditions.
- The highest numbers of child labourers are in the Asia/Pacific region, where there are 122 million working children.
- The highest proportion of child labourers is in Sub Saharan Africa, where 26% of children (49 million) are involved in work.

Development of Women through Education

Education is the process of instruction aimed at the all round development of boys and girls. Education dispels ignorance. It is the only wealth that cannot be robbed. Learning includes the moral values and the improvement of character and the methods to increase the strength of mind.

Once the first Prime Minister of India, Jawaharlal Nehru said, "you can tell the condition of a nation by looking at the status of its women". This is absolutely true. Woman of any nation is the mirror to its civilisation. If women enjoy good status it shows that the society has reached a level of maturity and sense of responsibility while a decadent image conjures up if the opposite is true. The story of Indian women is as old as the history of Indian civilisation.

Kumud Sharma of the Centre for Women's Development Studies in New Delhi traced the correlation between education and domestic violence to patriarchal attitudes. "Educated women are aware of their rights," she said. "They are no longer willing to follow commands blindly. When they ask questions, it causes conflicts, which, in turn, leads to violence. In many Indian states, working women are asked to hand over their paycheck to the husband and have no control over their finances. So, if they stop doing so or start asserting their right, there is bound to be friction."

Female Literacy in India

According to last census held in 2001, the percentage of female literacy in the country is 54.16%. The literacy rate in the country has increased from 18.33% in 1951 to 65.38% as per 2001 census. The female literacy rate has also increased from 8.86% in 1951 to 54.16%. It is noticed that the female literacy rate during the period 1991-2001 increased by 14.87% whereas male literacy rate rose by 11.72%. Hence the female literacy rate actually increased by 3.15% more compared to male literacy rate.

Women Universities in India

- **Andhra Pradesh :** Sri Padmavati University, Tirupati
- **Delhi :** Lady Shri Ram College for Women, Lajpat Nagar
- **Maharashtra :** SNDT Women's University, Mumbai
- **Rajasthan :** Banasthali Vidyapith, Banasthali

It is necessary to establish some more universities and colleges for women in India. Education is a solution for any type of problem in the society. Education gives strength, power and character. Education helps to improve economic position also in the society.

The number of women job seekers has increased from 99.3 lacs in 1999 to 106.1 lacs in 2004. Thus the percentage of women job seekers to the total job-seekers has also increased from 24.6per cent in 1999 to 26.2per cent in 2004.

Table 9.1. Number of Women Job Seekers

Year	Number of Women (in lacs)	Percentage to total
1999	99.3	24.6
2000	104.5	25.3
2001	108.8	25.9
2002	106.0	25.9
2003	107.5	26.0
2004	106.1	26.0

Number of Educated Women Job Seekers as on December 2004 was 7537.7 thousand. Educated Women at the end of 2004 accounted for 25.8per cent of the total educated job-seekers.

Table 9.2: Number of Educated Women Job Seekers

Year	Number of Women	Percentage to total
2000	7911.7	27.1
2001	8525.6	28.1
2002	7921.4	26.8
2003	8032.4	26.6
2004	7537.7	25.8

Vision of National Commission for Women

Dr.(Miss.) Girija Vyas took over as Chairperson of the National Commission for Women on 16th February, 2005.

The Indian Women of Today Culturally rooted, Globally-oriented Healthy, Educated, and Self Reliant Secure in her Home and Safe outside with Access to all the Rights of a Citizen with Opportunity to Contribute in all walks of life.

Modern Indian Women

The status of women in modern India is a sort of a paradox. If on one hand she is at the peak of ladder of success, on the other hand she is mutely suffering the violence afflicted on her by her own family members. As compared with past women in modern times have achieved a lot but in reality they have to still travel a long way. Their path is full of roadblocks. The women have left the secured domain of their home and are now in the battlefield of life, fully armored with their talent. They had proven themselves. But in India they are yet to get their dues. The sex ratio of India shows that the Indian society is still prejudiced against female. There are 933 females per thousand males in India according to the census of 2001, which is much below the world average of 990 females. There are many problems which women in India have to go through daily. These problems have become the part and parcel of life of Indian women and some of them have accepted them as their fate.

First Woman of India

Women had played an important role in the Modern World. Here are some of the most successful and first women of the world, who lead a Nation, a Party, a State, etc.

- First woman President of Indian National Congress — Annie Besant (1917)
- First Indian woman President of Indian National Congress — Sarojini Naidu (1925)
- First woman Ambassador from India — Vijay Lakshmi Pandit (to USSR from1947-49)
- First woman Governor of an Indian State — Sarojini Naidu (UP from 1947-48)
- First woman Minister of an Indian State — Vijay Lakshmi Pandit (UP)
- First Mayor of Delhi — Aruna Asif Ali (1958)
- First woman Central Minister — Rajkumari Amrit Kaur
- First woman Film star to be a member of Rajya Sabha — Nargis Dutt
- First woman Chief Minister of an Indian State — Sucheta Kriplani (UP from 1963-67)
- First woman Prime Minister of India — Indira Gandhi (1966-77 and 1980-84)
- First woman Speaker of an Indian State — Shano Devi
- First woman winner of the Bharat Ratna — Indira Ghandi (1971)
- First woman Judge of the Supreme Court — Justice M Fatima Beevi (1989)
- First woman Chief Justice of a High Court — Leila Seth (CJ of Himachal Pradesh 1991)
- India's officially recognised billionth citizen — Aastha (Born on May 11, 2000 at ND)

Conclusion

Indian women have mastered anything and everything which a woman can dream of. But she still has to go a long way to achieve equal status in the minds of Indian men. The desire of Indian women can be best summed up in the following lines of 'Song of an African Women':

I have only one request.
I do not ask for money
Although I have need of it,
I do not ask for meat . . .
I have only one request,
And all I ask is
That you remove
The road block
From my path.

Educate all the children in the family. Education is the most powerful instrument for the development of women and children in the society.8th March is observed as *International Women's Day.* It is necessary to celebrate International Women's Day every year in a grand manner. Our present president Pratibha Patil is also a woman. It is the power and credit of woman. It is also very important to celebrate Children's Day on November 14th and Mother's day.

REFERENCES

1. *Census of India*, (2001), Government of India, New Delhi.
2. *Child and Women Development Report*, (2006), Ministry of Women and Child.
3. *Development*, Government of India, New Delhi.
4. *Heilbroner,* R. L. (1995) *Visions of the Future: The Distant Past, Yesterday, Today, and Tomorrow* (New York: Oxford University Press).
5. *National Crime Records Bureau*, (2007), Government of India, New Delhi.
6. *National Family Health Survey*, (2006), Government of India, New Delhi.
7. *National Institute of Child Health and Human Development*. (2001). The National Reading Panel: Reports of the Subgroups.
8. *UNESCO Institute for Statistics: Literacy Rates, Youth (15-24) and Adult (15+),* by Region and Gender (September 2006 Assessment).

CHAPTER 10

Impact of Education on Ethno-Medicine and Healthcare Practices Among the Tribal People of India

—Dr. Naraginti Amareswaran

We must protect the forests for our children, grandchildren and children yet to be born. We must protect the forests for those who can't speak for themselves such as the birds, animals, fish and trees.

Introduction

Anthropology as an integrated science of man deals with biological and cultural aspects of man. Presently anthropologists are more involved in applying their knowledge and techniques for human welfare.

Ethno-medicine is a sub-field of medical anthropology and deals with the study of traditional medicines: not only those that have relevant written sources (*e.g.* Traditional Chinese Medicine, Ayurveda), but especially those, whose knowledge and practices have been orally transmitted over the centuries.

In the scientific arena, ethno-medical studies are generally characterised by a strong anthropological approach, more than a bio-medical one. The focus of these studies is then the perception and context of use of traditional medicines, and not their bio-evaluation.

Tribes in India

The Indian sub-continent is inhabited by 88.2 million tribal populations belonging to over 577 tribal communities that come under 227 linguistic groups. They inhibit varied geographic and climatic zones of the country. Their vocation ranges from hunting, gathering, cave dwelling nomadic to societies with settled culture living incomplete harmony with nature.

Forests have been their dear home and totally submitted themselves to forest settings. Their relationship with the forest was symbolic in nature. They have been utilising the resources without disturbing the delicate balance of the eco-system. Tribal thus mostly remained as stable societies and were unaffected by the social, cultural, material and economic evolutions that were taking place with the so called civilised societies. But this peaceful co-existence of the tribal has been disturbed in recent years by the interference in their habitats. Traditional communities living close to nature have, over the years acquired unique knowledge about the use of living biological resources. Modernisation, especially industrialisation and urbanisation has endangered the rich heritage of knowledge and expertise of age-old wisdom of the traditional communities.

A study on the utilisation of local tribal revealed that they hold precious knowledge on the specific use of a large number of agents of wild plant and animal origins, the use of many are hitherto unknown to the outside world.

Herbal History and Tradition in Indian Context

The Rigveda, the oldest document of human knowledge mentions the use of medicinal plants in the treatment of man and animals. Ayurveda gives the account of actual beginning of the ancient medical science of India, which according to western scholars was written between 2500 to 600 B.C. Charaka and Susruta wrote around 1000 B.C. Charaka concentrates more on medicine while Susruta deals with surgery in details along with therapeutics.

Tribes and Ethno-Medicine

Ethno-medicine refers to "those beliefs and practices relating to disease which are the products of indigenous cultural development and are not explicitly derived from the conceptual framework of modern medicine" (Hughes, 1968, cited from Misra et al, 2003). Various institutions are now concerned with the traditional health care system and means of traditional treatment.

The tribal people are the real custodians of the medicinal plants. Out of 45,000 species of wild plants, 7500 species are used for medicinal purposes. The World Health Organisation (WHO) has been promoting a movement for 'Saving plants for saving lives'. This is because of the growing understanding of the pivotal role medicinal plants play in providing herbal remedies to health maladies.

India is the home of several important traditional system of health-care like Ayurveda. This system depends heavily on herbal products. Several millions of Indian households have been using through the ages nearly 8000 species of medicinal plants for their healthcare needs. Over one and half million traditional healers use a wide range of medicinal plants for treating ailments of both humans and livestock across the length and breadth of the country. Over 800 medicinal plant species are currently in use by the Indian herbal industry.

In recent times with the increased knowledge of life and culture of the tribal communities, the social scientists are taking interest in ethno-medicinal studies. Many works have been reported especially from among the rural and tribal communities of India (Choudhury, 1986; Bhadra and Tirkey, 1997; Sharma Thakur, 1997).Ray and Sharma (2005) have given a description of ethno-medicinal beliefs and practices prevalent among the Savaras, a tribal community of Andhra Pradesh.

Kumari (2006) gave an account on the concept of illness and disease and the application of folk medicine among the Saureas of Jharkhand. However, ethno-medicinal studies are relatively less in Northeast India. Guha (1986) has reported from among the Boro-Kachari tribe of Assam. A glimpse of indigenous health practices among the plain tribes of Assam is given by Sharma Thakur (1999). The socio-economic condition of some of the tribes of Arunachal Pradesh and their problems of health and indigenous methods of treatment has been reported by Choudhury (2000), Duarah and Pathak (1997), Kohli (1999), Bhasin (1997, 1999, 2002, 2003, 2005).

Ethno-Medicine and Healthcare Practices among Sonowal Kacharis in Assam (India)

The Sonowal Kacharis is an endogamous group of Kachari tribe and a popular plain scheduled tribe population of Assam. Various types of locally available herbs and leaves of wild plants are used by them as medicine. Like many other communities of the region, there are few herbal specialists among the Sonowal Kachari. These specialists or medicine-men have considerable knowledge about the herbs and its medicinal use. Normally they learn about these medicinal plants and its uses from their ancestor. These medicine-men are referred by different term according to the cultural norms. Among the Sonowal Kachari's they are called as Bez (Barua and Phukan, 1958: 334). Of course in rural Assam, they are mainly known by this term.

It has been observed in the villages that use of herbal medicine for curing certain diseases are quite known to the people and besides medicine-men, many elderly persons known about the use of herbal medicines. Some of the diseases and their indigenous methods of treatment are given below:

(1) **Fever:** Lime (Citrus auran tifolia) juice mixed with sugar is applied on the forehead of the patient to get relief from fever.

(2) **Diarrhoea:** Dry goose berry (Emblica officinalis) powder and black salt mixed with cold water is taken. Bark of Long Pepper (Pipoli tree) mixed with Misiri water is also used to cure the disease.

(3) **Dysentery:** Lime (Citrus auran tifolia) juice with hot water and little salt is used in dysentery. The juice of black Tulsi leaves (Ocimum sanctum) and Sirata (Swertiachirata) is also used for the purpose. The juice of tender leaves (three numbers) of mango (Mangifera indica), black berry (S.cuminii) and goose berry (Emblica officinalis) (equal proportions) together with honey are mixed with goat milk and is taken to cure blood dysentery. Honey together with the juice of Dubari grass (Family-Gramineae) can cure blood dysentery and need to be taken for three/ four days. They also use a kind of wild herb, locally called Manimuni (Centila asiatica).The juice of this herb

mixed with sugar or honey should be taken continuously for a month to cure the disease. They also use limewater (Chun pani) mixed with juice of turmeric (Purcuma domestica) leave to get relief from blood dysentery and mucous.

(4) **Blood Vomiting:** A table spoon of carrot (Dancus carota) juice mixed with honey can cure blood vomiting.

(5) **Liver Disease:** Two to three raw or ripe Papayas (Carica papaya) daily can cure liver disease. A curry prepared from the bud of banana (Musa paradisiaca) and the meat of pigeon is also used as a medicine for the purpose.

(6) **Jaundice:** The medicine is prepared by pounding five or six number of Silikha (Myroballum) mixing with jaggery and it can cure jaundice. A glass of sugarcane (Saccharum officinarum) juice twice daily prescribed for the purpose. Boiled raw papaya (Carica papaya) is said to be good for curing the disease. Kardoi (Averrhoa carambola), Goose Berry (Emblica officinalis), Sugar cane (Saccharun officinarum), Neem leave (Azadirachta indica), a wild herb known as Duran ban (Lecas aspera), Brahmi sak (Herpestis monnieria), Purakol (Musa sapientum) are prescribed edibles for the patient.

(7) **Nose Bleeding:** Flower of Pomegranate (Punica granatum Linn) is crushed and 3-4 drops of juice is poured inside the nose to give immediate relief.

(8) **Tonsilities:** Juice is prepared by mixing one Amara seed (Sponolias mangifera), one Silikha seed (Mysoballum) and a piece of Turmeric (Purcuma domestica) and advice the patient gargles for a week regularly.

(9) **Worms:** Paste of five lemon seeds (Citrus aurantifolia) mixed with water and is prescribed to eat in empty stomach for a few days. The twigs of Chirata (Swertia chirata) are soaked in the water overnight and the water is prescribed to drink in empty stomach in the morning for one week regularly.

(10) **Scabies:** Lemon juice (Citrus aurantifolia) mixed with coconut oil is massaged for curing scabies. To remove scabies they take bath with hot water in which leaves of Neem (Azadirachta officinarum) were boiled. Twigs of Chirata (Swertia chirata)

arecrushed into paste with water to be used as an ointment and applied on the skin. Chirata water is prescribed to drink in the morning in empty stomach.

(11) **Pain in the Ear:** Juice of Tulsi (Ocimum sanctum) is boiled and put it in the ears to heal earache.

The patient is treated with available herbs, flora and minerals. Some of these are home remedies and some are specially prescribed by herbalist or folk medicine man available in the community. The practice of ethno-medicine is a complex multi-disciplinary system constituting the use of plants, spirituality and the natural environment and has been the source of healing for people for millennia. The spiritual aspects of health and sickness have been an integral component of the ethno-medicinal practice for centuries.

Diseases due to Wrath of the Supernatural

Disease	Supernatural agencies	Pujas (Rituals)
Dysentery, mental diseases, cancer	Deo	Propitiated by sacrificing two red cocks, one red hen, and one egg, besides other items of feast. Arrangement is made in the forest.
Asthama, Mental Disease, cancer	Lord of water	*Jalkhai puja*, worshipped by sacrificing one white duck and other items of feast, rice, salt vegetables, etc.
Accident, sudden illness	Burah-dangoria	No sacrifice. Only raw items, e.g. gram, rice, powdered rice, etc. are offered to propitiate Burah-dangoria.
Gastritis	Ancestral spirits	Ai puja, no sacrifice is made except offering of raw articles, powdered rice, gram with betel nut and leaves.
Epidemic and natural calamities	Mother goddess	Community level worship by arranging bhur-utuwa puja. One pair of betel nut and leaf is offered from each family. One red duck is offered on behalf of the villagers. All the offered articles are placed in a boat.
Epidemic and large scale death of men and animals	Mother goddesses of forest	A white goat is a must for the Puja besides other offering.

Present Position of Tribes

The tribal healthcare practices and system of treating diseases are based on their deep observation and belief in nature. But with the development of education and their awareness towards importance of health and health care and also with the advent of modern health care facilities, Government health measures these people are becoming more interested in taking modern medicine instead of traditional herbal medicine.

Saving the Plant is Saving the Life

According to the text of Vishnu Samhita, causing any harm to the plants/animals is a sin. Even purloining of parts/ products of any of these living beings is a crime. The sinner/ criminals are liable to chastisement in this life and also after death. The punishments are of diverse nature:—pecuniary, corporal, expiatory and donation of specific articles to Brahmins.

Conclusion

The growing disinterest in the use of the ethno-medicinal plants and its significance among the younger generation of the tribes will lead to the disappearance of this practice. Educated younger generation of the tribes should be encouraged by the Government to protect and cultivate these valuable herbal plants before they get lost due to the impact of modernisation and urbanisation and also due to deforestation.

The role of Anthropology is also very important in the field of saving herbal plants. By educating tribal people we can preserve all these things for future generation. It is the Government duty to take necessary steps to preserve all these things.

REFERENCES

1. Barua, I. and R. Phukan. 1990. "*Socio-religious Aspects of Health Among Sonowal Kachari*". The Eastern Anthropologist, 55: 4.
2. Bhasin, Veena. 1997. "*Medical Pluralism and Health Services in Ladakh.*" J. Soc. Sci., 1: 43-69.
3. Bhasin, Veena. 1997. "*The Human Settlements and Health Status of People of Sikkim*", (pp. 153-187), in K.C. Mahanta (ed.), People of the Himalayas: Ecology, Culture, Development and Change. Delhi:Kamla-Raj Enterprises.

4. Bhasin, Veena. 1999. *Tribals of Ladakh: Ecology, Human Settlements and Health.* Delhi: Kamla-Raj Enterprises.
5. Bhasin, Veena. 2002. "Traditional Medicine Among Tribals of Rajasthan." J. Soc Sci., 6(3): 153-172.Bhasin, Veena. 2003."*Sickness and Therapy Among Tribals of Rajasthan.*" Stud. Tribes and Tribals, 1(1): 77 -83.
6. Choudhury, S. 2000. "*Indigenous Beliefs and Practices of Herbal Medicine Among the Few Arunachalis*".Resarun, 26. 72-81, Govt. of Arunachal Pradesh, Department of Cultural Affairs.
7. Das, B. M. 2007. "*Sonowal Kachari Nigostiya Parichya*", (pp. 1-3) in M. Sonowal (ed.), Sonowal Saurav Smarak Granth. Assam: Sonowal Kachari Sanskritic Mahotsava.
8. Duarah, D. K. and S. D. Pathak. 1997. "*A Short Note on the Healthcare Practices Among the Nishis of Arunachal Pradesh.* (pp. 73-78) in F. Ahmed Dasand R. K. Kar (eds.), Health Studies in Anthropology. Department of Anthropology, Dibrugarh University, Dibrugarh.
9. Kumari, P. 2006. "*Etiology and Healing Practices: A Study in Primitive Societies of Jharkhand*", (pp. 487-499) P. Dash Sharma (ed.), Anthropology of Primitive Tribes in India. New Delhi: Serial Publications.
10. Guha, A. 1986. "*Folk Medicines of the Boro-Kacharis –A Plain Tribe of Assam*", (pp. 191-199) B. Choudhuri(ed.), Tribal Health. New Delhi: Inter-India Publications.

CHAPTER 11

Impact of Globalisation on Teacher Education

–Dr. K. Radhika
–Dr. Naraginti Amareswaran

A teacher who establishes rapport with the taught, becomes one with them, learns more from them than he teaches them. He who learns nothing from his disciples is, in my opinion, worthless. Whenever I talk with someone I learn from him. I take from him more than I give him. In this way, a true teacher regards himself as a student of his students. If you will teach your pupils with this attitude, you will benefit much from them. **—M.K. Gandhi**

Introduction

Education has been around for as long as man has been, though its structure and perception has varied over centuries and civilisations. Now we are living in the highly scientific and technological world. Enormous changes are occurring in the day to day life of human beings because of globalisation, privatisation and liberalisation. Education is seen as central to economic competitiveness, the reduction of poverty and inequality, and environmental sustainability. So, it is necessary to provide education for all; then only India will become developed country by 2020.

Globalisation

Globalisation is a term describing the increasing interdependence, integration and interaction among people, companies and corporations in disparate locations around theworld. This umbrella term refers to a complex medley of economic, trade, social, technological, cultural and political relationships. The term has been used as early as 1944;

however Theodore Levitt is usually credited with its first use in an economic context.

In defining and explaining globalisation, Nsibambi (2001), incorporated five concepts. He defined globalisation as "a process of advancement and increase in interaction among the worlds, countries and peoples facilitated by progressive technological changes in locomotion, communication, political and military power, knowledge and skills, as well as interfacing of cultural values, systems and practices". He noted that globalisation is not a value-free, innocent, self-determining process. It is an international socio-politico-economic and cultural permeation process facilitated by policies of governments, private corporations, international agencies and civil society organisations. It essentially seeks to enhance and deploy economic, political, technological, ideological and military power and influence for competitive domination in the world.

Globalisation is the worldwide process of homogenising prices, products, wages, rates of interest and profits. Globalisation relies on three forces for development: the role of human migration, international trade, and rapid movements of capital and integration of financial markets.

From the culture point of view, David (2002), states that globalisation is the process of harmonising different cultures and beliefs. Globalisation is the process that eroding differences in culture and producing a seamless global system of culture and economic values (Castells, 1997). The harmonisation, according to Awake (2002), is achieved due to advancement in communication and countries are increasingly being forced to participate. Therefore, globalisation can be viewed as a process of shifting autonomous economies into a global market. In other words, it is the systematic integration of autonomous economies into a global system of production and distribution.

The world of separate nation-states is said to be ending enabling the process of globalisation to run its logical course. The new technology, based on the computer and satellite communication have indeed revolutionised our traditional conception of the media, both print and electronic. Books, newspapers, radio, television and video programme are now being transposed into the multimedia world of the cyber space and available to all people of the world wherever they may live. Ajayi (2001) remarks that globalisation is about competition and struggle for dominance which encourages more than anything else, the continuation and expansion of western imperialism in the new millennium.

Importance of Education

During the Vedic and Upanishadic period, India had some of the prominent institutions of higher education, which attracted scholars from distant places located in different parts of the world to come to India in pursuit of knowledge. The ancient universities of Takshashila and Nalanda, which survived till the end of the fifth and twelfth Century AD respectively, imparted knowledge in different areas according to the requirements of the contemporary society.

The importance of education is quite clear. Education is the knowledge of putting one's potentials to maximum use. One can safely say that a human being is not in the proper sense till he is educated.

This importance of education is basically for two reasons. The first is that the training of a human mind is not complete without education. Education makes man a right thinker. It tells man how to think and how to make decision.

The second reason for the importance of education is that only through the attainment of education, man is enabled to receive information from the external world; to acquaint him-self with past history and receive all necessary information regarding the present. Without education, man is as though in a closed room and with education he finds himself in a room with all its windows open towards outside world.

Education means the gradual process of acquiring knowledge. Education is a preparation for life. Swami Vivekananda, the great thinker and reformer of India had remarked: "We want that education by which character is formed, strength of mind is increased, intellect is expanded and by which one can stand on one's own feet. Education is the manifestation of the perfection already in man." The great

Nobel Laureate and writer Rabindra Nath Tagore was one of the earliest educators to think in terms of the global education village, and his educational model has a unique sensitivity and aptness for education within multi-racial, multi-lingual and multi-cultural situations.

Development through Educational Institutions

Independent India has witnessed an upsurge in the growth of higher education. Yet from an international perspective, we are relatively slow, despite being steady in registering advancements in learning. Today India has the second largest education system in the world, next only to the USA. Yet, the total number of students represents hardly six per cent of the relevant age group, *i.e.* 18-23 years, which is much below the average of developed countries which is about 47 per cent. The gap is glaring. Hence the phenomenal challenge. The journey from being 'Good' to being 'Great' appears to be long and arduous.

India is a developing country. 70% of people are living in the villages. The rural area literacy percentage is very low when compared to urban area literacy rate. The main occupation of Indians is cultivation. The duty of higher educational institutions is to introduce courses which help to improve the rural people socio-economic status in the society. Through education it is possible to change the world. Because of globalisation now world become a village. We get any type of information with in the seconds. Educational institutions have prominent role in the development of rural people in the society.

The first citizen of India today, Dr. A P J Abdul Kalam, while envisioning India of 2020, recently observed — "Spirit of Inquiry, creativity, entrepreneurial and moral leadership are the capabilities central to nation building in a democracy. Educators should develop in our children these capacities and make them autonomous learners who are self-directed and self-controlled."

Earlier all over the world, education, especially higher education, was available only to a privileged few. In the context of a knowledge society and the goals of sustainable development, higher education/ teacher education needs to percolate to the masses, not only just in terms of quantity, but also quality. In the last few years, this shift has been slowly taking place. Still, glaring deficiencies remain in the access to higher education, overall development of the student, sensitivity to human needs and equality in our society.

Also come into play, concerns in teacher education that come with globalization and rapidity of change like fast rate of obsolescence of knowledge, quality, competitiveness of education services, networking of institutions and innovations and new practices in delivery, combined with this are the concerns for sustainable development of the world.

Role of Teacher in Building Modern India

The role of the modern teacher is not confined to teaching alone. He/she is expected to participate in the development programmes of the community life. The question arises as to how this could be integrated with the teacher education programmes. Mudaliar Commission (1952-53) Report stated rightly, "we are convinced that the most important factor in the contemplated education reconstruction is the teacher-his personal qualities, his educational qualifications, his professional training and the place that he occupies in the school as well as in the community". On similar lines Kothari Commission (1964-66) stated that, "Nothing is more important than securing a sufficient supply of high quality recruits to the teaching profession, providing them with the best possible professional preparation and creating satisfactory conditions of work in which they can be fully effective".

The importance of the teachers in the Educational Programme of a country is too great. The greatness of a country does not depend on lofty buildings, gigantic projects and large armies, but on the quality of its citizens. If a nation has young men of sterling character and unimpeachable patriotism, she is found to make rapid progress in all fields. Young men are entrusted to the care of the teacher and it is therefore the sacred duty of the teacher to impart the right type of knowledge and make them good citizens. It is the teacher who impresses his children with his personality.

The teacher, a national integrator as he is, is the backbone of society, particularly so in the remote villages. He stands as an outstanding figure among the illiterate and semi-literate families. He is their friend, Philosopher and guide. The teacher actively shares the responsibility of reconstructing a social order, with all the cherished values and traditional beliefs, which are being eroded by the surge of new ideals and practices. He acts as a social reformer and counsellor to the community.

Impact of Globalisation on Teacher Education

In the knowledge economy, the objectives of a society changes from fulfilling the basic needs of all round development to empowerment. The education system instead of going by text-book teaching will be promoted by reactive, interactive self learning, both formal and informal, with focus on values, merit and quality. The workers instead of being skilled or semi-skilled will be knowledgeable, self-empowered and flexibly skilled. Finally, the economy will be knowledge driven and not industry driven.

All fields of human activity, including education, have been influenced by the process of globalisation clubbed with unexpected advancements in information and communication technology. Within the various sectors of education, teacher education has been affected the most. It is now increasingly realised that knowledge is universal and its creation and dissemination cannot be confined within national boundaries. The world is now like a global village, and continuous international interaction has become an essential component of human survival. The globalisation of economy has led to internationalisation of higher education including teacher education, not merely for economic benefits, but also for increased social interaction and promotion of international understanding.

Positive impact of Globalisation on Teacher Education

1. A number of teacher educational institutions were increased.
2. Usage of technology increased in the educational institutions.
3. Information and communication technology were increased.
4. Teacher educational institutions were established in rural areas.
5. Government and private partnership in the field of teacher education.
6. Extension of Internet facilities even to rural areas educational institutions.

7. Teachers are less worried for government jobs as MNC's and private or public sector are offering more lucrative jobs.
8. Free education for bright students.

Negative Impact of Globalisation on Teacher Education

1. Indian youths leaving education in mid-way and joining MNC's.
2. There has been an increase in the violence, particularly against women in the educational institutions.
3. Quality in education is decreasing (liberalisation).
4. Degradation of values.
5. More availability of cheap and filthy material (CD's or DVD's of Hollywood movies, porn movies, sex toys, foreign channels like MTV) in the name of liberalisation. It affects the psychology of teachers. Some teachers are miss-behaving with students.
6. Values of teacher are decreasing.

Conclusion

It is left to one's discretion to use a knife either to cut a fruit or to kill a person/animal. In the modernised and globalised world, it is necessary to be very cautious. Every single step should be taken with utmost care. It is the first duty of policy makers, politicians, officials and leaders to give priority for mother society and well being of their people. Globalisation undoubtedly offers great opportunities for growth and development. However, no one can deny that its benefits are unevenly shared and its costs are unevenly spread among, across and within countries. This is particularly true with respect to developing and underdeveloped countries. Inspite of economic reforms the rates of unemployment and poverty in India are still high. Both in concept and practice, while globalisation has positive, innovative, dynamic aspects, it also has negative, disruptive and marginalising aspects (UNDP HDR 1999). Nsibambi (2001) suggested that globalisation must be seen as a change process full of opportunities and challenges that must be carefully and skilfully harnessed and managed to ensure human development.

Teacher is a national builder. According to Indian philosophy teacher is a third god. It is very important to take care about teacher education. Through education only it is possible to preserve values and culture. Through education it is possible to solve any types of problems in the society.

It is apt to quote Mahatma Gandhi "I do not want my house to be walled in on all sides and my windows to be stuffed. I want the cultures of all the lands to be blown about my house as freely as possible. But, I refuse to be blown off my feet by any".

REFERENCES

1. David F. (2002). *Why National Pride Still Has a Home in the Global Village*. Global Policy Forum. New York. The Scotsman May 18.
2. Gandhi, M. K. (1977), "*The Collected Works*, Ahmedabad: Navajivan.
3. Kumar, K. (1994), 'Mohandas Karamchand Gandhi' in Z. Morsy (ed.) *Thinkers on Education Volume 2*, Paris: UNESCO.
4. Nsibambi, A (2001). "*The Effects of Globalisation on the State in Africa: Harnessing the Benefits and Minimizing the Costs*. Paper presented at UN General Assembly, Second Committee: Panel Discussion on Globalisation and the State, November 2, 2001.
5. Ruggie, John Gerard (1993), "*Territoriality and Beyond: Problematising Modernity in International Relations*," International Organisation 47; 139-74.
6. Scholte, Jan Aart (2000), "*Globalisation: A Critical Introduction*" (New York: St. Martin's).

CHAPTER 12

Importance of Values in Teacher Education

–Dr. Naraginti Amareswaran

- Be good, see good and do good. That is the way to God.
- Money comes and goes; but morality comes and grows!
- Good and bad, peace and agony, pain and pleasure, all these originate within man and not outside him.
- The past is beyond recovery. We are not sure of the future. The given moment is the right time. Do not delay; do right action.

—Sri Sathya Sai Baba

Introduction

The development of any nation depends mainly on the standards of its educational institutions. Education is the most powerful and effective instrument for inducing radical changes in the behaviour of students. Education is a powerful instrument of national development—social, economic and cultural. The teacher occupies pivotal position in the system of education. Teaching has been one of the oldest and most respected professions in the world.

According to Indians, Teacher is the third god. Today we are living in the technological world. India developed in the fields of Science and Technology. It is possible to know each and every thing with in seconds through out the world.

Today's children are tomorrow's citizens. It is necessary to give quality and value based education to each and every student in the society. Then only all children will become good citizens in the future.

Values

Values are the guiding principles, decisive in day to day behaviours as also in critical life situations. Values are a set of principles or standards of behaviour. Values are regarded desirable, important and held in high esteem by a particular society in which a person lives. Thus values give meaning and strength to a person with character by occupying a central place in his life. Values reflect one's personal attitudes and judgments, decisions and choices, behaviour and relationships, dreams and vision. They influence our thoughts, feelings and actions. They guide us to do the right things.

Values are the guiding principles of life which are conductive to all round development. They give direction and firmness to life and bring joy, satisfaction and peace of life. Values are like the rails that keep a train on the track and help it move smoothly, quickly and with direction. They bring qualities to life.

Value Education

Value education means inculcating in the children a sense of humanism, a deep concern for the well being of others and the nation. This can be accomplished only when we instill in the children a deep feeling of commitment to values that would build this country and bring back to the people pride in work that brings order, security and assured progress.

Through value education, we like to develop the social, moral, aesthetic and spiritual sides of a person which are often undermined in formal education. Value education teaches us to preserve whatever is good and worthwhile in what we have inherited from our culture. It helps us to respect the attitude and behaviour of those who differ from us. Value education does not mean value imposition or indoctrination.

Value education has the capacity to transform a diseased mind into a very young, fresh, healthy, natural and attentive mind. The transformed mind is capable of higher sensitivity and a heightened level of perception this leads to fulfillment of the evolutionary role in man and in life. Values in general, could be classified broadly under five headings—personal, social, moral, spiritual and behavioural.

Education in general and value education in particular occupies a prestigious place in the modern context of the contemporary society. The problem of value education of the young has assumed increasing prominence in educational discussions during recent times. Parents, teachers, administrators and society at large are concerned of about values and value education of children.

"The destiny of India is now being shaped in her class rooms". This is the opening sentence of the Kothari Education Commission report (1964-66). What kind of destiny has been actually shaped during the last sixty years? There are thousands of schools without primary needs. The position of teacher's economic condition is also poor when compared to USA teachers.

Nature of Values

- Values relate to the aims of human life. For the achievement of aims man frames certain notions and these notions are called values.
- Our conduct is motivated by our values.
- Value is the act of cherishing something. A person who values justice will spend a lot of energy in search for it.
- Values are masterminds which give direction to one's strivings. Values represent feelings, wants, interests, attitudes, preferences and opinions about what is right, just fair or desirable.

Classification of Values

There are so many classifications of values. According to Plato's classification, there are three types of values: (1) Truth, (2) Beauty and (3) Goodness.

Gandhi's Classification

In order to create new social order Gandhiji introduced Nai Talim in the year 1937, which is popularly known as Basic Education.

1. Truth
2. Non-violence

3. Freedom
4. Democracy
5. Sarva Dharma Smabhava
6. Equality
7. Self-realisation
8. Purity of ends and means
9. Self-discipline
10. Suddhi

The numbers of values are unlimited. The NCERT listed 83 values. It is unmanageable to deal with so many values in schools. Under the Sathya Sai Organisation, these 83 values are classified and grouped under the five well known prime values. These five are: Sathya (Truth), Dharma (righteousness), Prema (Love in its broadest Sense), Shanti (Peace) and Ahimsa (Non-violence in various forms and actions, thoughts, feelings etc).

We have the constitution of India which we are bound to follow: major values embedded there in are: (1) Justice, Equality, liberty and Fraternity; and (2) Democracy, Secularism, and Social Justice.

Next we have individual and personal values: Cleanliness, Neatness, Punctuality, Regularity, Industriousness, Healthcare, honesty, Self respect, Self reliance etc.

We must add values necessary for Peace and Harmony. These are concern and compassion for others, co-operation, self-sacrifice, national integrity and unity and world/ universal brotherhood. For all values, the approach has to be through a spirit of enquiry, persuit of truth, logical thinking, open mindedness, sharing and a scientific bent of mind.

Characteristics of a Real Teacher

Teacher is a national builder. He has a power to change the society. In the 13th chapter of the "Bhagavadgita" the characteristics of a real teacher are laid down as follows: absence of pride, free from hypocrisy, non-violence, forgiving nature, straight forwardness, service of the preceptor, purity of mind and body, steadfastness and self-control. Centuries ago in this land of Vedas the teacher devoted all his time for the upliftment of his pupils in all directions-knowledge, morals, values etc. He was called the 'Guru or Acharya'.

According to V.S.Mathews "No system of education, no syllabus, no methodology, no text book can rise above the level of its teachers. If a country wants to have quality education it must have quality teachers". So, it is necessary to give importance for values in the teacher education.

Teacher Education

"Values are to be caught and not taught', is a very old saying. It was perhaps true in days gone by when parents at home and leaders in community in various walks of life were all value-based people. Therefore younger children and growing adolescents could catch values of elderly people and either by imitation or by special efforts developed appropriate values accepted and respected in society. Much water has flowed under the bridge since then and there is a grave deterioration both among parents and community leaders in terms of their being value models for the younger generation. We cannot there fore expect values to be caught from undesirable situations and persons in society. In today's world, therefore values have got to be taught in addition to being caught from selected situations and personalities.

According to V.S.Mathews "No system of education, no syllabus, no methodology, no text book can rise above the level of its teachers. If a country wants to have quality education it must have quality teachers". So, it is necessary to give importance for values in the teacher education.

Let we observe the teacher education system in the state of Andhra Pradesh, India. There are 24 Government D.Ed. colleges for the academic year 2006-07 with 2565 students, 324 B.Ed. colleges with 36009 students, 3B.Ed. institution in distance mode with 1500 students, 17 Telugu Pandit colleges with 1700 students, 10 Urdu Pandit Colleges with 480 students, 35 Hindi Pandit colleges with 2090 studens, 5 D.P.Ed. colleges with 400 students, 7 B.P.Ed. colleges with 435 students and 20 M.Ed. colleges with 457 students both in Government and Private sectors.

It is necessary to take care in the framing of teacher education curriculum. Teacher is a national builder. So, it is important to give good quality and value based education to the teacher in teacher education. It is necessary to provide all types of labs and library facilities to improve quality education in teacher education.

Need for value based Teacher Education

Today we are in a technological world where things are happening fast. Parents and teachers would like to be getting results fast. India has kept pace in science and technology with forward nations but we have shown slower pace in our value system even when we have a strong heritage of human values. India was quoted by great visionaries and saints as a punya bhumi. Swami Vivekananda reiterated in his powerful words: " *If there is any land on this earth that can lay claim to be the blessed punya bhumi, to be land to which souls on this earth must come to account for karma, the land to which every soul is wending its way Godward must come to attain its lost home, the land where humanity has attained its highest towards gentleness, towards generosity, towards purity, towards calmness, above all, the land of introspection and of spirituality—It is India.*" Thus value Education has been elucidated by swamiji. From such a state, we are in the Pythonic Grip of deepening Value crisis. How unfortunate it is!!!

How can we overcome this? When can we become capable of training the young citizens to be the carriers of the noble human resources? What value, value has changed to? Present scenario and surroundings looms large with terroristic acts, violence, negative thoughts, anti-social acts, many an immoral qualities are all seen every where and the world looks a big booming , buzzing confusion. Such is the case in all fields, braving such conditions the wise men of our country has been trying to put forth issues like a national system of education and a national policy of education which should focus and bridge the gaps that are widening .

The NPE (1986) and subsequently the POA's have been emphasising the faith in *vidya dadati vinayam, vinayat yati patratam, patratwat dhanamapnoti, dhanat dharmam tataha sukham*—it is learning and knowledge that gives capability to earn, and earning the ability to do dharma for a noble cause and this results in gaining peace. The analysts and educationists of our country have consciously changed the curriculum and prioritized universalisation of primary education, the girl child education, and inculcating value-based education in their recent policy recommendations like—the Eshwarbhai Patel's; Ramamurthy commission; Prof .Yashpal's commission and the present focus on the same issues through the national curriculum framework. All these commissions, reports and recommendations have one thing in common and that is, changing curriculum at different levels for capacity building among teachers. Further, recent studies and analysis of evaluation of achievements at different levels have clearly shown the quality concerns and that teacher factor and his / her performance is poor but his responsibilities are more and there is need to train teachers in several of the new techniques and bring him to the frontline in this task of building a national system of education with a focus on value education. Thus educating the whole child and developing values assumed importance in recent years.

Implementation Process

The following points may be considered for implementing the value education in in-service and pre-service teacher training programmes and at different stage of educational institutions.

In-service Teacher Training

As a first step, three training camps may be arranged for teachers—(1) coaching camp, (2) evaluation camps and (3) refresher courses. A minimum of two teachers from each school must be covered by this programme. The above programmes for the teachers should be in such a way that it kindles the vast potentialities lying dormant in a teacher resulting in the teacher developing his/her own ways of imparting VE. These courses should enable the teacher to have his perspective in all the activities of school *viz.* classes on subjects, sports and games, cultural activities, youth festivals and all other extra-curricular activities. *In other words, moral education will not get confined to one moral class only.*

A teacher's manual of guidelines may be prepared, based on the values listed above, containing portions from the existing textbooks that deal with values, to help them give a special thrust to values while teaching the students.

Progammes

- Conduct periodically essay writing, elocution, story telling, poems recital, quiz on value-based subjects.
- Teach life stories of eminent characters in the epics and history, poems that would spur national fervour and devotion, patriotic songs, environmental hygiene etc.
- Motivate children to write short notes on value-based topics from the school library books. This will also encourage the development of reading habit.
- Organise special programmes on value-based subjects on every January 26, August 15 and October 2, and give awards to all the participants in the form of leaflets/pamphlets/books containing value-oriented articles and stories.
- Conduct a class exclusively for moral instruction, based on Gandhian lines, in every school once a week to focus the student's attention on the observance of a proper code of conduct and good behaviour at home, in school, in public places, and while moving about in the society.
- Begin the classes every day with a universal peace prayer.
- Display every day, messages and sayings of Mahastmas and great thinkers related to values at a prominent place in the schools under the caption 'Thought for the Day'. Such sayings may be read out and explained in the morning school assembly.
- Invite distinguished persons to talk to the students and parents on the need for importance of leading a value-based life.
- Organise occasionally common gatherings of students of government, aided and unaided schools to bridge the gap in the level of their awareness and absorption capacity.

- Institute recognition and bravery awards for those students whose assimilation of values outshines that of their fellow-students.
- Observe once a year a Parents' Day; to enable the children to express their abiding love, reverence and gratitude for all that their parents have been doing for them.
- Celebrate Teachers' Day in the true spirit to enable children to remember with great reverence and abiding gratitude what their teachers have done for them.
- Arrange debates, speeches and skits on the life and teachings of outstanding national leaders, who can be considered as role models for the young generation.

Outdoor camps

- Conduct periodical outdoor camps for selected children from a group of schools. This is an easy way to enable the children to understand the gifts of nature and to study the infallible laws of nature.
- In this context, it may be most appropriate to arrange for at least one outdoor self-contained campsite in each of the approximately 50 districts in the country. This site may also provide facilities for nature cure, organic farming and yoga as it is felt that there is growing importance given to this in many countries and therefore, students may be trained in this at an early age itself. Such a facility would basis in the outdoor camps that may be conducted every weekend in each district.

Conclusion

According to Sarvepalli Radhakrishnan teacher is a national builder. He has a power to change the society. It is government duty to provide quality education for prospective and in-service teachers. Teacher is a back bone for national development. Through education we can change the world. Teacher is a good resource to develop values in the society. Without teacher the education have no meaning. Value oriented education is necessary for today's situation.

REFERENCES

1. *Achievement of B.Ed. Students*, Dr. C. Manchala, Discovery Publishing House, New Delhi-110002.
2. *Value Education in India*, Usha Rai Negi, Editor, Published by Association of Indian Universities, AIU House, 16 Kotla Marg, New Delhi-110 002, 2000.
3. *Value Education*, Dr. Venkataiah, Editor, APH Publishing Corporation, 5, Ansari Road, Daryaganj, New Delhi-110 002, First Edition, 1998.

CHAPTER

13

Inculcation of Ethics Through Education and Globalisation Effects on Ethics

—Dr. Naraginti Amareswaran
—Dr. B. Ramchandra Reddy
—Dr. C. Manchala

Introduction

'The care of human life and happiness, and not their destruction, is the first and only object of good government'.

—Thomas Jefferson

'When I give food to the poor, they call me a saint. When I ask why the poor have no food, they call me a communist'.

—Dom Helder Camara

Now we are living in the technological modern world. Science and Technology have a prominent role in the development of the any nation in the world. India is a developing county in the world. Indian economy is the fourth largest economy in the world. According to 2001 census the literacy rate of India is 64.84%. It is very less when compared to developed county in the world. The Planning Commission made a survey for finding out the number of persons below poverty line and estimated that 18.96% of the total peoples live below poverty line as of the year 1993-94. It is necessary to take care about poor and illiteracy.

Ethics

Ethics is a major branch of philosophy, encompasses right conduct and good life. It is significantly broader than the common conception of analysing right and wrong. A central aspect of ethics is "the good life", the life worth living or life that is satisfying, which is held by many philosophers to be more important than moral conduct. The major problem is the discovery of the *summum bonum,* the greatest good.

Ethics are related to institutions and rights. The Universal Declaration of Human Rights and human rights accordingly stem from ethics even if no moral grounds can be adduced. Yet moral grounds are to be found everywhere, including science. From the point where, in the name of ethics, science itself does not fall outside this domain, morals, similarly, do not lie outside the realm of ethics as ethics are a profoundly human, secular construction in so far as they represent a conscious choice or plan and a legal endeavour in terms of the law. The confusion that exists between rights and values on the one hand and between morals and ethics on the other lie at the heart of the debate on universal ethics, that is to say, universal ethics based on recognition of human rights.

Morals are linked to the very definition of ethics. Moral principles are extremely diverse. As it happens, morals, historically speaking, have come to be increasingly connected with religion as human society has developed. Therefore, the moral debate has also become a religious one and, as many religious phenomena do not lie beyond the scope of laws, between majorities and minorities, nor the ideological choices involved, it may be difficult to find the same moral values for all societies. Moral values are very diverse. A number of values are universal.

In generally, values may be classified as:

- Personal Values
- Social Values
- Moral Values
- Spiritual Values, and
- Behavioural values.

All these values are necessary for all types of persons in the society.

Why Ethics?

To enable young people to appreciate themselves and others, and to take greater responsibility for their actions and for the world around them.

Ethics and Economics

There are three ways in which ethics enters economics. First, economists have ethical values that help shape the way they do economics. This builds into the core of economic theory a particular view of how the economy does work and how it should work. Second, economic actors (consumers, workers, business owners) have ethical values that help shape their behaviour. Third, economic institutions and policies impact people differentially and thus ethical evaluations, in addition to economic evaluations, are important.

Economists have Ethical Values

The issue of ethical value judgments in economics is at least as old as the John Neville Keynes argument which divided economics into three areas: positive (economic theory), normative (welfare economics), and practical (economic policy). The first deals with 'what is', the second with 'what ought to be', and the third with how to get from one to the other. Although the majority of economists admit that ethical values permeate welfare economics and economic policy, they proceed with some confidence in the belief that their work in pure and applied economic theory is ethically neutral. Methodologists studying the question are more cautious.

Ethics in the relationship between developed and less developed countries dictates that the developed countries treat the less developed countries fairly, aware of their disadvantaged economic position, and acknowledging that taking advantage of one's own economic power inevitably will hurt the poor with indeveloping countries.

What is Unethical?

- Economic institutions, rules, practices which disadvantage the poor will be viewed as unethical
- Ethical behavior requires "progressivity": the poor should benefit disproportionately
- Hypocritical behaviour viewed as unethical
- Advisers who are not "fully honest" viewed as unethical

Ethics and Globalisation

The world has been utterly transformed in recent years by a phenomenon affecting us all, what we call globalisation. Although there was a time when it was possible for citizens of one country to think of themselves as owing no obligation to the people of other nations, admittedly that was long ago. Today national borders have less meaning as issues of trade, environment, and health, along with incredible technological advances of the last century, have left us with a legacy of connectedness we cannot ignore.

We know globalisation involves complete economic liberalisation, *i.e.*, opening doors to big businesses. Multinational corporations are at the forefront. Globalisation wants the governments around the world to create an environment that is as conducive as possible to its growth of business. Regional groupings like APEC, GATT and WTO are totally committed to the same goal. The connection between big businesses, governments and regional and international institutions to create an environment for globalisation is not an accident. It has historic roots in colonisation, and as such, the dominant forces behind globalisation are based in the developed world. Nonetheless, it would be wrong to describe globalisation today as a replica of the Western colonial experience only. This is because one of the centres of power is based in Japan. Other centres of control in Northeast and Southeast Asia are emerging.

In reflecting on the good and bad sides of globalisation we find that whatever good has come out of it is actually a by-product. The very motive, maximising profit is responsible for its bad sides. So, globalisation may well be one of the most serious challenges ever to the integrity of human civilisation. Since society and culture hold some positive aspects it is important that it is not completely rejected. Ethics and moral standards should be injected into some economic activities as a short-term and medium-term strategy. The market should be regulated by ethical principles. The challenge is to devise ethical economically-sound policies built into the globalisation process that are in keeping with values. I mean, the economic dimensions of globalisation are not the only factors that need reconsidering. Culture should be guided by moral universal values whereby a strong ethic of restraint is within one culture is applied to prevent the dominance of another culture. The internationalisation of the ethical values within the consciousness of the individual and the community could be the only hope for humanity. It is almost impossible to effectively censor all information through the Internet, satellite, etc. The individual who derives his/her value-system should be guided by time-honoured principles of what is right and wrong. Such individuals are the real antidotes to the bad effects of globalisation.

Positive Aspects of Globalisation

- Foreign Direct Investment (FDI) has helped to reduce poverty by creating jobs and improving incomes.
- The expansion of trade and foreign investment has accelerated social mobility and strengthened the middle class.
- New communications and information technology have helped disseminate knowledge in many fields of study and disciplines.
- Communication is cheaper and easier. Costs of telephone calls as well as travel have fallen. This makes it easier to understand one another. Communities although heterogeneous, can be more cooperative now that are more means of understanding each other.
- Globalisation makes it possible for humanity to have compassion for each other when calamities, natural or man-made, affect others.
- Issues such as human rights and public accountability are brought to the fore.
- The rights of women are highlighted and the problems many women face are now addressed.

Negative Aspects of Globalisation

- Environmental degradation due to unrestrained activities of multinational corporations whose sole aim is to multiply profits.
- Although poverty has been reduced to a certain extent, new economic disparities have been created. There are stark regional disparities in poverty.

- Basic necessities in life are set aside in favour of profits. Many developing countries have been occupied with facilitating foreign investment in industries that are lucrative to foreign markets and discarding the most fundamental needs of the people.
- Globalisation aids the removal of national controls over cross-border financial flows. Dramatic outflows of capital from one country to another have caused havoc in some currencies, particularly in Southeast, and South Asia including Bangladesh.
- Advances in technology aggravated by the outflow of capital to low cost production sites in the developing countries has caused growing unemployment in the developed countries, which is an cause offence to human dignity.
- Globalisation has popularized the consumer culture. Consumerism has given birth to materialism where people are more interested in what they have rather than the essential aspects of humanity.
- Global consumerism is now forming a homogeneous global culture where rich indigenous cultures of many developing countries are being replaced by cultures with vibrant economies.
- Formal education systems are emphasizing technical and managerial skills responding to market demands and leaving aside traditional academic subjects. This means that education is nothing more than acquiring specific skills and techniques to do business and less emphasis on development of social or basic sciences.
- Although the IT boom has given rise to an expanse of information there is a lot of information that is useless and meaningless causing people to be pre-occupied with unimportant things.
- Double standards are present in the human rights aspect of the present world where they are used as part of many governments' policy but only when it suits them.

Because of globalisation we have some advantages and disadvantages. We are human beings. Take good things and leave bad things. The policies of some developed countries are not good for developing countries. The ethical value decreases day by day. The business person gives more important for profit only. Organisational ethics is very important.

Centre for Globalization

The Yale Center for the Study of Globalisation uses a variety of means to explore globalization and promote the flow of ideas pertinent to our core issues. The activities organised by the YCSG are designed to interconnect in ways that will further the Center's mission and enable us to achieve our goals. It is necessary to establish this type of centre in our university also. In the modern generation also computer literacy is very low in our community. It is very sad thing that our students have no interest to learn computer education. It is very necessary in the scientific and technological world.

Inculcation Ethics though Education

Value education means inculcating in the children a sense of humanism, a deep concern for the well being of others and the nation. This can be accomplished only when we instill in the children a deep feeling of commitment to values that would build this country and bring back to the people pride in work that brings order, security and assured progress.

Value education has the capacity to transform a diseased mind into a very young, fresh, healthy, natural and attentive mind. The transformed mind is capable of higher sensitivity and a heightened level of perception this leads to fulfillment of the evolutionary role in man and in life.

By saying autobiography of good persons like Gandiji, Vivekananda, Ramakrishna Paramahamsa, Ramananda, Tagore and Sathya Sai Baba; we can easily inculcate values in the students and in the people.

Thinking with love is truth
Feeling with love is peace
Acting with love is right conduct
Understanding with love is non-violence

—Sathya Sai

According the Sathya Sai Baba the following five values are necessary for students:

- Right Conduct
- Peace
- Truth
- Love
- Non-Violence

Gandhi's Values

In order to create new social order Gandhiji introduced Nai Talim in the year 1937, which is popularly known as Basic Education.

11. Truth
12. Non-violence
13. Freedom
14. Democracy
15. Sarva Dharma Samabhava
16. Equality
17. Self-realisation
18. Purity of ends and means
19. Self-discipline
20. Suddhi

If there is no place for values education in the curriculum, we can inculcate values through other subjects like Social Sciences and Technology. Learning takes place through lesson plans based on practical, meaningful and fun activities using the five *components* of:

- **Stories** — about life, identity and relationships;
- **Quotations, poems and prayers**;
- **Songs and music**;
- **Silent sitting** - exercises leading to inner calm and peace;
- **Activities** *e.g.* drama, discussion, games, role play, community service, etc.

Conclusions

Swamy Vivekananda said *"We want that education by which character is formed, strength of mind is increased, the intellect is expanded, and by which one can stand on one's own feet"*. It is true. It is our Government duty to give such type of education for each and every student in the country. Through education only we can solve all types of problems. Through education it is easy to motivate people about Ethical value and Moral values and human rights. Education gives knowledge, strength and creativity. India is a fourth largest economy in the world. The youth population is also very high. By proper using of science and technology and human and natural resources India will become developed country in the world.

> *We must protect the forests for our children, grandchildren and children yet to be born. We must protect the forests for those who can't speak for themselves such as the birds, animals, fish and trees.*

REFERENCES

1. Amrtya Sen. '*On Ethics and Economics*'.
2. Peter Singer. '*One World—The Ethics of Globalisation*', 2004.
3. *Value Education in India*, Usha Rai Negi, Editor, Published by Association of Indian Universities, AIU House, 16 Kotla Marg, New Delhi – 110 002, 2000.
4. *Value Education*, Dr. Venkataiah, Editor, APH Publishing Corporation, 5, Ansari Road, Daryaganj, New Delhi – 110 002, First Edition, 1998.

CHAPTER 14

Inculcation of Human Values Through Education

—Dr. Naraginti Amareswaran
—Dr. C. Manchala
—Dr. C. B. Ramchandra Reddy

Introduction

"If human values take root in the educational system, the emerging individuals will have the following attributes:

They will want peace and justice in a world that acknowledges the rule of law and in which no nation or individual need live in fear;

Freedom and self reliance to be available to all;

The dignity and work of every person to be recognised and safeguarded;

All people to be given an opportunity to achieve their best in life; and

They will seek equality before the law and the equality of opportunity for all".

—Sathya Sai

Now we are living in the Modern, Scientific and Technological world. Science and Technology have brought enormous changes in the society. The attitudes of the people are also changes in the day to day life of human beings.

Man is a unique creation in this universe that under certain parameters is free to make his own destiny. Now, if man has to make his destiny, the question of values in life comes up. He has to think naturally as to what should be the guiding norms of life process. It is therefore clear that the guiding factors for man, which provide the prime motivating force behind his thought, emotion and action, have to be moral and spiritual. The socio-cultural and spiritual life of man has to bring peace, progress and welfare for both the individual and the society. This is precisely the reason why the modern society is worried about the deterioration of values.

Having diagnosed the present problem, we have to find the remedy for this situation before there is further deterioration of values in the wider interest of the mankind. With the help of Science (Exhibitions) and Technology (Print and Electronic Media and Mass Media) including social awareness programmes we can inculcate the values in the people.

Importance of Values

In today's multi-cultural and multi-racial society, with its changing social norms and expectations, it can be difficult for a young person to know what is right. To enable young people to appreciate themselves and others, and to take greater responsibility for their actions and for the world around them. Sri Sugunendra Tirtha Swamiji of Puthige Math has said that it is necessary to give importance to human values in the present era of globalisation.

Classification of Values

In generally, values may be classified as:

- Personal Values
- Social Values
- Moral Values
- Spiritual Values, and
- Behavioural values

All these values are necessary for all types of persons in the society.

Inculcation of Values through Education

Thinking with love is truth
Feeling with love is peace
Acting with love is right conduct
Understanding with love is non-violence

—*Sathya Sai*

According the Sathya Sai Baba the following five values are necessary for students:

- Right Conduct
- Peace
- Truth
- Love
- Non-Violence

These values are specific because they are in line with a human being's make up. They are also heavily interrelated (*e.g.* right conduct is action with love and according to conscience).These five values are inter-related and inherent in human beings, raising them above the level of the animal kingdom.

Right Conduct

Information is received through the five senses i.e. smell, taste sight, touch and hearing. When this information is referred to the conscience, the resulting action will be beneficial. Every action is preceded by thought. If the thought is consciously seen and noted, aims to help and is unselfish, the action will be good for oneself and others. If our mind is busy, or we are daydreaming, the action may be useless, clumsy or harmful to ourselves or others.

Right conduct is also concerned with how we look after and use our bodies. The body needs to careful maintenance to be strong, healthy and well co-coordinated to serve us in performing the tasks of life. Students need to understand the importance of exercise, such as gymnastics, yoga and sports combined with good rest. Good thoughts and good company (which includes everything imbibed by the five senses) are essential for healthy and well balanced development. Right conduct is taught through: Silent Sitting, Story telling and Group Activities.

Values Relate to Right Conduct

Self-help Skills

- Care of Possessions

- Diet
- Hygiene
- Modesty
- Posture
- Self-reliance
- Tidy appearance

Social Skills

- Good behaviour
- Good manners
- Good relationships
- Helpfulness
- Not wasting

Ethical Skills

- Code of conduct
- Courage
- Dependability
- Duty
- Efficiency
- Ingenuity
- Initiative
- Perseverance
- Punctuality
- Resourcefulness
- Respect for all
- Responsibility

Peace

We smile when we are happy and contented. Contentment is gained when we cease to want for us all the apparent 'good' things conveyed to us through our five senses. When our willpower is sufficiently strong to enable us to discern the difference between real needs and superfluous desires, we cease to be driven by the urge to own more and more things.

Inner agitation stops and we are left feeling peaceful. When there is peace in the individual, there will be peace in the family. When there is peace in the family, there will be peace in the community. In order to learn, self-esteem, calmness and freedom from anxiety are necessary.

These qualities are fostered by two of the Programmes components, namely silent sitting and the self-reflective exercises in some of the group activity sessions.

Values Related to Peace

- Attention
- Calm
- Concentration
- Contentment
- Dignity
- Discipline
- Equality
- Equanimity
- Faithfulness
- Focus
- Gratitude
- Happiness
- Harmony
- Humility
- Inner silence
- Optimism
- Reflection
- Satisfaction

- self-acceptance
- Self-confidence
- Self-control
- Self-discipline
- Self-esteem
- Self-respect
- Sense control
- Surrender
- Understanding
- Virtue

Truth

The desire to know truth has prompted mankind to ask some of the great questions such as: Who am I? What is the purpose of life? How can I know my inner self/ God/ the Creator of the universe? How can I live fully in the present moment?

Learning to speak the truth is a first and vital step in the formation of a strong character. Voicing an untruth is an anti-social act and causes confusion in the mind of both the speaker and listener and leads to anti-social behaviour. Telling lies hurts us as well as others in a subtle, but very real way.

One great distinction between humankind and the rest of the animal kingdom is the ability to choose how to behave, rather than just to follow the lower instincts (the law of the jungle). A human being is also able to recognise past, present and future and to take note of changes occurring over time.

A quotation used in the lesson to stimulate thought and questions may later come to mind to provide guidance and choice in a life situation. Short Term Pain for Long Term Gain: Choosing to refer to this higher level of awareness and to consciously exercise moderation in our behaviour leads to better health and greater contentment. The value of truth can also be taught through story telling which promotes curiosity, optimism, fairness to all and noble ideals. It also aids the understanding of the value of honest speech and self-analysis.

Values Related to Truth

- Accuracy
- Curiosity
- Discernment
- Fairness
- Fearlessness
- Honesty
- Integrity
- Intuition
- Justice
- Optimism
- Purity
- Quest for knowledge
- Reason
- Self Analysis
- Self Awareness
- Sincerity
- Spirit of enquiry
- Synthesis
- Trust
- Truthfulness
- Determination
- Unity of thought
- Word and deed

Love

Love is not an emotion, affected by the sub-conscious mind, but is a spontaneous, pure reaction from the heart.

It is the power of love which causes one person to wish happiness for another and take pleasure in their well-being. A beneficial energy (love) is directed towards the other person. As this energy flows through our own body first, it also enhances our own health.

It is the power of love which causes one person to wish happiness for another and take pleasure in their well-being. A beneficial energy (love) is directed towards the other person. As this energy flows through our own body first, it also enhances our own health. Love is unconditional, positive regard for the good of another. It is giving and unselfish. Love is essential if children are to grow up healthy in mind and body. Love is the unseen undercurrent binding all the four values.

When the mind is turned away from selfishness, the 'heart' opens, and love flows. Love is energy, not an emotion, and is inherent in every breath. It is the motive force of the physical body and is enhanced through breathing exercises. The component of group singing in the Programme promotes harmony, co-operation and joyfulness. In singing a child may experience the sweetness of love. Love may also be fostered through story telling and activities which provide young people with the opportunity to care for other people, animals, plants and objects.

Values Related to Love

- Acceptance
- Affection
- Care
- Compassions
- Consideration
- Dedication
- Devotion
- Empathy
- Forgiveness
- Friendship
- Generosity

- Gentleness
- Humanness
- Interdependence
- Kindness
- Patience
- Patriotism
- Reverence
- Sacrifice
- Selflessness
- Service sharing
- Sympathy
- Thoughtfulness
- Tolerance
- Trust

Non-Violence

For the non-violent person, the whole world is his family When the former four values are practiced (*i.e.* the conscious mind is keenly aware, love is flowing, there is peace and actions are right) life is lived without harming or violating anything else. It is the highest achievement of human living encompassing respect for all life -living in harmony with nature, not hurting by thought, word or deed.

Non-violence can be described as universal love. When truth is glimpsed through intuition, love is activated. Love is giving, rather than grasping and in allowing our stream of desires to subside, inner peace develops and right conduct is practiced. This results in nonviolence *i.e.* the non-violation of the natural laws which create harmony with the environment.

Non-violence is taught through quotations, story telling and group activities. True knowledge is that which establishes harmony and synthesis between science on the one hand and spirituality and ethics on the other.

Values Related to Non-Violence

Psychological

- Benevolence
- Compassion
- Concern for others
- Consideration
- Forbearance
- Forgiveness
- Good Manners
- Happiness
- Loyalty
- Morality
- Universal Love

Social

- Appreciation of other cultures and religions
- Bother/Sisterhood
- Care of Environment
- Citizenship
- Equality
- Harmlessness
- National Awareness
- Perseverance
- Respect for Property
- Social Justice

Spiritual knowledge is also very importance for students and people in the society. Living in a way which causes as little harm as possible to oneself, other people, animals, plants and the planet, is a sign of a well-integrated, well-balanced personality. Such a person is well tuned to the spiritual aspect of humanity and is in touch with an inner happiness which is permanent and part of one's real nature.

It is through our universal or spiritual aspect that we may experience:

- A feeling of awe and wonder for the universe
- A feeling of the unity of all
- The desire to improve the quality of life for everyone
- A sense of being part of a larger whole
- A feeling of oneness of the planet and love for everything on it
- An awareness of an underlying order to Creation
- Love and respect for the diversity of the human family

Learning takes place through lesson plans based on practical, meaningful and fun activities using the five *components* of:

- **Stories** — about life, identity and relationships;
- **Quotations, poems and prayers**;
- **Songs and music**;
- **Silent sitting** — exercises leading to inner calm and peace;
- **Activities** *e.g.* drama, discussion, games, role play, community service, etc.

In working through the lessons that comprise these components, the importance of the triple partnership (Student, Teacher and Parents) for education becomes apparent:

- Teachers will inspire children in their schools, if they are value conscious adults;
- Parents' example affects the conduct of their children; and
- Children when reaching a certain age need self-discipline to balance their generally natural exuberance.

Conclusion

According to our Indian tradition and culture teacher is the third God. He has a pivotal role in the process of teaching and learning. He is a guide, philosopher, mother, father, god, architecture and model. Education is the solution for all types of problems. With the help of education we can solve any types of problems in the society. Through education it is easy to inculcate values in the students and in the people. Without human values we can't survive in the world in the peaceful manner and we can't enjoy life. So give importance for human values.

REFERENCES

1. *National Institute of Child Health and Human Development.* (2000). The National Reading Panel: Reports of the Subgroups.
2. *Value Education in India,* 2000 Usha Rai Negi, Editor, Published by Association of Indian Universities, AIU House, 16 Kotla Marg, New Delhi-110002.
3. *Value Education*, Dr. Venkataiah, Editor, APH Publishing Corporation, 5, Ansari Road, Daryaganji, New Delhi – 110 002, First Edition, 1998.
4. www.sathyasaieh v.org.uk.

CHAPTER 15

Inculcation of Organisational Ethics in Management Students Through Education

–Dr. Naraginti Amareswaran
– B. Ramchandra Reddy
–Dr. C. Manchala

If you want to build a ship, then don't drum up men to gather wood, give orders, and divide the work. Rather, teach them to yearn for the far and endless sea.

—Antoine de Saint-Exupery

Introduction

India is a developing country. We have thousands of years of tradition and culture. 'Unity in diversity' is the greatness of Indian culture. According to the latest World Developing Report of World Bank, Indian Economy is the fourth largest economy in the world. The *population* of India is *1,129,866,154* (July 2007 est.). The *literacy* of India is 61%. (73% male and 48% female literacy) according to 2000 report. *Adult literacy* rate is *61.3%* for the age group 15 years and above. *Youth literacy* rate is *76.4%* (2000-2004) for the age group 15-24 years. There are *268.42 million illiterates* in India (2000). The *unemployment* rate in India is *10.1%* out of the total population (2004).

The Planning Commission made a survey for finding out the number of persons *below poverty line* and estimated that *18.96%* of the total peoples live below poverty line as of the year 1993-94. It is necessary to take care about poverty and illiteracy. By minimising poverty ratio and increasing literacy ratio, we will reach the developed country position in the future. Because of globalisation it is easy for government to do these things with the help of corporate companies. Today they are participating seriously in social service activities. We have largest youth population in the world. It is necessary to take care about them. Then only they will become good citizens in the future.

Organisational Ethics

Organizational ethics is a tool that shapes an organisation as a community. In every organisation, there is something that works well, which can serve as a foundation for significant progress toward a desired future. Organisational ethics pays special attention to the best of an organisation's past and present to ignite its collective imagination of what might be. It builds from what is working well now toward where the organization and its stakeholders truly desire to go. Organisational ethics sees an organisation as a community to be valued and explored. It strives to quicken and intensify existing individual capabilities and organisational capacities, extend their number and scope, organise them so that their conflicts will be harmonised, and mobilise their energies of will and intellect to bring them to self-realisation. Organisational integrity is the end sought. It is a dynamic state of being and process; it both shapes and improves. It is about moving the organisation toward its guiding image of the future.

Organisational ethics is one of the most important, yet perhaps one of the most overlooked and misunderstood concepts in corporate America and schools of business. Organisational ethics initiatives have not been effectively implemented by many corporations, and there is still much debate concerning the usefulness of such initiatives in preventing ethical and legal misconduct. Simultaneously, business schools are attempting to teach courses and/or integrate organisational ethics into their curricula without general agreement about what should be taught, or how it should be taught. Ethics has been termed the study and philosophy of human conduct, with an emphasis on the determination of right and wrong. For managers, ethics in the workplace refers to rules (standards, principles) governing the conduct of organisation members. Most definitions of ethics relate rules to what is right or wrong in specific situations. For present purposes, and in simple terms, organisational ethics refers to generally accepted.

Importance of Organisational Ethics

As the speed of decision making in organisations increases we are becoming more dependent on our values to guide our judgments. Although rules are still important in guiding ethical decision making, they can also be a burden to developing timely and innovative responses.

On the other hand organisations have seldom had greater exposure to ethical risk. Contemporary organisations, and the products and services they produce are more complex and more likely to have unforeseen consequences in production, delivery, and consumption. When mistakes happen in an increasingly interdependent world the repercussions can be far reaching. Whether the issue is employee, consumer, or public safety, or fairness in the way we treat our stakeholders, organisations which are proactive in addressing ethical concerns are much better positioned to deal with problems once they arise. The benefits of being proactive are enormous: improvements in organisational reputation, stakeholder good will, employee recruitment and retention, organisational effectiveness, and cost savings associated with minimising ethical mistakes.

Organizational ethics is important in developing ethical leadership. An individual's personal values and moral philosophies are but one factor in decision-making processes involving potential legal and ethical problems. True, moral rules can be related to a variety of situations in life, and some people do not distinguish everyday ethical issues from those that occur on the job. Of concern, however, is the application of rules in a work environment.

Employees with only limited work experience sometimes find themselves making decisions about product quality, advertising, pricing, hiring practices, and pollution control. The values that they bring to the organization may not provide specific guidelines for these complex decisions, especially when the realities of work objectives, group decision making, and legal issues come into play. Many ethics decisions are close calls. Years of experience in a particular industry may be required to know what is acceptable, and what is not acceptable.

Inculcation of Organisational Ethics in Management Students Through Education

The development of any nation depends mainly on the standards of its educational institutions. Education is the most powerful and effective instrument for inducing radical changes in the behaviour of students. Education is a powerful instrument of national development-social, economic and cultural. The teacher occupies pivotal position in the system of education. Teaching has been one of the oldest and most respected professions in the world.

Education is the process of instruction aimed at the all round development of boys and girls. Education dispels ignorance. It is the only wealth that cannot be robbed. Learning includes the moral values and the improvement of character and the methods to increase the strength of mind.

In this era of global economy, education has emerged as significant important factor of economic development. The general opinion is that countries at which invest more on education will have higher growth rates of national economy since educated people may provide more productivities. Therefore, many people tend to seek sophisticated and excellent education in order to obtain technically competent. However, the current concern is that the ethical behaviour of business has become a major issue in the workplace. The major reason of this concern is that some educated people have deficient in understanding their responsibilities in managing a company and interacting in society. The illustrations of this include political and business scandals, sexual harassment. It is necessary to overcome these things. With the help of moral and ethical education, it is possible to change the behaviour of the management students (any type of students).

We know *'today's children are tomorrow's citizens'*. In the same manner today's management students are tomorrow's managers, executive officers, policy makers and professors. By inculcating organizational ethics through education, the management students will become good citizens in the future. Then, India will become developed county in the world. Value and Ethics oriented education is necessary for management students. It is better if there is any separate ethics subject in the curriculum.

The six ethical decision-making steps are as follows: Issue clarification, Stakeholder analysis, Values identification, Issue resolution, Addressing objections, and Resolution implementation. Social responsibility is critical for organisation's to succeed ethically and to be seen as good corporate citizens.

The organisational ethics programmes are recommended by:

- The World Bank
- The Organisation for Economic Cooperation and Development
- The U. S. Federal Sentencing Guidelines
- The Public Service of Canada's Modern Management Programme

Excellent ethics programmes contain the following characteristics in one form or another:

- Goals clear and linked to a realistic time-frame.
- Finances, other indicators of support
- Well-planned design, with ethics in mind
- Relevance for employees' work, linking the desired goals to the work
- Ethical programme consistency and accountability
- Measurable outcomes with documentation

Through Organisational Ethics education it is easy to give answers to the following questions:

1. How to design a comprehensive and successful ethics programme tailored to your organisational environment?
2. How to avoid common pitfalls in designing and sustaining ethics programmes?
3. How to measure programme effectiveness and conduct social audits?
4. How leaders and managers can shape and sustain organisational ethical culture?

5. How to recognise ethical problems and apply situation specific ethical decision making tools to resolve such problems?
6. How to develop customised ethical awareness sessions for employees, managers and different communities of practice?
7. How to align the organisation with ethical initiatives?
8. How to identify and reduce ethical risks?
9. What are the sources and differences in personal, cultural, and organisational ethical values?
10. What employees value and why some ethics programmes are counterproductive?

Stages of Moral Development

Stages of Moral Development have been proposed by Lawrence Kohlberg. Kohlberg contended that different people make different decisions when confronted with similar ethical situations because they are at different stages of what he termed cognitive moral development (Kohlberg 1969). He believed that people progress through the following three stages:

- The pre-conventional stage of moral development, in which individuals focus on their own needs and desires.
- The conventional stage of moral development, in which individuals focus on group-centered values and conforming to expectations.
- The principled stage of moral development, in which individuals are concerned with upholding the basic rights, values, and rules of society.

Conclusion

There is no universal agreement on the correct moral philosophy to use in resolving ethical and legal issues in the workplace. Moreover, research suggests that employees may apply different moral philosophies in different decision situations (Fraedrich and Ferrell 1992). And, depending on the situation, people may even change their value structure or moral philosophy when making decisions.

Individuals make decisions under pressure and may later feel their decisions were less than acceptable, but they may not be able to change the consequences of their decisions.

Education is a solution for all types of problems in the society. Through education it is easy to motivate any type of person in the society. By inculcating organisational ethics in the curriculum of management students, we can get a lot of change in the behaviour of the management students in the society. Write valuable quotations in the campus of companies and colleges.

REFERENCES

- Charlotte McDaniel(2004), '*Organisational Ethics—Research and Ethical Environment*' Ashgate Publishing Ltd.
- *Economic Survey 2004-05*, Economic Division, Ministry of Finance, Government of India, quoting UNDP Human Development Report 2004.
- *National Institute of Child Health and Human Development* (2000). The National Reading Panel: Reports of the Subgroups.
- Robert Allen Peterson, O. C. Ferrell, '*Business Ethics: New Challenges for Business Schools and Corporate Leaders*".
- UNESCO *Institute for Statistics: Literacy rates, youth (15-24) and adult (15+) by Region and Gender* (September 2006 Assessment).

CHAPTER 16

Pioneering Institutions in Adult Eudcation—Aicmed, AMS, IAEA, Literacy Hous, RDT, Sevamandir

– Dr. K. Sudha Rani
– Dr. Naraginti Amareswaran

'Literacy Education is of no values, if it is not build up a Sound Character'
—M.K.Gandhi

Introduction

The contribution of the human factor towards progress both in the urban and rural areas, can't be over emphasised, more so in a world of ever-changing social systems and values. Such an endless task – like the development of educational activities for innumerable farmers and workers, illiterate and semi-illiterate adults, men and women, boys and girls—needs a deep involvement of all national forces, government and non-governmental. From even before 1947, voluntary organisations have been playing a significant role in the reconstruction of education and their success has been in no small measure owing to the dedication of social workers and the larger academic and administrative freedom they enjoy to conduct new experiments.

Voluntary organisations are initiating and developing activities and programmes which can be considered to be of relevance to adult education directly or indirectly. This trend needs to be encouraged and supported. Many of them are closely linking their out-of school activities or programmes of social education with other socio-economic or socio-cultural goals which are part of their objectives.

The contribution of voluntary organisations in general has been encouraging, promising and stimulating. It is fervently hoped, that voluntary organisations, both from their headquarters and in the field will expand their interest for adult and youth education, as well as channelise their efforts to common national goals.

The contribution of the following six voluntary agencies to the development of adult education, non-formal education is briefly described.

1. All India Council for Mass Education and Development (AICMED), West Bengal.
2. Andhra Mahila Sabha (AMS), Hyderabad.
3. Indian Adult Education Association (IAEA), New Delhi.
4. Literacy House, Lucknow
5. RDT, Anatapur.

   Sevamandir, Udaipur.

ALL INDIA COUNCIL FOR MASS EDUCATION AND DEVELOPMENT (AICMED), WEST BENGAL

Introduction

All India Council for Mass Education and Development (AICMED), established in 1987 (Regn. No. S/56626 1987-88) is a voluntar non-profiteering registered organisation. It is also covered by Foreign Contribution Regulation Act (FCRA) of the Government of India (Regn. No. 147120474).

It had its genesis in the formation, in 1965, of the West Bengal Students' Council to Eradicate Illiteracy, which was the culmination of large-scale mobilisation of students and youth from the colleges and universities of Calcutta to the villages of West Bengal to launch a mass literacy campaign. The vision of the organisation is to develop an enlightened, empowered and self-sustained rural community—both materially and morally. The mission of AICMED is 'enlightenment' and 'empowerment', particularly of the poor and the underprivileged, with special emphasis on women and the tribal people.

Aims and Objectives

- To encourage and develop adult education programme as a part of the development programme.

- To encourage and promote voluntary actions in the rural areas in favour of rural development and introduction of advanced technology.
- To organise workshop and prepare teaching and learning materials for various programmes.
- To orient adult education functionaries and development activists of different levels so that they can undertake adult education and developmental programmes independently.
- To undertake research and promotional work to develop and sharpen existing technologies and methodologies of rural development. The structure of the organisation provides opportunities to involve people of different kinds drawn from a wide spectrum of the society.

Activities

In the course of implementing National Adult Education Programme, AICMED has developed people's organisation in 13 of the 17 districts of West Bengal and elsewhere. However, presently it has concentrated activities in several districts of West Bengal, Andhra Pradesh, Jharkhand, Orissa and Tripura in other rural development programmes.

AICMED conducts projects, holds seminars & camps, organises exhibitions, runs awareness and training programmes, and such other activities lead to the empowerment of the poor and the underprivileged of our society.

It has successfully completed, and has been continuing, the projects in the following domains in West Bengal and Tripura.

- **Mass Education Programmes:** Adult Education, women's education, early childhood education and non-formal education.
- **Gender and Health Programmes:** Health and Family Welfare especially mother and child health, Family Planning, awareness and different aspects of women's/men's awareness.
- **Livelihood Generation Programmes:** Training in modern fishery activities, poultry farming, piggery, weaving etc. especially among the rural people.

- **Environment Programme:** Safe drinking water, use of eco-friendly organic fertilisers, smoke-less chulhas etc. among villagers.
- **Herbal Programmes:** Capacity building workshops on Herbotherapy, kitchen-gardening of relevant herbs, cottage-scale preparation of herbal products (like spices, pickles, jam), preservation, containerisation and micro-marketing of the products.
- **Arsenic Programmes:** Mass awareness generation and mitigation of arsenic pollution through community participation in forty villages of two districts of West Bengal. The mitigation devices include Arsenic Removal Plants, Rainwater Harvesting Units and Domestic Filters.
- **Other Programmes:** AICMED, through its central resource centre in Calcutta (which houses a modest library of relevant books, documents, pamphlets, handbills etc.) continually disseminates useful information among potential users.

ANDHRA MAHILA SABHA (AMS), HYDERABAD

Introduction

Andhra Mahila Sabha, a unique institution dedicated to the up-liftment of women, was established by Padma Vibhushan Dr.(Smt) Durgabai Deshmukh in 1948 as a registered society under Indian Societies Act (XXI) of 1860 and a Trust in the same year. With its Central Office located in Hyderabad, Andhra Mahila Sabha has 30 units working under its flag – 9 of them in Chennai and rest in the State of Andhra Pradesh. The institutions run by Andhra Mahila Sabha cater to care of Women, Children, Senior Citizens, Disabled, Health and Education.

Aims and Objectives

Andhra Mahila Sabha is a non-profitable voluntary organisation with the specific objective of promoting education and training of women to overcome their socio-economic and political backwardness and empower them to participate in all aspects of national development. It has also established a regional handicraft training institute for the women. AMS runs a hospital and research centre providing various services including out patient services in eye care, general surgery, orthopaedics and in patient services including neo-natal unit and well equipped air conditioned operation theatres. It also runs a vocational training and rehabilitation centre, girls high school and colleges and legal aid centre for women.

Activities

Andhra Mahila Sabha is the premier Women's organisation in the country, with around 40 units functioning under its logo. These units focus on education, health care, upliftment, empowerment, old age care of the downtrodden of the society, in particular women, causes dear to Dr Durgabai Deshmukh's legendary figure of 20th Century. The major services provided by the various institutions established under this organisation are:

- Education
- Health
- Rehabilitation
- Training
- Women's issues

Education Provides training and education to women and children and enable them to harness their services for building the nation. Dr Durgabai Deshmukh was inspired by the work done by Welthy H Fisher, a Canadian literacy worker at Lucknow, Uttar Pradesh. This led to the establishment of Literacy house at Andhra Mahila Sabha during 1967.

The Progammes/Courses under Andhra Mahila Sabha Literacy House

- Computer Courses
- Fabric Painting
- Glass Painting
- Embroidery
- Tailoring and Maggam work

- Basic Art designers Drawing Grade I and II
- Pre Primary Teacher Training
- Hand Writing
- Speed Mathematics
- Concentration and Memory
- Personality Development

Andhra Mahila Sabha has publications to its credit. AMS, Chennai releases a bi-monthly newsletter. AMS, Hyderabad releases a quarterly newsletter.

- Health Care Outreaches giving free treatment to the needy and dedicated to the rehabilitation and integration of disabled children.
- Upliftment and Empowerment Spreads literacy among women, counsels them on matrimonial and property matters, conducts training for trainers of teachers and teachers and also in various mass media of communication.
- Old Age Care Provides shelter and food at affordable price to the needy senior citizens who desired to live the remaining years of respectably.

INDIAN ADULT EDUCATION ASSOCIATION, NEW DELHI

Introduction

Indian Adult Education Association was established on 2nd Dec. 1939, Under the Indian Societies Registration Act. 1860. With unflinching faith in the effective participation of every citizen in social, economic, religious and political life of the country and consequent there to the imperative need for every citizen to have access to the expanding realms of knowledge through adult and life-long education, IAEA is specially committed to ceaselessly work towards raising the literacy level in its overall bid to safeguard the interests of the illiterates, down-trodden and deprived sections of population so as to enable them to take their rightful place in society.

In the beginning, IAEA's major emphasis was on creation of public opinion for a public policy on adult education, besides mobilising support from government and other public institutions for literacy movement. Today, when adult education has been duly recognised as an essential component of national reconstruction, IAEA functions as a federation of some 500 affiliated organisations spread throughout the length and breadth of the country, supporting their activities by bringing them together in its conferences, seminars, workshops and discussion groups. Through its publications, both periodic and otherwise, IAEA disseminates research findings and field experience on adult/non-formal and life-long continuing education to its more than 2500 'life' and yearly individual members coming from its 16 state branches, and others.

Aims and Objectives

1. Spread knowledge among the people of India on all subjects related to their all-round development, welfare and culture in a popular and attractive manner through suitable agencies.
2. Initiate, wherever necessary, adult education activities in cooperation with various organisations and individuals interested in the work, and to encourage and coordinate local efforts and organisations engaged in promoting the cause of adult education.
3. Serve as a 'Clearing House' for exchange of ideas, information and advice concerning adult education in different States of India.
4. Cooperate with movements aiming at removal of illiteracy and ignorance, and promotion of civic, economic and cultural interests of the people.
5. Serve as a connecting link for inter-State cooperation and coordination among the State Governments and NGOs.
6. Prepare and supply, if necessary, slides, charts, films, booklets, suitable literature, etc., and to undertake publication of bulletins, newsletters and journals. Arrange public lectures, demonstrations, seminars, etc., in furtherance of the objectives of the Association.

7. Organise All India Adult Education Conferences, Zonal, Regional and State level Conferences in furtherance of its objective.
8. Persuade universities, Govt. Depts.; NGOs; colleges and other educational bodies in the country to take up adult education work and to do all other acts that are incidental to fulfillment of the above mentioned aims and objectives of the Association.

Activities

Functions of IAEA are as varied and wide-ranging as its aims and objectives. The following is a brief account of its activities over the years.

As Catalytic Agent

Being a pioneer, promoter, catalyst and leader, IAEA advises Central/State Governments, Universities, State Resource Centres, Jan Shikshan Sansthans, Zilla Saksharta Samitis (ZSSs), its member-institutions and other organisations on adult, non formal and population education programmes.

As 'Clearing House'

IAEA has been functioning as a 'Clearing House' to disseminate information on growth and development of adult education through its periodicals, books, correspondence, etc., for the benefit of individuals and organisations.

Training

IAEA accords high priority to training of adult education functionaries. Since 1948, it has been organising training for adult education functionaries and public opinion leaders. It organises intra-state and inter-state training for key-level functionaries of Government Departments, NGOs, Universities, Colleges and trade union workers in different parts of the country, including the far flung areas.

IAEA also provides hands-on training in computer and information technology to women. The Association is recognised as a Study Centre of Makhanlal Chaturvedi University, Bhopal for DCA and PGDCA courses and Accredited Vocatlional Institute of National Institute of Open Schooling (Previously National Open School). The Association has started Library Science and CCA courses.

Research

IAEA accords high priority to research in adult education to strengthen the programme of adult education. It undertakes surveys and research projects on its own as well as in collaboration with other institutions.

Research Methodology Courses

IAEA also organises Research Methodology Courses for budding researchers in collaboration with Jawaharlal Nehru University, Directorate of Adult Education, Government of India and other agencies. So far 10 courses have been organised by the Association.

Research Fellowship

IAEA instituted Mohan Sinha Mehta Research Fellowship in 1986 in honour of its late President Dr. Mohan Sinha Mehta. This fellowship is awarded every year to individuals to carry out research in the field of Adult Education.

Monitoring and Evaluation

IAEA has, over the years, been engaged in monitoring and evaluation of literacy programmes. Empanelled by the National Literacy Mission for this purpose, IAEA has undertaken external evaluation work of the Total Literacy Campaigns/Post Literacy Programmes in about 22 districts in the country.

Other Activities

Under UNFPA-assisted project on Population Education in Adult Literacy Programme, IAEA houses the National Documentation Centre on Literacy and Population Education (DCLPE). Its activities were given below:

- Publication of quarterly Indian Journal of Population Education containing information on health education, adolescent education and gender issues, family welfare and population education in India

- Bringing out quarterly bibliography/accession list of latest acquisitions on population and population education.
- Publication of bi-monthly Newsletter on Population Education.
- Repackaging and dissemination of information through networking arrangements with various agencies, institutions and persons.
- Acquiring books and periodicals on the subject from national/ international organisations.

IAEA has established an International Institute of Adult and Life Long Education. The mission of the Institute is to professionalise adult education by strengthening and promoting it as a distinct but distinguished field of practice and discipline of study.

LITERACY HOUSE, LUCKNOW

'Literacy is an idea whose time has come. Local, national and international programmes—public and private—are hard at work on one of the most stubborn problems facing mankind—the development of an articulate and informed citizenry in a free society'.

—Welthy Honsinger Fisher

Introduction

Literacy House was founded in 1953 by Dr. Welthy H. Fisher. Mahatma Gandhi, Six weeks before his assassination said, "Cities have every thing. Our villages have nothing. Go and help the villages". This was the first step shown to Mr. W.H. Fisher. She took the first step in 1953 when she started her literacy work for the villages near Alhabad. At the request of the Governor, the literacy House was moved to Lucknow in 1956 and literacy work began on the present campus. Literacy house is the creation of the Ford Foundation. It is situated six miles from the City on the Luknow-Kanpur Road.

Aims and Objectives

- To develop through its programmes of education and training, the techniques of communication with the masses.

- To produce educational materials-books, pamphlets, periodicals and simple audio-visual aids such as flash cards, khaddargraphs, puppets and puppet stages etc. for illiterate and literate adults.
- To produce professional literature for adult education and literacy workers.
- To publish books in Hindi, English and other languages dealing with problems such as those of citizenship, cottage industries, folk literature, health and agriculture.

Activities

Illiteracy is strongly linked to poverty, poor health, disadvantage and exclusion, and education is not an issue that stands in isolation from the many challenges that face the poor. As a result, Literacy House has developed a highly integrated approach to literacy that includes community programs that focus on women's rights, social justice, and healthcare, access to public services, advocacy, and community building.

Adult Literacy Programme

In UP, according to census 2001 survey, the literacy rate in Male are 68.8% and among adult women literacy rates are 42.98% only. In India the overall literacy rate is 64.8 % (Male: 75.3%; Female: 53.7%). Historically, a variety of factors have been found to be responsible for poor female literate rate,*viz* gender based inequality, social discrimination and economic exploitation, occupation of girl child in domestic chores, low enrolment of girls in schools and low retention rate and high drop-out rate.

Children's Education Programme

In India, only 62% of children reach grade 5 and one-third of all children aged 6 to 14 do not attend school. Presently 62 Balwadi Kendras are running either through literacy house directly or rural NGO partners in 9 districts of eastern UP where over 1600 kids are receiving informal education.

Health Awareness Programme

Major Activities of Health Program are: Clinical Support, House Visit, Immunization, Health Awareness Meeting, Pregnant women check up and distribution of Iron / Folic acid tab, Health awareness Camp, Sterilization and distribution of family planning material, Networking for health facilities, Special Cases, Health Staff Training etc.

Health Awareness Meetings

A combined total of 300 Health awareness meeting were held in the period April 2005 to March 2006.

Social Enterprise Programme

The term 'Social Enterprise' implies a linking of business ventures to achieving social good. 'Social enterprise' program consists of assisting poor women in developing new methods of income generation, especially through small business ventures, in order to improve the income and quality of life of their families.

Advocacy Programme

The advocacy programme works to actively engage targeted communities on issues of human rights, women's empowerment, literacy, democratization and good governance. Our goal is to help these people understand the larger issues that affect the quality of their lives, and to enable them to make their voices heard for change.

RDT, ANATAPUR

Introduction

The Rural Development Trust (RDT) is a voluntary organisation working in Anantapur District of Andhra Pradesh, India. Fr. Vincent Ferror was established RDT in the year 1969. Anantapur district is the second most drought prone district in India due to failure of monsoons coupled with untimely and erratic rains and also high wind velocity and extreme heat. The average rainfall in the district is around 520 millimeter per annum, ranging from 120 millimeters in some parts to 650 millimeters in some other parts of the district.

Temperatures normally upto 45 degrees centigrade in summer and wind velocity reaches 50 to 60 kilometers per hour during the wind season. The district lies between 13'-40' and 15'-15' northern latitude and 76'-50' and 78'-30' eastern longitude.

Aim and Objective

The main and fore most aim and objective of RDT is overall rural development in Anatapur Distcit.

Activities

- Rural Development
- Women empowerment
- Child Education
- Health Facility
- Cultural Development
- Old age Homes

SEVA MANDIR

Introduction

Dr Mohan Singh Mehta a social worker and an educationalist, founded Seva Mandir. Udaipur, in the pre-independence period 1900-1947, was witness to an increasing awareness among educationalists and liberal thinkers of the particular backwardness and political stagnation of Rajasthan.This realisation provoked a move to change, and inspired certain individuals, who had imbibed ideas of voluntarism, to seize the initiative. Dr Mehta, not only played a very important role in founding Seva Mandir in 1966, but also was an inspiration to progressive change throughout Udaipur District. He was a true liberal influenced by the thoughts of Tagore, Gandhi, Dr. Kunzru, and Pandit Madan Mohan Malviya and by tenets of the scout movement. In pre-independence time he served as education minister and Prime Minister of Banswara in the State of Mewar and later as an Ambassador of independent India and as Vice Chancellor of Rajasthan University. He set up Vidya Bhavan at Udaipur in 1931, one of the pioneer co-educational institutions, with the philosophy of treating every child as a unique individual and molding them into citizens with sound moral character and a deep sense of social responsibility.

Aims and Objectives

- To create and strengthen institutions for development (at the village, organisation and society levels)
- To enhance people's capabilities for self-development (both at individual and community level); and
- To create sustainable improvements in the livelihoods base;

These three objectives form the basis for Seva Mandir's three program sectors.

Activities

- Natural Resources Regeneration
- Non Farm Income Generation
- Education
- Health
- Women's Empowerment
- Child and Youth Development
- Village Institution
- Building
- People's Management School

Each of these programmes, in achieving its respective goals, is also designed to build values and social capacities needed to achieve development and democracy for the poor.

Note:

- At present there are 165 Balwadi centres in Seva Mandir's work area, reaching out to a total of 3,806 children.
- Today some 9,307 women have managed to amass a total saving of Rs. 6,172,957 at women's groups.

Conclusion

India is a democratic country. We have freedom to do any type of good work. The literacy rate of India very less when compared to any other developed country or developing in the world. The roles of NGOs' are very important to increase literacy rate. They have a prominent role to do all the activities like literacy improvement, empowerment etc. Education in general, Adult Education in particular gives strength to human beings. Educate all the human beings.

REFERENCES

- All India Council for Mass Education and Development (AICMED).
- Annual Reports. Lucknow, India: Literacy House, 1958, 1959, 1960, 1961, 1962, and 1963.
- Anuradha Prasad et.al., (2005): "*Living in Diversity*", External Review.
- Complete Puppet Kit. A leaflet, Ibid. Undated.
- "Eleventh Anniversary of Literacy House," National Herald. New York. February 14, 1964.
- Fisher, Welthy M. *To Light A Candle.* London: Peter Davies, Ltd. 1963.
- Go to Ramon Magsaysay Award Foundation Online.
- Grimes, Paul. "*Literacy Village Near Lucknow Keeps Promise of Aid to Gandhi*," New York Times. April 2, 1961.
- Imprint. Bombay: F & S Distributors Private Ltd. Vol. 3, no. 7, October 1963.
- Koshy, T. A. *Five Year Plan—A Summary*. Lucknow India: Literacy House. November 22, 1960.
- Lederer, William J: and Eugene Burdick. "*Some Non-ugly Americans*," Life International. New York. March 14, 1960.
- Lekhak. Lucknow, India: Literacy House, Vol. 2, no. 2, April 1962; Vol. 3, no. 3, 4, January 1964.
- "*Light for the Illiterate*," Asia Magazine. Hong Kong. December 3, 1961.
- Literacy House, The First Decade. Delhi: Publications Division, Indian Cooperative Union. 1963.
- Messages Received on the 10th Anniversary of the Founding of Literacy House, Lucknow, India. February 15, 1963.
- News Circle. Delhi: American Women's Club. Vol. 4, no. 9, May 1959.
- Shah, M. A. Hyder. "*The Literacy Village in Lucknow*," The Asian Student. San Francisco: Asia Foundation. May 13, 1961.

- Siddiqi, Abdur Rashid. *An Approach to Educating Adults for Functional Literacy in India.* A thesis presented to the Faculty of the Graduate School of Cornell University for the Degree of Master of Science, September 1963.
- *Simple Visual Aids on Development Problems*. Lucknow, India: Literacy House. Undated.
- "*Teaching People to Read and Write,*" Yojana. India. February 19, 1961.
- *Visit to Literacy House and Its Fieldwork in the Villages*. Interviews with persons acquainted with Mrs. Fisher and her work.
- www.andhramahilasabha.com
- www.sevamandir.com

CHAPTER 17

Poverty, Education and Health in India

–Dr. Naraginti Amareswaran
–Dr. N. Koteeswari
–Dr. K. Sudha Rani

Introduction

Poverty is hunger. Poverty is lack of shelter. Poverty is being sick and not being able to see a doctor. Poverty is not having access to school and not knowing how to read. Poverty is not having a job, is fear for the future, living one day at a time. Poverty is losing a child to illness brought about by unclean water. Poverty is powerlessness, lack of representation and freedom. Education and Health are two faces of an Economic Growth coin. Through education it is possible to minimise or eliminate poverty in the society with good health.

Poverty and Its Reduction in India

Poverty eradication has been a key objective of India's development strategy. Both economic growth and the specific target of poverty eradication have been tied together as major development tools (Gupta, 1995). 'Growth with social justice' has been the main strategy of development since the beginning of the 1970s, though in recent years the relative focus tends to shift in favour of growth. 'Balancing of economic growth and social development' has been a difficult challenge. Along with strategies for growth a large number of poverty alleviation programmes have been launched, some of which originated in the 1960s.

According to government estimates, in 2007 there were nearly 220.1 million people living below the poverty line. Nearly 21.1% of the entire rural population and 15% of the urban population of India exists in this difficult physical and financial predicament.

Table 17.1. Poverty Line in India

Year	Poverty Line in India (Rs. per capita per month)	
	Rural	Urban
1973-74	49.63	56.76
1983-84	89.50	115.65
1993-94	205.84	281.35
1999-00	327.56	454.11
2005-06	365.00	580.00

Table 17.2. Incidence of Poverty in India

	Incidence of Poverty in India (Population below poverty line)					
	Rural		Urban		Total	No. of People
	%	No (min)	%	No (min)	%	No (min)
1970-71	57.30	251.70	45.90	50.10	55.10	301.80
1983-84	45.65	251.90	44.79	70.90	44.48	322.89
1987-88	39.10	231.40	40.10	78.70	39.30	310.10
1993-94	32.27	244.03	32.26	76.33	35.97	320.36
1999-00	27.89	193.27	23.62	67.01	26.10	260.25

Source: National Human Development Report 2001 (New Delhi: Government of India, Planning Commission, 2001).

India has made significant progress in reduction in poverty over the years. The percentage of population below the poverty line has declined from 55 per cent in 1970-71 to 26 per cent by 1999-2000. But still 260 million people are estimated to be living below the poverty line—193 million in rural areas and 67 million in urban areas, some of whom may have been living in 'chronic poverty' in 1999-2000. During the 30 year period, *i.e.*, between 1971 and 1999-2000, in absolute numbers the number of people in poverty could be reduced by a meager 40 million. Increase in population has been a big hindrance to several development efforts, including to the poverty alleviation programmes. It is important to note, according to these official estimates, that a substantial decline in the number of poor has happened only between 1993-94 and 1999-2000.

Programmes Launched to Reduce Poverty

- Integrated rural development programmes that include provision of subsidy and bank credit for productive employment opportunities
- Training rural youth for self employment (TRYSEM)
- Development of Women and Children in Rural Areas (DWACRA)
- Supply of Improved Toolkits to Rural Artisans
- Drought Prone Area Programme
- Self employment and Wage employment programmes
- Creation of Rural Infrastructure (roads, etc.,) for employment generation
- Employment assurance schemes,
- Social Security programmes—national social assistance programme—that include old age pension scheme, family and maternity benefit schemes, food and nutrition security, public distribution system etc.
- Land reforms

Health

"If wealth is lost nothing is lost
If health is lost something is lost
If character is lost everything is lost"

—M. K. Gandhi.

Approximately 1.2 billion people in the world live in extreme poverty (less than one dollar per day). Poverty creates ill-health because it forces people to live in environments that make them sick, without decent shelter, clean water or adequate sanitation. The total health expenditure in India for the year 2001-02 was Rs. 1,057,341 million, which accounted for 4.6 per cent of its gross domestic product. As a proportion to total health expenditure, public expenditure constituted 20.3 per cent, private sector expenditure 77.4 and external support 2.3 per cent. Health care provider data reveal that 70 per cent of the financial resources is flowing to health care providers in the for profit private sector. Another 23 per cent of resources is spent on public providers of health care services.

Table 17.3. Per Capita Expenditure on Health in India

Year	Per Capita Expenditure on Health in India(1993-1994 to 2003-2004)	
	Real	
	Health Expenditure (Rs. In Core)	Per Capita Expenditure
1993-1994	7938.36	89
1994-1995	7921.58	87
1995-1996	8521.14	91.82
1996-1997	8876.16	93.83
1997-1998	9772.64	101.38
1998-1999	10884.42	110.73
1999-2000	12068.52	120.56
2000-2001	12078.79	118.54
2001-2002	11795.52	113.75
2002-2003	12790.28	121.23
2003-2004	13091.7	122.01

(**Source:** Planning Commission, Govt. of India)

The Indian Finance Minister said in his Budget 2007-08 speech, all districts to complete preparation of District Health Action Plans by March 2007; major emphasis to be on mother and child care and on prevention and treatment of communicable diseases; convergence sought to be achieved among various programmes such as immunisation, ante natal care, nutrition and sanitation through Monthly Health Days (MHD) organised at Anganwadi centres; 320,000 Associated Social Health Activists (ASHAs) recruited with over 200,000 given orientation training; 90,000 link workers selected by the States; AYUSH systems being mainstreamed into health delivery system at all levels; increase in allocation for NRHM from Rs.8,207 crore to Rs. 9,947 crore.

Education

"Economic development naturally makes growing demands on human resources and in a democratic set-up it calls for values and attitudes in the building up of which the quality of education is an important element" (Government of India, 1956, p. 500).

"Education is the most important single factor in achieving rapid economic development and technological progress ... in all branches of national life education becomes the focal point of planned development" (Government of India, 1961, p. 573).

The State shall endeavour to provide, within a period of ten years from the commencement of this Constitution, for free and compulsory education for all children until they complete the age of fourteen years. (Article- 45).

The role of education in development has been recognised ever since the days of Plato. Education, Plato believed, is indispensable to the economic health of a good society, for education makes citizens 'reasonable men'. Since education has high economic value, Plato argued that a considerable part of the community's wealth must be invested in education. Major contribution to the discussion on the relationship between education and economic growth was made first by Adam Smith, followed by a long honourable tradition of classical and neo-classical economists until Alfred Marshall (1890) who emphasised that "the most valuable of all capital is that invested in human beings". However, "in line with the biased postwar approach it was largely forgotten" (Myrdal, 1968, p. 167), and no systematic study on the contribution of education to economic growth could be found in the literature, until Schultz's (1961) Presidential Address to the American Economic Association in 1960, which created what is later aptly described as "human investment revolution in economic thought" (Bowman, 1966). Schultz's pioneering research followed by a mammoth growth of research in the area of Economics of Education, and the untiring research has clearly established that education is not merely a consumption activity, but for the most part of an investment. It leads to the formation of human capital, comparable to physical capital, making a significant contribution to economic growth.

Synchronising with the human investment revolution in economic thought, many countries around the world, and more particularly the newly independent developing countries expanded their educational systems and made heavy investments in education. The rates of growth of educational systems in many countries exceed the rates of economic growth. This is not surprising, as "during the process of economic modernisation the rate of increase in human capital is higher than that of reproducible physical capital" (Schultz, 1986, p. 5). India stands as an outstanding classic example of massive expansion of educational systems among the third world countries. In the post-independent India, particularly since the inception of the plan era (since 1951), an educational explosion has taken place, which may be described as an "educational miracle". The 'miracle' is particularly important when one examines in the context of the colonial legacy.

The 73rd and the 74th amendments to the Constitution had placed greater role on local bodies on the development of education, among others. Elementary education has been made a fundamental right with the 86th amendment to the Constitution in 2002. Several foreign aided projects have been launched in primary education since the mid-1990s. Some of these efforts, including decentralization, specifically aimed at not only improving the education situation, but also targeted at reducing poverty and empowerment of the poor.

Table 17.4. Growth of Education in India

Year	Primary	Upper Primary	Secondary & Higher Secondary	Higher	
				University	Colleges
Institutions					
1950-51	209,671	13,596	7,416	27	578
1960-61	330,399	49,663	17,329	45	1,819
1970-71	408,378	90,621	37,051	82	3,277
1980-81	494,503	118,555	51,573	101	6,943
1990-91	560,965	151,456	79,796	184	5,748
2000-01*	638,738	206,269	126,047	254	10,152
2002-03*	651,382	245,274	137,207	304	15,000

(Cont...)

Year	Primary	Upper Primary	Secondary & Higher Secondary	Higher University Colleges
Enrolment	*in 10 million*		*in thousands*	
1950-51	1.92	0.31	0.15	174
1960-61	3.50	0.67	0.34	557
1970-71	5.70	1.33	0.76	1956
1980-81	7.38	2.07	1.10	2752
1990-91	9.74	3.40	1.91	4924
2000-01*	11.38	4.28	2.76	8399
2002-03*	12.24	4.69	3.32	9516
Teachers *(in thousands)*				
1950-51	538	86	127	24
1960-61	742	345	296	62
1970-71	1060	638	629	190
1980-81	1363	851	926	244
1990-91	1616	1073	1334	271
2000-01*	1896	1326	1761	350
2001-02*	1928	1488	1777	

* Provisional

Source: Selected Educational Statistics 2001-2002; Annual Report, UGC 2002-03 for enrolment and teachers in higher education.

The above table shows the growth of Education in India from 1950 to 2003.

Major Issues

- 27.5 per cent of Indians live below the national income poverty line
- More than 60 per cent of women are chronically poor, as are 43 per cent of Scheduled Tribes and 36 per cent of Scheduled Caste groups
- More than 90 per cent of the overall workforce is employed in the informal economy; for women, it is even higher, at 96 per cent

Table 17.5. Educational Level in India

S. No.	India/ State	Educational Level	Population		
			Persons	Males	Females
1	India	Total	1,028,610,328	532,156,772	496,453,556
2	India	Illiterate	467,922,531	195,623,056	272,299,475
3	India	Literate	560,687,797	336,533,716	224,154,081
4	India	Literate but below Matric/ secondary	381,798,166	220,614,002	161,184,164
5	India	Matric/secondary but below graduate	117,432,082	76,056,459	41,375,623
6	India	Technical diploma or certificate not equal to degree	3,666,680	2,900,839	765,841
7	India	Graduate and above other than technical degree	32,615,751	21,891,181	10,724,570
8	India	Technical degree or diploma equal to degree or post-graduate degree	5,054,396	3,642,127	1,412,269

Source: Census of India 2001.

- 48.6 per cent of farmer households are in debt, and only 27 per cent access formal credit
- 296 million people are illiterate and 233 million are undernourished, particularly children younger than age 3.
- Educational expenses formed 3% of total consumer expenditure in rural India and 5% in urban India.
- Post-elementary education makes a significant contribution to reduction in absolute as well as relative poverty.
- Medical expenses formed 7% of total consumer expenditure in rural India and 5% in urban India.
- In 2004-05, 5% of the Indian rural population belonged to households with monthly per capita consumer expenditure (MPCE) in the range "Rs. 0-235", that is, spending less than Rs. 8 per person per day on consumption.

- Another 5% of the Indian rural population belonged to households with monthly per capita expenditure in the range "Rs. 235-270", that is, spending about Rs. 8-9 per person per day on consumption.
- Maternal mortality—an indicator not only of the quality of maternal health care services but also of the general level of empowerment of women—stands at 301 per 100,000 live births, compared to a target of 108 per 100,000.

Source: Poverty Estimates for 2004-2005, Government of India, NSS 61st round 2004-05, Government of India, New Delhi.

Poverty, Health, Education and Development

Poverty is a state of deprivation. In absolute terms it reflects the inability of an individual to satisfy certain basic minimum needs for a sustained healthy and a reasonably productive living. The proportion of population not able to attain the specified level of expenditure is then segregated as poor. Poverty is hunger. Poverty is lack of shelter. Poverty is being sick and not being able to see a doctor. Poverty is not being able to school and not knowing how to read.

In India Rao (1964; see also Rao, 1970) and the Education Commission (1966) are first of their kind to have emphasised the links between education and development. Though the earlier research in India and abroad concentrated more on the role of education in economic growth, the impact of education on poverty and well being of the masses was also clearly recognised and of late this began receiving more serious attention in the wider framework of human development.

Available research in the last couple of decades (*e.g.*, Fields, 1980a, 1980b; Tilak, 1978, 1986, 1989a, 1994) clearly shows that education and poverty are inversely related: the higher the level of education of the population, the lower would be the proportion of poor people in the total population, as education imparts knowledge and skills that are associated with higher wages.

Economics of Education is abundant with studies that firmly established the correlation between education and earnings—earnings rising with increase in education levels, not rarely but almost universally and quite steeply and systematically, in case of the general population and also of sub-groups of the population—males, females, rural, urban, socially backward sections, etc. (Psacharopoulos and Tilak, 1992). As Blaug (1972) noted, the universality of this relationship is well recognised beyond doubt.

In addition to this direct effect of education, the effect of education on poverty could be indirect through its fulfillment of basic needs like better utilization of health facilities, shelter, water and sanitation, and its effects on behaviour of women on decisions relating to fertility, family welfare and health etc., (Noor, 1980; Cochrane, 1988; Jeffery and Basu, 1996) which in turn enhance the productivity of the people and yield higher wages, taking them above the poverty line.

The relationship between health and poverty or health and development is complex multifaceted and multidirectional. Poverty in its various dimensions could be a manifestation, as well as a determinant of an individual's health. In its most basic from—as a state of food deprivation and nutritional inadequacy – poverty has a direct bearing of the morbidity and longevity of people. How does health relate to development? The first point to is that the enhancement of health is a constitute part of development; second given other things good health and economic prosperity tend to support each other. Better health, also contributes directly to economic growth as it reduces production losses on account of illness of workers or, potentially, also in terms of higher work productivity for healthy workers.

Improvements in educational attainments have invariably been accompanied by improvement in health and longevity of the population and in their economic well-being. Educated people are likely to be more productive and hence better-off. They are also likely to contribute more to a country's economic growth. Lack of education robs an individual of a full life. It also robs society of a foundation for sustainable development because education is critical to improving health, nutrition and productivity. Income poverty may pull children from out of the school system, thus denying them the opportunity of participating in school education, even at the basic level, as evidenced in the third world country situations.

It is known fact that illiteracy, one of the key factors contributing to poverty is a fall out of the poor participation of children in elementary education. Some of the main issues of human deprivation are hunger, illiteracy, epidemics and the lack of health services or safe water. Improving health outcomes not only improves well-being but also increases income—earning potential. Increasing education not only improves well-being-it also leads to better health outcomes and to higher incomes. Health, along with education, is seen as one of the key ultimate goals of development and increasingly seen as a dimension of poverty in its own right.

Suggestions and Conclusion

India is a developing country. We have lot of human resources after China. In the recent years we find that economic growth is also high. Still we are facing poverty, ill health and illiteracy. Health and Education are two faces of an economic growth coin. Though growth tends to reduce poverty, significant improvements in health status are also necessary for poverty to decrease. Also, economic growth and health status are positively correlated and have a two-way relationship, suggesting that better health enhances growth by improving productivity and higher growth allows better human capital formation. Health expenditure is an important determinant of both higher growth and better health status, and is therefore a key tool available to policy-makers. Among other exogenous variables, literacy and industrialisation seem to improve both health outcomes and growth, and to reduce poverty.

REFERENCES

1. Barro, R. (1996), "*Health and Economic Growth*", Annex I of the Convocatoria para propuestas de investigacion sobre Inversion en Saludy Crecimiento Economico de la Organizacion Panamericana de la Salud.
2. *Census of India* 2001, Government of India, New Delhi.
3. Dev, S. Mahendra and Jos Mooij (2002), "*Social Sector Expenditure in the 1990s: An Analysis of Central and State Budget*", Economic and Political Weekly, Vol. 37 No. 9, March 2.
4. Indrani Gupta and Arup Mitra (2004). "*Economic Growth, Health and Poverty: An Exploratory Study for India*" Overseas Development Institute.

5. Janadyala B. G. Tilak (2005). "*Post-elementary Education, Poverty and Development in India*".
6. *NSS 61st Round* 2004-05, Government of India, New Delhi.
7. Planning Commission of India—2008, Government of India, New Delhi.
8. *Poverty Estimates for 2004-05*, Government of India, New Delhi.
9. Saravalingam, A., Siva Kuma, M. (2004). "*A Study About Poverty, Health, Education and Human Development in India*".

CHAPTER 18

Poverty, Illiteracy and Alcoholism in India and Solutions Through Education

–Dr. Ramachandra Reddy
–Dr. Naraginti Amareswaran
–Dr. C. Manchala

Introduction

The development of any nation depends mainly on the standards of its educational institutions. Education is the most powerful and effective instrument for inducing radical changes in the behaviour of students. Education is a powerful instrument of national development—social, economic and cultural. The teacher occupies pivotal position in the system of education. Teaching has been one of the oldest and most respected professions in the world.

Education is the process of instruction aimed at the all round development of boys and girls. Education dispels ignorance. It is the only wealth that cannot be robbed. Learning includes the moral values and the improvement of character and the methods to increase the strength of mind.

Now India is facing so many problems like Terrorism, Poverty, High-population, Alcoholism and Illiteracy. With the help of Science and Technology India have developed in all the fields. Different types of religions and castes people are living in India. The greatness of India is 'Unity in Diversity'.

Poverty in India

Poverty in India can be defined as a situation only when a section of people are unable to satisfy the basic needs of life. The definition and methods of measuring poverty differs from country to country. According to an expert group of Planning Commission, poverty lines in rural areas are drawn with an intake of 2400 calories in rural areas and 2100 calories in urban areas. If the person is unable to get that minimum level of calories is considered as being below poverty line.

The Planning Commission made a survey for finding out the number of persons below poverty line and estimated that 18.96% of the total peoples live below poverty line as of the year 1993-94.

The poverty in India can be defined on the basis of rural poverty as well as urban poverty.

Rural Poverty in India

India is a more rural based country highly dependent on agricultural sector. There is higher concentration of poverty in the rural India as to the given statistics. Government's plans and procedures have failed in many times. The important reasons for country's poverty are as follows:

- Alarming population Growth
- Lack of Investment
- Lower Literacy Rate
- Regional inequalities
- Failure of PDS system

The Government of India has taken various steps from time to time to reduce Rural poverty in India. The recent steps are as follows:

- Small Farmers Development Programme
- Draught Area Development Programme
- Food For Work Programme
- Minimum Needs Programme
- Integrated Rural Development Programme
- National Rural Employment Programme
- Rural Labour Employment Guaranty Programme
- Assurance on Employment

Urban Poverty in India

India is stepping forward for becoming a country with more urbanized. The recent experiences tell that the urban areas are facing the same problem of poverty as of the rural areas. The reasons behind urban poverty are as follows:

- Improper Training
- Growing population
- Slower job Growth
- Failure of PDS System

Government's policy initiatives for eradicating the problem of urban poverty are as follows:

- Nehru Rozgar Yojana
- Prime Minister Rozgar Yojana
- National Social Assistance Programme
- Urban Basic Services for the Poor Programme

The following table shows the over all *poverty in India* over various years given by Tenth Five Year Plan.

Year	Poverty Ratio (Per cent)			Number of Poor (Millions)		
	Rural	Urban	Combined	Rural	Urban	Combined
1977-78	53.1	45.2	51.3	264.3	64.4	328.9
1983	45.7	40.8	44.5	252.0	70.9	322.9
1987-88	39.1	38.2	38.9	231.9	75.2	307.1
1993-94	37.3	32.4	36.0	244.0	76.3	320.3
1999-00	27.1	23.6	26.1	193.2	67.1	260.3
2007*	21.1	15.1	19.3	170.5	49.6	220.1

Steps to Minimise Poverty Ratio through Education

We know through education we get strength of mind and knowledge. Strength of mind and knowledge gives solutions for different problems. Through education we can motivate any type of person in the society.

- Take proper steps to use advanced technology for caste based occupation people in the society.
- Good training for formers to use advanced technology and hybrid seeds.

- Conduct good programmes for all type of people to proper utilisation of natural sources.
- Take care about health and clean and green.

Illiteracy in India

The Constitution of India advocates free and compulsory education of children below the age of 14. There are so many commissions and committees to increase literacy rate in India. But we failed to improve literacy rate when compared to other countries in the world.

Adult literacy rate is 61.3% for the age group 15 years and above. Youth literacy rate is 76.4% (2000-2004) for the age group 15-24 years. Overall literacy rate of India is 61 %.(73% male and 48% female literacy) according to 2000 report. There are 268.42 million illiterates in India (2000).

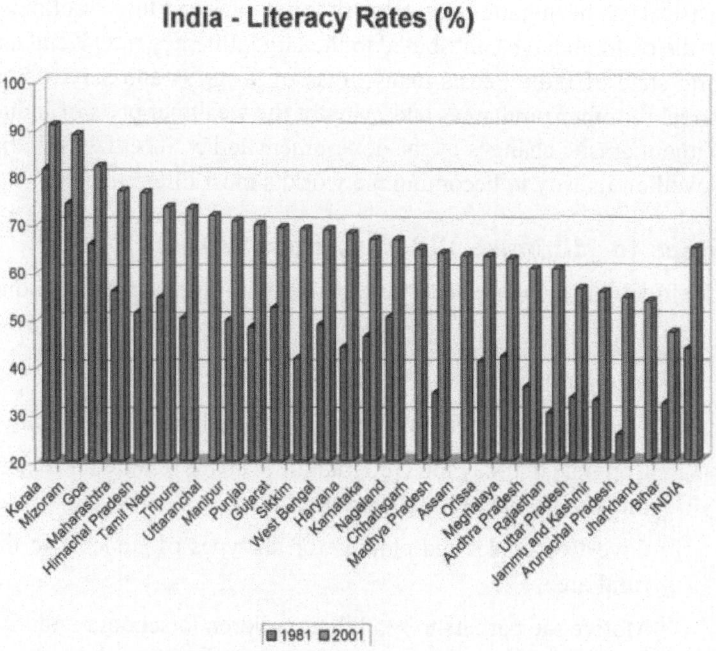

The above graph shows the literacy rates of different states in India in 1981 and 2001.

Life in India or in that case in any part of the world is easy if you have resources (money and infrastructure). Moreover, a social and economic factor slows you down. While driving back home you must have seen children selling books or flowers. Estimates cite figures of between 60 and 110 million working children in India. Child labor is a source of income for poor families. Is it poverty responsible for child labor or is it the inadequacy of school system in India?

Because of poverty and illiteracy some people participating in the anti-social activities. These activities can't help national development. Rural illiteracy rate is very high when compared to urban illiteracy rate.

A high illiteracy rate in rural parts of India is an area of the Indian education system that cannot be overlooked. Hampered by the government and by other factors the quality of education in rural districts has been quite poor. High dropout rates and low enrollment by the children have contributed to the large illiteracy rate. Kerala, a rural state of India boasts many areas of progress and serves as a model for other rural areas and many of the wealthier parts of India. Without drastic changes by the government and by its citizens, India is well on its way to becoming the world's most illiterate nation.

Steps to Minimise Illiteracy Rate in India

The following steps are necessary to minimise illiteracy rate in India.

- Minimise wastage and stagnation in the schools.
- Increase teacher-student ratio in the class (1:20).
- Give quality education for both rural and urban students.
- Continue mid-day food programme in all the schools and extent this programme to higher classes also.
- Give free books and clothes for all types of students in the rural area.
- Motive the parents to send their children to school regularly.
- Arrange Parent, Teacher and Student (PTA) meetings alteast twice in every three months.

- Increase school numbers.
- Use advanced technology in the school at the time of teaching and learning.
- Continue adult education programmes perfectly.

Alcoholism in India

Prevalence of alcohol use India is generally regarded as a traditional 'dry' or 'abstaining' culture. A recent National Household Survey of Drug Use in the country, the only systematic effort to document the nation-wide prevalence of drug use, recorded alcohol use in only 21% of adult males. Expectedly, this figure cannot accurately mirror the wide variation that obtains in a large and complex country like India. The prevalence of current use of alcohol ranged from a low of 7% in the western state of Gujarat (officially under Prohibition) to 75% in the Northeastern state of Arunachal Pradesh. There is also an extreme gender difference. Prevalence among women has consistently been estimated at less than 5 per cent but is much higher in the Northeastern states. Significantly higher use has been recorded among tribal, rural and lower socioeconomic urban sections.

Indian society is currently undergoing another tectonic shift in its socio-economic fabric. The impact of globalization and economic liberalisation (exposure to satellite television, rapid socio-economic transition and growing disposable incomes) appears to have influenced a widespread attitudinal shift to greater normalization of alcohol use.

The social welfare system and the criminal justice system, often the first to come into contact with alcohol related problems, can be sensitised in identifying and assisting individuals and families at risk from heavy drinking and acting as early referral systems. Extensive opportunities exist to lessen alcohol problems through community education and the prevention of drink driving, domestic violence, public disorder, unintentional injuries and criminal damage.

Community programmes supporting healthier lifestyles, mass media campaigns that present the advantages of reduced consumption rather than the dangers of heavy alcohol and community development in general, (job creation, skills development and upgrading infrastructure or recreational facilities in communities with high levels of alcohol abuse) should be utilised to encourage alternatives to drinking among the young and disadvantaged. Community action can also serve to shape attitudes, values and norms about drinking. Recently, several effective temperance campaigns have been led by heads of certain Hindu religious orders, though the impact has been limited to their immediate followers.

The Official Response to the Alcohol Problem

Unfortunately, the official response remains focused on the visible tip of the alcohol problem, – persons with alcohol dependence (around 4% of the adult male population) instead of on the emerging crisis due to hazardous drinking in more than 20% of the adult population. This is reflected in the approach to alcohol control policies at federal and state levels. The focus is exclusively on supply reduction (prohibition-centric) and tertiary prevention.

Steps to Minimise Alcohol use Through Education

Through education it is easy to minimize alcohol users and heavy alcohol users in India. The following steps are necessary.

- Lessons about good health are provided in the curriculum at both school and college levels.
- Number of counselling centers should increased for heavy alcohol users both in rural and urban areas.
- Tell disadvantages of alcohol with the help of print and electronic media and use technology.
- Write good quotations in the campus of schools, colleges, bus and railway stations and other heavy movable places.

REFERENCES

1. *Economic Survey 2004-05*, Economic Division, Ministry of Finance, Government of India, quoting UNDP Human Development Report 2004.
2. *National Institute of Child Health and Human Development.* (2000). The National Reading Panel: Reports of the Subgroups.
3. *National Institute of Child Health and Human Development.* (2001). The National Reading Panel: Reports of the Subgroups.
4. *UNESCO Institute for Statistics: Literacy Rates, Youth (15-24) and Adult (15+), by region and gender* (September 2006 Assessment).

CHAPTER 19

Preservation of Indian Values and Culture Through Education

–Dr. Naraginti Amareswaran
–Dr. Koteeswari

"The central task of education is to implant a will and facility for learning; it should produce not learned but learning people. The truly human society is a learning society, where grandparents, parents, and children are students together." **—Eric Hoffer**

"The only purpose of education is to teach a student how to live his life—by developing his mind and equipping him to deal with reality. The training he needs is theoretical, i.e., conceptual. He has to be taught to think, to understand, to integrate, to prove. He has to be taught the essentials of the knowledge discovered in the past—and he has to be equipped to acquire further knowledge by his own effort." **—Ayn Rand**

"The aim of education should be to teach us rather how to think, than what to think rather to improve our minds, so as to enable us to think for ourselves, than to load the memory with the thoughts of other men." **—Bill Beattie**

Introduction

India is a land of different religions, communities and languages. Though each has its own tradition and culture, they co-exist. 'Unity in diversity' is the greatness of Indian culture. The development of any nation depends mainly on the standards of its educational institutions.

Education is the most powerful and effective instrument for inducing radical changes in the behaviour of students. Education is the process through which an individual is developed into individuality and a person into a personality. Education should be individualised and personalised to the utmost and should constitute preparation for self-learning.

Education, according to Indian tradition, is not merely a means to earn a living, nor is it only a nursery of thought or a school for citizenship. It is an initiation into the life of spirit, a training of human soul in pursuit of truth and the practice of virtue. Aristotle, however, held that education exists exclusively to develop man's intellect in a world of reality, which men can know and understand.

Man and Education

Man has created education, yet it has become indispensable in his life; for man seeks education for betterment of his life, both inward and outward, and even for survival. It is no wonder, therefore that the U.N.O., in its Universal Declaration of Human Rights, proclaims: "Everyone has the right to education" (Article 26). Not only is this, 'educability' now considered as one of the capacities which distinguish man from other species. Man is educable, whereas other animals and birds etc., are not, although some of them can be trained to do certain things. Hirst and Peters rightly state: "We distinguish now between 'training' and 'education', whereas previously people did not. We would not now naturally speak of educating animals and we would never speak in this way of plants. But we do speak of training animals and of training roses and other sort of plants.

Man can, not only create objects, machines, institutions and ideas, but also can envision a life which he can be or become if he wills. To elaborate a little more—man imagines the concept of a chair or a machine with some particular form, qualities or functions and builds it with a degree of perfection, approaching that of the concept, depending on his ability. Similarly man can envision a life with certain qualities: truthfulness, love, tolerance, peace etc., and can become the being he envisions. To explain in the words of Maslow, "being" is "that which the person is" and "becoming", "that which the person could be", Gordon W. Allport can be aptly quoted in this connection. He writes:

> "If the prejudiced style of life can be learned and certainly it is not innate—then surely the tentative style or in Gandhi's term, 'equi-minded outlook' can also be acquired".

Thus man can envision lives with different styles, virtues, states etc., and can become like those. Creativity of this kind, envisioning a life and devising ways for becoming the envisioned personality can very well be termed as "creativity in the field of being and becoming".

In ancient India, the highest conception of education was: *Sâ Vidyâ Yâ Vimuktaye*—Learning or education is that which liberates or makes one liberated. Although other aims were there, certainly there had been a stress on 'to-be'—to be a liberated person (jivanmukta) and to be completely free in ultimate sense. In modern age, quite for a long time education has been conceived as that which helps to achieve—mostly outward things. But it seems, there is a revival of the interest in a kind of education that helps 'to be'—kind of person. The emphasis on 'to be'—to be a 'lifelong learner' and to be a 'complete man' by the International Commission on the Development of Education, and naming of their report as 'Learning to Be', symoblises such an interest.

In the 13th chapter of the "BHAGAVAD GITA" the characteristics of a real teacher are laid down as follows : absence of pride, free from hypocrisy, non-violence, forgiving nature, straight forwardness, service of the preceptor, purity of mind and body, steadfastness and self-control.

In line with this, centuries ago in this land of Vedas the teacher devoted all his time for the upliftment of his pupils in all directions—knowledge, morals, values etc. He was called the **'Guru or Acharya'**.

Guru Brahmo Gurur Vishnu
Gurur Devo Maheshwara
Gurur Saakshat Param Brahma
Tasmai Sree Gurave Namaha

Guru is verily the representative of Brahma (Creator), Vishnu (Preserver) and Shiva (Transformer). He creates, sustains knowledge and destroys the weeds of ignorance. Every person can salute such a Guru.

The Concept of Value

According to Cambridge dictionary of philosophy, the value is the worth of something that philosophers discerned these main forms of intrinsic, instrumental, inherent and contributory value.

Values are described as the socially defined desires and goals that are internalised through the process of condition, learning and socialisation.

Values are goals set for achievement and they motivate, define and colour all our activities cognitive, affective and co-native. When education builds up true values in the life of our student, it has equipped the ship of students with RADAR and compass to sail clear on the stormy sea of life.

Values reflect different philosophical positions. The concepts of values are closely associated with the concept of man.

According to Jules Henry in "Culture against Man" (1963), values are something that we consider good such as love, kindness, quietness, contentment, fun, honesty, decency, relaxation and simplicity.

According to Carl Rogers in "Freedom to Learn" (1969), valuing is the tendency of a person to show preference.

According to Louis Raths, Merril and Harmin and Sidney B. Simon (1966) in "Values and Teaching", values are due to the out of experiences may come certain and guides to behaviour. These tend to give direction to life.

According to Shepard B. Clough (1960) in "Basic Values of Western Civilisation", in a summary states that values have been variously viewed as preferences, criteria, objects and possessions, personality and status characteristics and states of mind that are absolutes, inherent in objects present in man and stages of mind and identical with his behaiour.

According to John Dewey "the value means primarily to prize, to esteem, to appraise, to estimate; it means the act of cherishing something, holding it dear and also the act of passing judgment upon the nature and amounts of values as compared with something else".

According to Parker, "values belong wholly to the inner world of mind. The satisfaction of desire is the real value; the thing that serves is only an instrument. A value is always an experience never a thing or an object".

According to Mukerjee "values are socially approved drives and goals that are internalised through the process of conditioning, learning or socialisation and that becomes subjective preferences, standards and aspirations".

According to Alloport's "the term value means the relative prominence of the subject's interest or the dominant interest in personality".

According to Derek Rowntree's (1960), "Dictionary of Education" that the moral and aesthetics, principles, believes and standards that give coherence and direction to a persons decisions and actions. Where such values are held by or are imposed upon the majority of people in a society they may be known as social values.

In statistics, the different quantitative and qualitative in which an entity can be with respect to some variable that is different categories and measurement.

Values simply stated, are the determiners in the man that influence his choices in life and that decide his behaviour.

Values as indicated are inherent, in individual man but they are additionally inherent although perhaps less definably so, in collective man in a given culture that is or in a combination of cultures. Whatever the exact nature of human society, values exist in some form. In a primitive society, they reside in developed society they reside in written documents as well as in the intangible of social mores and expectances.

The Concept of Culture

Culture comes from the Latin word *cultura* stemming from colere, which means to cultivate. There are many various definitions of culture, some define it as the behaviours, ways of life, arts, beliefs and the institutions of a population that are passed down from generation to generation. Another definition of culture can be and has been called the way of life for an entire society which includes codes of manners, dress, language, religion, rituals, norms of behaviour such as law and morality.

Culture has been defined differently by people. The different definitions attached to culture are based on the differences in the orientation of the people. According Ekeh (1989), culture is constructing, used in an attempt to analyze and integrate events and ideas in broad spectrum of areas of society. Culture is complex which includes knowledge, belief, arts, morals, laws, customs, and any other capabilities and habits acquired by man as member of the society.

Schein (2003) defined culture as, "a set of basic solutions—shared solutions to universal problems of external adaptation (how to survive) and internal integration (how to stay together)—which have evolved over time and are handed down from one generation to the next".

Culture is not an abstraction. It evolves by constantly integrating individual and collective choices that are taken in interaction with other, similar wholes. It expresses itself in diverse ways without being reducible to 'works'. Culture is the product of a complex inheritance constantly submitted to scrutiny and the need to adapt a constant conquest to achieve (Jean, 2002).

In the modern day third world countries, absolute kneeing down may be fading as noted by Tardif (2002). He opines that culture is not genetically transmitted rather it takes place by process of absorption from the social environment or through deliberate instruction. This is to say that culture is learned. Such learning does not occur through natural inheritance. Probably that is why Jekayinfa (2002) maintains that the man learns culture through the process of socialisation, enumeration, personal experience and through deliberate teaching. It should be noted that learning of culture is a life long process. That is, learning of culture is from birth of death. Jekayinfa (2002) further observes that what is learnt differs from society to society and from one stage to another. However, all that is learnt is geared towards the realisation of the goal of the society.

Culture is the totality of the way of life of a group of people that has been developed, shaped and practiced over the years. The development of these cultural norms and practices are shaped by the environment and the needs of the people. Over the years as societies develop and modernise, these cultural practices undergo changes to reflect the changing times to better serve the needs of the people. This means that culture is not stagnant. It is constantly undergoing evolutions based on the changes in the environment in which it exists (Baffoe 2005).

According to Obiora (2002) the transformation of culture is gradual and not sudden. Obiora (2002) contends that culture is a continuous process of change. Inspite of the change culture continues to give a community a sense of dignity, continuity, security and binds society together. Another attribute of culture is that it is learned, acquired, transmitted or diffused through contact or other means of communication flow from one generation to another. The fact that we are human does not mean we are the same. However, it is noted that every moment, we are being transformed, always growing like the cell in our bodies. Culture changes exactly the same way as the human being change. In other words, culture is dynamic.

Preservation Value and Culture through Education

"Today, it is no longer desirable to undertake educational reforms in piecemeal fashion, without a concept of the totality of the goals and modes of the educational process. To find out how to reshape its component parts, one must have a vision of the whole" (UNESCO, 1972).

The National Policy on Education has laid considerable emphasis on value education by highlighting the need to make education a powerful tool for cultivation and preservation of social and Moral Values. Keeping in view the pluralistic base of our society, the education system besides preserving our cultural heritage has also to nurture our youth to be more adaptable to life in the changing environment. An inter-linking of education and culture has also been emphasised in the Programme of Action for implementation of National Policy on Education.

People say that "Values cannot be taught but caught". Against this belief educationists strongly advocate that values could be taught with sufficient care and caution.

The National Council for Educational Research and Training (NCERT) in its publication documents on Social, Moral and Spiritual Values in Education (1979) has drawn up 84 values to be inculcated through education.

The cultural values need to be identified for standard curricula all over the country. Respect for the old, care for poor and up-privileged and tolerance should be some of the values. Value based inter-personal relations, importance of racial and religious harmony and concern for humanity should form the basis for friendship and cooperation amongst the people.

Fine arts, music, creative writing, puppetry and theatre are to be given due place in the curricula right from school to the university level.

The curriculum should strike a balance between theory and practice. Creative work in fields of music, dance, literature, drama, visual arts is essential to cultivate the inherent tolerance of children.

Value/moral education should be thought as a compulsory subject up to the high school level. It should be made an examinable subject at the school level. Evaluation of value education should be based on compassion, self-reliance, respect and honesty.

Language is an importance medium for inculcating, fostering and propagating of moral vales and national cultural heritage. Education through mother tongue needs to be ensured.

Co-curricular activities play a very significant role in preserving different values in the students. For all-round development of personalities of the students co-curricular activities are considered to be very important now-a-days. Previously the term "extra-curricular activities" was used for outdoor activities and other cultural programmes organised in the school. But now-a-days this term has been discarded keeping in view the importance of these activities. In many progressive schools there is an allotment of certain periods for these co-curricular activities in their regular time table.

Through these activities, many values can be inculcated profitably. Co-curricular activities form an integral part of the modern school curriculum. They should be made more and more purposive and fruitful as well as value oriented with the democratic base and purposeful pursuit. This can be done, provided children have an opportunity of having living experience of moral life through these activities.

In programmes of outdoor activities, the children are taken out of the school to the areas of adventure, appreciation of art and culture and the places of historical values. They can be brought avenues in the training of initiative, team-work, self-discipline and learn much about our cultural heritage and historical details. Besides games and sports, there are several outdoor activities, namely, NCC, Scouting and Guiding, Mountaineering, Trekking, Excursion, Field trips etc., which may serve the purpose of inculcation of desired values among the students and formation of character.

Almost in all the schools and colleges various festivals are organised at different levels. Festivals may be classified into three heads:

1. National Festivals
2. Religious Festivals
3. Birth/Death anniversaries of great persons

Besides these, there are so many occasions like Sports Day, Teachers' Day, Parents' Day, Annual Day, UNO Day, etc., in the school. Through these activities, the qualities of leadership, self-discipline, co-operation, team-work, etc., can be easily developed. Through these activities, new dimension can be given to the personalities of the students.

Conclusion

Values and culture are two faces of a single coin. They are co-existing. Through culture we can preserve values. Today there is lot of degradation of values in every walk of human life. Individuals are crazy for material wealth. Money making is the main motive of the majority of the individuals even through immoral ways. Proper foundation will be laid on Moral Values at the initial stages of the child. Schools and colleges are the institutions which can shoulder the responsibility of inculcating Moral Values among the people and students. Through games and sports, essay writing, elocution, quiz competition, drama and seminars and conferences we can inculcate and protect our values and culture.

REFERENCES

- Allport, G.W. (1951): "*New Knowledge in Human Values*", Houghton Mifflin Co., Boston.
- Allport, G.W. Vernon. P.E. and Lindzey, G (1951): "*A Manual of Study of* Values", Houghton Mifflin Co., Boston.
- Baffoe M. (2005). "These *Obsolete Customs and and Traditions Must Be* Scrapped"! www.ghanaweb.com.
- Carl Rogers (1969): "Freedom to Learn", Merill, Ohio.
- Jean T. (2002). *The Hidden Dimension of Globalization: What is at Stake Geoculturally*? Global Policy Forum, New York, ATTAC May 29.
- Jean, T (2002). "*Intercultural Dialogues and Cultural Security*". September 2005 planat Agora, www.planetagora.com.
- Ministry of Education (1964): "Report of the Committee on Religious and Moral Instructions", GOI, New Delhi.
- Ministry of Education (1964-66): "*Report of the Indian Education Commission*", Kothari Commission.
- Ministry of Education (1966): "*Education and National Development*", NCERT, New Delhi.
- Ministry of Education (1971): "*Report of the Indian Education Commission*", NCERT.
- Obiora, A. L. (1996). "*Feminism, Globalisation and Culture* After Beijing" Paper presented at a Symposium Organised by Indiana Journal of Global Legal Studies.
- Seshadri, C.S. (1981): "*The Concept of Moral Education Column*", Comparative Education Vol. 17, No.3.

CHAPTER

20

Preservation of Medicinal Plants by Tribes Through Education in India

—Dr. Naraginti Amareswaran

Introduction

"Health is not valued till sickness comes". —***Thomas Fuller***

"To insure good health: eat lightly, breathe deeply, live moderately, cultivate cheerfulness, and maintain an interest in life". **—William Londen**

"Use your health, even to the point of wearing it out. That is what it is for. Spend all you have before you die; do not outlive yourself". **—Bernard Shaw**

All of you know that 'Health is Wealth' and 'A Sound Mind in a Sound Body'. A person has a lot of money and relatives without health he can't enjoy the life. A patient knows the value of health. Man is a greatest animal in the world. Because of Education, Science and Technology he has been becoming a strongest person in the world. Because of internal and external environmental effects some times we got diseases. With the help of practiced knowledge we can treat diseases by using medicinal plants.

Medicinal Plants in India

Human beings have been utilising plants for basic preventive and curative health care since time immemorial. Recent estimates suggest that over 9,000 plants have known medicinal applications in various cultures and countries, and this is without having conducted comprehensive research amongst several indigenous and other communities (Farnsworth and Soejarto 1991).

Medicinal plants are used at the household level by women taking care of their families, at the village level by medicine men or tribal shamans, and by the practitioners of classical traditional systems of medicine such as Ayurveda, Chinese medicine, or the Japanese Kampo system. According to the World Health Organisation, over 80% of the world's population, or 4.3 billion people, rely upon such traditional plant-based systems of medicine to provide them with primary health care (Bannerman et. al. 1983).

India is the home of several important traditional system of health care like Ayurveda. This system depends heavily on herbal products. Several millions of Indian households have been using through the ages nearly 8000 species of medicinal plants for their health care needs. Over one and half million traditional healers use a wide range of medicinal plants for treating ailments of both humans and livestock across the length and breadth of the country. Over 800 medicinal plant species are currently in use by the Indian herbal industry.

Herbal History in Indian Context

The Rigveda, the oldest document of human knowledge mentions the use of medicinal plants in the treatment of man and animals. Ayurveda gives the account of actual beginning of the ancient medical science of India, which according to western scholars was written between 2500 to 600 B.C. Charaka and Susruta wrote around 1000 B.C. Charaka concentrates more on medicine while Susruta deals with surgery in details along with therapeutics.

Tribes in India

The Indian sub-continent is inhabited by 88.2 million tribal populations belonging to over 577 tribal communities that come under 227 linguistic groups. They inhibit varied geographic and climatic Zones of the country. Their vocation ranges from hunting, gathering, cave dwelling nomadic to societies with settled culture living incomplete harmony with nature.

The tribal people are the real custodians of the medicinal plants. Out of 45,000 species of wild plants, 7500 species are used for medicinal purposes. The World Health Organisation (WHO) has been promoting a movement for *'Saving plants for saving lives'*. This is because of the growing understanding of the pivotal role medicinal plants play in providing herbal remedies to health maladies.

Forests have been their dear home and totally submitted themselves to forest settings. Their relationship with the forest was symbolic in nature. They have been utilizing the resources without disturbing the delicate balance of the eco-system. Tribal thus mostly remained as stable societies and were unaffected by the social, cultural, material and economic evolutions that were taking place with the so called civilized societies. But this peaceful co-existence of the tribal has been disturbed in recent years by the interference in their habitats. Traditional communities living close to nature have, over the years acquired unique knowledge about the use of living biological resources. Modernisation, especially industrialisation and urbanisation has endangered the rich heritage of knowledge and expertise of age old wisdom of the traditional communities.

A study on the utilisation of local tribal revealed that they hold precious knowledge on the specific use of a large number of agents of wild plant and animal origins, the use of many are hitherto unknown to the outside world.

Preservation of Medicinal Plants by Tribes Through Adult Education in India

According to 2001 census the literacy rate of schedule castes was 54.69% and that of. Schedule tribe was 47.10% as against the national average of 64.84%. We know majority of the tribes living in the deep forest area. They are for away from the rural and urban communities. Now a day also majority of tribal communities have no current facility. They do not using modern technology in the field of cultivation. Their livelihood is also different. The tribal children are not interest to come the school. Majority of the medicinal plants are occurring in the deep forest. The following steps are necessary to preserve medicinal plants.

- Educate all types of people in the tribal area.
- Provide advanced technology for tribes.

- Tell the importance of medicinal plants for world people.
- Increase Teacher-Student ratio in the tribal community area.
- Collect valuable medicinal plants with the help of tribes in the deep forest area.
- Give training about photography for tribes for documentation of medicinal plants and herbal products.
- Provide all types of facilities with advanced communication system.
- Conduct awareness programmes about diseases and un-believable things.
- Give lectures about modern world, universe, marketing system and population in the world.
- Give encouragement for cultivation of medicinal plants.
- Arrange medicinal plans garden in the forest.
- Conduct seminars, workshops and exhibitions about medicinal plants both in the agency and rural/urban areas.

Preservation of Medicinal Plants by Farmers Through Education in India

We know India is a developing country. The majority of the people occupation in India is cultivation. 70 per cent of the total population is living in the rural area and their main occupation is cultivation. The farmers' gives importance for food based agriculture. Because of globalisation and industrialisation and economic reforms, the attitude of the farmer is also changed, the State and Central Governments encouraging the farmers for cultivation of medicinal plants by giving subsidy. The recent allocations in the XI five year plan over Rs. 970 Crores (from 93.50 Crores during X Plan) for the sector is an indication on the importance given by the Government for the development of medicinal plants in the country.

According to National Medicinal Plants Board and Department of AYUSH there are 344 Medicinal plants garden in India. Through these institutions/gardens it is possible to give training for farmers about cultivation of medicinal plants.

The literacy rate of rural people in India is 58.74%. It is very less when compared to national average 64.84%. We know education is a solution for all types of problems. The following steps are important in the preservation of medicinal plants in India by the farmers.

- Educate all the people in the villages.
- Provide advanced technology in the field of agriculture, transport and communication system.
- Provide good market system for their products.
- Arrange regular awareness programmes about cultivation of medicinal plants for farmers.
- Tell the importance of medicinal plants.
- Tell the value of medicinal plants in the international market.
- Establish Ayurved colleges in the rural areas.
- Give subsidy for farmers and provide good marketing system.
- Arrange medicinal plants garden in the rural areas.
- Conduct workshops, seminars and exhibitions.

Uses of Medicinal Plants

Since ancient times, plants have been an exemplary source of medicine. Ayurveda and other Indian literature mention the use of plants in treatment of various human ailments. India has about 45000 plant species and among them, several thousands have been claimed to possess medicinal properties.

There has been resurgence in the consumption and demand for medicinal plants. These plants are finding use as pharmaceuticals, neutraceuticals, cosmetics and food supplements. Even as traditional source of medicines and they continue to play pivotal rule.

The World Health Organisation (WHO) estimated that 80% of the population of developing countries still relies on traditional medicines, mostly plant drugs, for their primary health care needs. Also, modern pharmacopoeia contains at least 25% drugs derived from plants. Many other are synthetic analogues built on prototype compounds isolated from plants. Demand for medicinal plant is increasing in both developing and developed countries due to growing recognition of natural products, being non-toxic, having no side-effects, easily available at affordable prices. Medicinal plant sector has traditionally occupied an important position in the socio cultural, spiritual and medicinal arena of rural and tribal lives of India.

The below table gives full information about some medicinal plants; Common Name, Maturity period, Botanical name or Family, Parts used, Average price (Rs./Kg) and Medicinal use.

NB: (Fam - Family, T – Tree, H – Herb, C – Climber, S- shrub)

Plant	Common name/ Maturity period	Botanical Name or Family	Parts Used	Average Price (Rs. Kg)	Medicinal Use
	Amla (T) After 4th year	Emblica officinalis Fam-euphorbiaceac	Fruit	Rs. 15–45/kg	Vitamin – C, Cough, Diabetes, cold, Laxative, hyper acidity.
	Ashok (T) 10 years onward	Saraca Asoca Fam: Caesalpinanceac	Bark Flower	Dry Bark Rs 125/kg	Menstrual Pain, uterine, disorder, Diabetes.
	Aswagandha (H), One year	Withania Somnifera Fam: Solanaccac	Root, Leafs	Rs 140/ Kg	Restorative Tonic, stress, nerves disorder, aphrodisiac.
	Bael/Bilva (T) After 4-5 year	Aegle marmelous Fam: Rutaccac	Fruit, Bark	Fruit – Rs 125 / kg Pulp – Rs 60 / Kg	Diarrhoea, Dysentery, Constipation.
	Bhumi Amla (H), within one year	Phyllanthous amarus Fam : euphorbiaccac	Whole Plant	Rs 40 / Kg	Anaemic, jaundice, Dropsy.
	Brahmi (H) Indian penny worth/one year	Bacopa, Monnieri Fam: Scrophulariaccac	Whole plant	Rs 20 per kg	Nervous, Memory enhancer, mental disorder.
	Chiraita (high altitude) with-in one year (H)	Swertia Chiraita Fam : Gentianaccac	Whole Plant	Rs 300-350/per kg	Skin Disease, Burning, cessation, fever.
	Gudmar/ madhunasini, after Four year (C)	Gymnema Sylvestre Fam: Asclepiadaccac	Leaves	Rs 50 – 75 per kg	Diabetes, hydrocil, Asthama.
	Guggul (T) after 8 years	Commiphora Wightii Fam: burseraccac	Gum rasine	Rs 80 – 100 per kg	Rheumatics, arthritis, paralysis, laxative.

	Guluchi/Giloe (c) Within one year	Tinospora Cordifolia Fam	Stem	Rs 20 – 25 per kg	Gout, Pile, general debility, fever, Jaundice.
	Calihari/ panchangulia Glori Lily Five years	Gloriosa superba Fam: Liliaccac	Seed, tuber	Rs 60	Skin Disease, Labour pain, Abortion, General debility.
	Kalmegh/ Bhui neem (H) within one year	Andrographis Paniculata Fam : scanthaccac	Whole Plant	Rs 12 - 20	Fever, weakness, release of gas.
	Long peeper/ Pippali (C) after two to three years	Peeper longum Fam : Piperaccac	Fruit, Root	Rs 100 – 150 per kg Root– 150 per kg	Appetizer, enlarged spleen, Bronchitis, Cold, antidote.
	Makoi (H) Kakamachi/ Within one year	Solanum nigrum Fam: Solanaccac	Fruit/ whole plant	Rs 40 per kg Seed– 200 per kg	Dropsy, General debility, Diuretic, anti dysenteric.
	Pashan Bheda/ Pathar Chur (H) One year	Coleus barbatus Fam : Lamiaccac	Root	Rs 40-50 per kg	Kidney stone, Calculus.
	Sandal Wood (T) Thirty years onward	Santalum Album Fam: santalinaccac	Heart wood, oil	Rs 350 per kg	Skin disorder, Burning, sensation, Jaundice, Cough.
	Sarpa Gandha (H) After 2-year	Ranwolfia Serpentina Fam: apocynaccac	Root	Root– Rs 60 per kg Seed– Rs 300 per kg	Hyper tension, insomnia.
	Satavari (C) After 2-3 year	Asparagus Racemosus Family: liliaccac	Tuber, root	Rs 20 – 50 per kg	Enhance lactation, general weakness, fatigue, and cough.
	Senna (S) Within 1 year	Casia augustifolia Fam: Liliaceae	Dry Tubers	Rs 500/ kg seed Rs1200/ kg dry	Rheumatism, general debility tonic, aphrodisiac.
	Tulsi (perennial) Each 3 months	Ocimum sanclum Fam: Lamiaccac	Leaves/ Seed	Leaves Rs 10/ kg	Cough, Cold, bronchitis, expectorant.
	Vai Vidanka (C), 2nd year onward	Embelia Ribes Fam: Myrsinaccac	Root, Fruit, Leaves	Rs 40- 50 per kg	Skin disease, Snake Bite, Helminthiasis.
	Pippermint (h) Perennial	Mentha pipertia Fam: Lamiaccac	Leaves, Flower, Oil	-	Digestive, Pain killer.

	Henna/Mehdi (S) 1/25 years	Lawsennia iermis Fam: lytharaceae	Leaf, Flower, Seed	L-50/ kg Powder- Rs. 75 per kg	Burning, Steam, Anti Inflammatory.
	Gritkumari (H) 2nd-5th yr	Aloe Verra Fam: Liliaceae	Leaves	Fresh L- Rs 5 kg Juice 90 Per Kg	Laxative, Wound healing, Skin burns and care, Ulcer.
	Sada Bahar (H) Periwinkle/ Nyantara	Vincea rosea/ catharanthus Roseus Fam: apocyanace	Whole Plant	R-Rs 50 per kg L- Rs 25S- Rs 10 kg	Leukemia, Hypertensive, Antispasmodic, Antidote.
	Vringraj (H)	Eclipta alba Fam: Compositae	Seed/ whole	Powder- Rs 60/kg	Anti-inflammatory, Digestive, hair tonic.
	Swet chitrak Perennial (h)	Plumbago Zeylanica Fam: Plumbaginaceae	Root, Rootbar	-	Appetiser, Antibacterial, Anticancer.
	Rakta Chitrak (H)	Plumbago Indica Fam: plumbaginaceae	Root, Root bar	-	Indyspeipsia, colic, inflammation, cough.
	Kochila (T) 15 yrs	Strychinos nuxvomica Fam: loganiaceae	Seed	-	Nervous, Paralysis, healing wound.
	Harida (T)	Terminalia Chebula Fam: Combretaceae	Seed	Rs. 80 per K Powder	Trifala, wound ulcer, leprosy, inflammation, Cough.
	Bahada (T)	Terminalia Bellerica Fam:comretaceae	Seed, Bark	Fruit – Rs 20/ kPowder- Rs 100/k	Cough, Insomnia, Dropsy, Vomiting, Ulcer, Trifala.
	Gokhur (H) Crawling Puncture Vine/1 yr	Tribulus Terrestris Fam: Lygophyllaceae	Whole Plant	Plant-Rs 10/KFruit –Rs 15/k	Sweet cooling, Aphrodisiac, appetiser, Digestive, Urinary.
	Neem (T)	Azardirchata–indica Fam : Mahaceae	Rhizome	Rs 45/k	Sedative, analgesic, epilepsy, hypertensive.
	Anantamool/ sariva(S) Indian Sarap sarilla	Hemibi smus Indicus Fam: Asclepiadaceae	Root/ Leaf	Rs 45/k root Rs 90/k Powder	Appetiser, Carminative, aphrodisiac, Astringent.
	Bach (H) Sweet Flag/ 1 yr	Acorus Calamus Fam : araceae	Rhizome	Rs 45/K	Sedative, analgesic, epilepsy, hypertensive.

	Vasa (S)	Adhatoda vesica Fam : Sacanthaceae	Whole Plant	Leaf– Rs 25/ k	Antispasmodic, respiratory, Stimulant.
	Nageswar (T) Nag Champa	Mesua Ferrea Fam : Guttiferae	Bark, Leaf, Flower	Flower – Rs 120/ kPowder Rs 175/k	Asthma, Skin, Burning, Vomiting, Dysentery, Piles.
	Benachar (S) Khus/khus	Vetiveria Ziziinoides Fam : Toaceae / Graminae	Root	Flower – Rs 120/k Powder Rs 175/k	Hyperpiesia, Burning, ulcer, Skin, Vomiting.
	Mandukparni (H)Indianp-ennywort	Centella asiatica Fam : Umdelliferae	Whole plant	-	Anti-inflammatory, Jaundice, Diuretic, Diarrhoea.
	Kaincha/ Creeper Baidanka	Mucuna Truriens Fam : Fabaceae	Root, Hair, Seed, Leaf	-	Nervous, Disorder, Constipation, Nephropathy, Strangury, Dropsy.
	Dalchini Perenial Shrub	Cinnamomum Zeylanicum Fam : Lauraceae	Bark, Oil	-	Bronchitis, Asthma, Cardiac, Disorder, Fever.
	Kurai (S)	Holorheena antidysentrica Fam:apocyaceaceae	Bark, Seed	-	Scabies, Antipyretic, Amoebic dysentery.
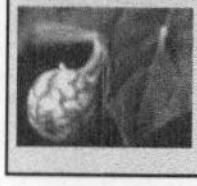	Kantakari/ Akranti Perennial (H)	Solanum Xanthocarpum Fam : Solanaceae	Whole Plant, Fruit, Seed	-	Diuretic, Anti-inflammatory, Appetiser, Stomachic.

Saving the Plant Is Saving the Life

According to the text of Vishnu Samhita, causing any harm to the plants/animals is a sin. Even purloining of parts/ products of any of these living beings is a crime. The sinner/ criminals are liable to chastisement in this life and also after death. The punishments are of diverse nature:—pecuniary, corporal, expiatory and donation of specific articles to Brahmins.

Conclusion

Since ancient times, plants have been an exemplary source of medicine. Ayurveda and other Indian literature mention the use of plants in treatment of various human ailments. India has about 45000 plant species and among them, several thousands have been claimed to possess medicinal properties. It is our duty to preserve all these medicinal plants for the purpose of future generation. Through Adult Education only it is possible.

- Educate all types of tribes in India.
- Educate all types of people in the society.
- Establish some more Medicinal Plants Boards in the rural and forest areas.
- Take care about marketing system of medicinal plants.
- Conduct awareness programmes about medicinal plants every month regularly.

REFERENCES

1. Andrew Chevallier. "*The Encyclopaedia of Medicinal Plants: A Practical Reference Guide to Over 550 Key Herbs and Their Medicinal Uses*".
2. Barua, I. and R. Phukan. 1990. "*Socio-religious Aspects of Health Among Sonowal Kachari*". The Eastern Anthropologist, 55: 4.
3. Bhasin, Veena. 1997. "*Medical Pluralism and Health Services in Ladakh.*" J. Soc. Sci., 1: 43-69.
4. Bhasin, Veena. 1997. "*The Human Settlements and Health Status of People of Sikkim*", (pp. 153-187), in K.C. Mahanta (ed.), People of the Himalayas: Ecology, Culture, Development and Change. Delhi:Kamla-Raj Enterprises.

CHAPTER 21

Privatisation of Professional Education

–*Dr. B. Ramachandra Reddy*
–*Dr. C. Manchala*
–*Dr. Naraginti Amareswaran*

Introduction

The development of any nation depends mainly on the standards of its educational institutions. Education is the most powerful and effective instrument for inducing radical changes in the behaviour of students. Education is a powerful instrument of national development—social, economic and cultural. The teacher occupies pivotal position in the system of education. Teaching has been one of the oldest and most respected professions in the world.

Importance of Education

Education is the process of instruction aimed at the all round development of boys and girls. Education dispels ignorance. It is the only wealth that cannot be robbed. Learning includes the moral values and the improvement of character and the methods to increase the strength of mind.

Higher and Professional Education in India

Higher education in India is gasping for breath, at a time when India is aiming to be an important player in the emerging knowledge economy. With about 300 universities and deemed universities, over 15,000 colleges and hundreds of national and regional research institutes, Indian higher education and research sector is the third largest in the world, in terms of the number of students it caters to.

However, not a single Indian university finds even a mention in a recent international ranking of the top 200 universities of the world, except an IIT Kharagpur ranked at 41, whereas there were three universities each from China, Hong Kong and South Korea and one from Taiwan.

On the other hand, it is also true that there is no company or institute in the world that has not benefited by graduates, post-graduates or Ph.D.s from India be it NASA, IBM, Microsoft, Intel, Bell, Sun, Harvard, MIT, Caltech, Cambridge or Oxford, and not all those students are products of our IITs, IIMs, IISc/TIFR or central universities, which cater to barely one per cent of the Indian student population. This is not to suggest that we should pat our backs for the achievements of our students abroad, but to point out that Indian higher educational institutions have not been able to achieve the same status for themselves as their students seem to achieve elsewhere with their education from here.

While many reasons can be cited for this situation, they all boil down to decades of feudally managed, colonially modeled institutions run with inadequate funding and excessive political interference. Only about 10 per cent of the total student population enters higher education in India, as compared to over 15 per cent in China and 50 per cent in the major industrialised countries. Higher education is largely funded by the state and central governments so far, but the situation is changing fast. Barring a few newly established private universities, the government funds most of the universities, whereas at the college level, the balance is increasingly being reversed.

The Privatisation Experience

The experience over the last few decades has clearly shown that unlike school education, privatisation has not led to any major improvements in the standards of higher and professional education. Yet, in the run up to the economic reforms in 1991, the IMF, World Bank and the countries that control them have been crying hoarse over the alleged pampering of higher education in India at the cost of school education. The fact of the matter was that school education was already privatised to the extent that government schools became an option only to those who cannot afford private schools mushrooming in every street corner, even in small towns and villages.

On the other hand, in higher education and professional courses, relatively better quality teaching and infrastructure has been available only in government colleges and universities, while private institutions of higher education in India capitalised on fashionable courses with minimum infrastructure.

Nevertheless, successive governments over the last two decades have only pursued a path of privatisation and deregulation of higher education, regardless of which political party ran the government. From the Punnaiah committee on reforms in higher education set up by the Narasimha Rao government to the Birla-Ambani committee set up by the Vajpayee government, the only difference is in their degree of alignment to the market forces and not in the fundamentals of their recommendations.

With the result, the last decade has witnessed many sweeping changes in higher and professional education: For example, thousands of private colleges and institutes offering IT courses appeared all across the country by the late 1990s and disappeared in less than a decade, with devastating consequences for the students and teachers who depended on them for their careers. This situation is now repeating itself in management, biotechnology, bioinformatics and other emerging areas. No one asked any questions about opening or closing such institutions, or bothered about whether there were qualified teachers at all, much less worry about teacher-student ratio, floor area ratio, class rooms, labs, libraries etc. All these regulations that existed at one time (though not always enforced strictly as long as there were bribes to collect) have now been deregulated or softened under the self-financing scheme of higher and professional education adopted by the UGC in the 9th five-year plan and enthusiastically followed by the central and state governments.

This situation reached its extreme recently in the new state of Chattisgarh, where over 150 private universities and colleges came up within a couple of years, till the scam got exposed by a public interest litigation and the courts ordered the state government in 2004 to derecognise and close most of these universities or merge them with the remaining recognised ones. A whole generation of students and teachers are suffering irreparable damage to their careers due to these trends, for no fault of theirs. Even government-funded colleges and universities in most states started many "self-financing" courses in IT, biotechnology etc., without qualified teachers, labs or infrastructure and charging huge fees from the students and are liberally giving them marks and degrees to hide their inadequacies.

It is not that the other well established departments and courses in government funded colleges and universities are doing any better. Decades of government neglect, poor funding, frequent ban on faculty recruitments and promotions, reduction in library budgets, lack of investments in modernisation leading to obsolescence of equipment and infrastructure, and the tendency to start new universities on political grounds without consolidating the existing ones today threatens the entire higher education system.

Another corollary of this trend is that an educational institution recognised in a particular state need not limit its operations to that state. This meant that universities approved by the governments of Chattisgarh or Himachal Pradesh can set up campuses in Delhi or Noida, where they are more likely to get students from well off families who can afford their astronomical fees. What is more, they are not even accountable to the local governments, since their recognition comes from a far away state. Add to this a new culture of well-branded private educational institutions allowing franchisees at far away locations to run their courses, without being responsible to the students or teachers in any other way. This is increasingly becoming a trend with foreign universities, especially among those who do not want to set up their own shop here, but would like to benefit from the degree-purchasing power of the growing upwardly mobile economic class of India. Soon we might see private educational institutions getting them listed in the stock market and soliciting investments in the education business on the slogan that its demand will never see the sunset.

The economics of imparting higher education are such that, barring a few courses in arts and humanities, imparting quality education in science, technology, engineering, medicine etc. requires huge investments in infrastructure, all of which cannot be recovered through student fees, without making higher education inaccessible to a large section of students. Unlike many better-known private educational institutions in Western countries that operate in the charity mode with tuition waivers and fellowships (which is one reason why our students go there), most private colleges and universities in India are pursuing a profit motive. This is the basic reason for charging huge tuition fees, apart from forced donations, capitation fees and other charges. Despite huge public discontent, media interventions and many court cases, the governments have not been able to regulate the fee structure and donations in these institutions. Even the courts have only played with the terms such as payment seats, management quotas etc., without addressing the basic issue of fee structure.

Privatisation of Teacher Education

"The destiny of India is now being shaped in her class rooms". This is the opening sentence of the Kothari Education Commission report (1964-66). What kind of destiny has been actually shaped during the last sixty years? There are thousands of schools without primary needs. The position of teacher's economic condition is also poor when compared to USA teachers. Majority of teacher educational institutions are under the control of private sector. The main aim of private organisations is to get profit.

It is not only students but also teachers who are at the receiving end of the ongoing transformation in higher and professional education. The nation today witnesses the declining popularity of teaching as a profession, not only among the students that we produce, but also among parents, scientists, society and the government. The teaching profession today attracts only those who have missed all other "better" opportunities in life, and is increasingly mired in bureaucratic controls and anti-education concepts such as "hours" of teaching "load", "paid-by-the-hour", "contractual" teachers etc. With privatisation reducing education to a commodity, teachers are reduced to tutors and teaching is reduced to coaching. The consumerist boom and the growing salary differentials between teachers and other professionals and the value systems of the emerging free market economy have made teaching one of the least attractive professions that demands more work for less pay. Yet, the society expects teachers not only to be inspired but also to do an inspiring job!

Present Status of Teacher Education

Permission is granted by the NCTE regional centres to number of teacher education institutions/colleges especially in the private unaided sector. Take for example, in Andhra Pradesh, there are more than 300 B.Ed Colleges in the private unaided sector and there are less than 20 B.Ed colleges in Government and aided sector. Is there any kind of supervision either by the university authorities or by the government officials or by the officers of NCTE with regard to availability of the staff during college days, proper attendance of the students, proper organisation and running of different programmes of B.Ed Course? It is a doubtful validity. The first and foremost supervising authority for running B.Ed programme is the concerned University. The concerned officials of the university have to make frequent surprise visits to the B.Ed Colleges under its Jurisdiction. If any loopholes identified, necessary steps may be taken for rectifying them at the earliest possible time; then only the quality of B.Ed programmes can be improved.

In most of the private B.Ed. colleges in the state of Andhra Pradesh, there is two or three teaching staff only. In some of the universities, there are no selection committees for these colleges. The managements will run the colleges according to their whims and fancies. In majority of the situations, they are charging Rs.6000/- for a set of B.Ed. records which cost about Rs.300/- in the market. They will pay less than Rs. 5000/- to the teaching staff. They are collecting huge amounts from the students under the heads; 'practical examinations', 'study tours', etc. they allow less than 20% attendance students to the examinations by collecting huge amounts from them. Some private management resort to all types of fraud activities. Then, who will set right these things? The first and foremost is the concerned affiliating university, then the state government and NCTE at the regional level and national level. Honesty persons with surprise visits can make the situation better.

Conclusion

India is a developing country. Different types of religious people are living in the country. We have thousand years of tradition and culture.

Now we are living in the technological and modern world. Because of globalisation a lot of change occurring. Education is a primary need for all in the society. It is the duty of government to provide free education for all up to 14 years. All people have no opportunity to study higher and professional education. Now majority of professional educational institutions are under the control of private organisations. Especially all teacher educational institutions are in the private sector. The main aim of private sector is to get profit. How it is possible to expect quality education? It is not possible to study Medicine or Engineering course for a poor student in the society. It is necessary to establish more and more professional and higher educational institutions in the country. Teacher is a national builder. He has a capacity to change the world. There are some benefits and losses due to privatisation of professional education. But India is a developing country. It is better to establish all professional educational institutions under the government sector. Then only it is possible to study all types of courses for poor section children and India will become developed country in the world.

CHAPTER

22

Research in Teacher Education

– *Dr. B. Ramachandra Reddy*
– *Dr. Naraginti Amareswaran*

Introduction

The role of the teacher is changing so fast that no amount of pre-service or in-service teacher education can probably cope with the expectations of the society. The teacher needs to be conceived as a 'changing agent' and not as a mere transmitter of knowledge and culture. He can work wonders provided he feels like doing so. From where can that feeling come? Surely, from within. But is it feasible? Can he live isolated from the beliefs, customs, manners, aspirations, etc. of the society of which he is a part? And if yes, in which respect? Can he ever get back the lost status?

Are our teacher preparation programmes competent to inculcate among the trainees the qualities, abilities, attitudes, ideals, etc. expected of a 'good teacher'? Have we pin-pointed the objective of different teacher preparation programmes so that we can at least try to achieve them? The meaning and concept of teaching has changed a lot. Nowadays, it is believed that there is no need for 'teaching', what we want is 'learning'.

In the process of learning, the emphasis is on 'help' rendered occasionally and at appropriate times. How many of our teachers are competent to do this? Can any teacher preparation programme help in this? A lot of research in teacher education is necessary in this direction.

Importance of Teacher

Teacher plays an important role in the field of education. Today's education is child-centred. But the child centred education cannot be successful without the teacher. The teacher is the maker of the future of the child. The children of today are the citizens and leaders of tomorrow. It means that the teacher is the maker of the leaders or rulers of the nation.

Like a master architect, the teacher has a very thorough knowledge of all the details essential to his work. He knows the real nature of the objectives of his work and the ends to be attained. Besides an understanding of the nature of the outcomes desired, he understands the nature of the different kinds of learning experiences necessary to attain them. He also knows how to organise and direct such learning experiences. Further, to do this satisfactorily he knows how to use effectively the best teaching techniques and devices available. He guides learning and gives suggestions and directions to the students in order to make them able to attain the desired knowledge. In any system of education, teacher has a pivotal role to play. The responsibility of making the education work successful lies with the teacher. He is undoubtedly the key point in all educational programmes and the quality of education depends on the quality of teachers. The teacher today is required to be able to cope up with the aspirations of rising generations of youth and the changing needs of the society and has to play a multidimensional role.

Teaching has always been considered to be essential for preservation and development of all intellectual life. Among other agencies, teachers are considered to be the major transmitters of accumulated knowledge and experience of human race from one generation to the next. The very foundation of the social order rests on citizens who are taught and trained in the classroom with or without walls. Teachers thus, determine to a great extent the character and destination of a nation.

Place of Teacher in any Educational System

"No system of education, no syllabus, no methodology, no text book can rise above the level of its teachers. If a country wants to have quality education it must have quality teachers"

—V.S. Mathews

"Of all the different factors which influence the quality of education and its contribution to national development; the quality, competence and character of teachers are undoubtedly the most significant...."

—Kothari Education Commission (1964-66)

The importance of the teachers in the educational programme of a country is too great. The greatness of a country does not depend on lofty buildings, gigantic projects and large armies, but on the quality of its citizens. If a nation has young men of sterling character and unimpeachable patriotism, she is found to make rapid progress in all fields. Young men are entrusted to the care of the teacher and it is therefore the sacred duty of the teacher to impart the right type of knowledge and make them good citizens. It is the teacher who impresses his children with his personality.

The framers of Second Five Year Plan in India observed, "At all times the teacher is pivot in the system of education". This is especially true in the case of a nation in its transition. The Secondary Education Commission (1952-53) also points out that every teacher and educationist of experience knows that even the best curriculum and the perfect syllabus remain dead unless quickened into life by right methods of teaching and the right kind of teachers. For imparting good education a good teacher is needed. All other things related to infrastructure are secondary.

The teacher, a national integrator as he is, is the backbone of society, particularly so in the remote villages. He stands as an outstanding figure among the illiterate and semi-literate families. He is their friend, Philosopher and guide. The teacher actively shares the responsibility of reconstructing a social order, with all the cherished values and traditional beliefs, which are being eroded by the surge of new ideals and practices. He acts as a social reformer and counsellor to the community.

The role of the modern teacher is not confined to teaching alone. He/she is expected to participate in the development programmes of the community life. The question arises as to how this could be integrated with the teacher education programmes. Mudaliar Commission (1952-53) Report stated rightly, "we are convinced that the most important factor in the contemplated education reconstruction is the teacher-his personal qualities, his educational qualifications, his professional training and the place that he occupies in the school as well as in the community". On similar lines Kothari Commission (1964-66) stated that, "Nothing is more important than securing a sufficient supply of high quality recruits to the teaching profession, providing them with the best possible professional preparation and creating satisfactory conditions of work in which they can be fully effective".

The Concept of Teacher Education

Teacher Education has been defined as, "All formal and informal activities and experiences that help to qualify a person to discharge his responsibilities as a member of the teaching profession and to discharge his responsibilities more effectively". The concept of "Teacher Education" is not new. However, scholarliness was considered the sole criterion for becoming a teacher. The concept that teachers are born and not made was also prevalent in olden days.

It has been aptly remarked, "If you educate a boy, you educate one individual. If you educate a girl, you educate the whole family and if you educate an individual as a teacher, you educate the whole community".

The contention that teacher are born, not made, can be true only in a few rare cases. It is also not contended that training, by itself, is sure to make a good teacher. But it is generally observed that a teacher with training becomes more mature and confident to perform his task more efficiently. Proper training and education enables the teacher to have knowledge of how children grow, develop and learn how they can be taught best and how their innate capacities can be brought out and developed.

Teacher Education is not mere pedagogy or acquisition of a training qualification. It is preparation of persons for family, for society and for the country. It is nurturing of creativity, inculcation of commitment and generation of a strong will to contribute at the highest level of efficiency through a value-based approach. Teacher Education is a process of unearthing the treasure within every learning centre. It is the process, which makes the individuals realize the magnitude and potentialities, which, if nurtured and inculcated in the right direction, could make significant contribution to the identified sectors.

Need and Significance of Teacher Education

The quality of a nation depends upon the quality of its citizens; the quality of citizens depends upon the quality of their education; the quality of education depends upon the quality of teachers; and the quality of teachers depends upon the quality of Teacher Education among many other factors.

The 21st century has been acknowledged as the century of learners and teachers, and we have to demonstrate that every teacher every day is performing the miracle of teaching. The learning society offers many and varied opportunities for learning at school and in economic, social and cultural life. The teachers are now required to update their knowledge. The teacher will have to be essentially a learner and the learner in his turn will also act as a teacher.

Teacher Education is needed for kindling the initiatives of the teacher, for keeping it alive, for removing the evils of 'hit and miss' process, for according a process, for according a professional status to the teaching profession and above all for making the optimum use of time and energy of the teacher and the taught.

Kothari Education Commission (1964-66) observed; "A sound programme of professional education of teachers is essential for the qualitative improvement of education. Investment in Teacher Education can yield very rich dividends because the financial resources required are small when measured against the resulting improvement in the education of millions".

In the light of this basic need, teacher education, as it stands today in India, is in dire need of rejuvenation, not just of a tinkering with a topic here and a topic there, or the provision of gadgets like 'computer' and other hardware and software, but a total overhauling of the entire system. This is reflected in five significant aspects in the National Policy on Education (NPE), 1986 and Programme of Action, 1992, namely: (*i*) Education as investment for the present and future; (*ii*) Five-fold role of teachers (teaching, aids preparation, extension, research and management); (*iii*) Value development to deal with value crises in society; (*iv*) Merit as the only basis of recruitment of teacher and to meet all these four; and (*v*) Overhauling of Teacher Education.

National Policy on Education (NPE), 1986 calls for the overhauling of Teacher Education as the first step towards educational reorganisation.

In this context effective Teacher Education becomes a core condition to ensure high proficiency and quality school education. In other words effective school education anticipates effective Teacher Education.

Review of Research in Teacher Education

Mehrotra (2006) reviewed the research in India in Teacher Education from 1993 to 2000. Studies on which this trend is based can be classified as follows:

Teacher Education

Area	Number of studies
A. Pre-service	
1. Admissions	3
2. Programmes	18
3. Teacher Trainees/Educators	16
4. Affective Domain	4
5. Outcome/Output	9
	50
B. In-service	
6. Programmes and their Evaluation	22
7. Training Needs	14
8. Higher Education – Academic Staff Colleges	5
Miscellaneous	7
Total	**48**
	98

Some of the Studies are Mentioned Hereunder

Shukla (1995) made a comparative study of state level selecton procedure of admission to the B.Ed. courses institutions in Rajasthan and Madhya Pradesh, on the basis of a survey of the opinions of teacher educators, B.Ed., students and administrations. Kaur and Kaur (2000) intended to investigate the relationship between the entrance test scores as predictors and achievement of teacher trainees of correspondence courses of Punjab University, Patiala. Pant, Bhatnagar and Prakash (1998) made a review of the researches about the validity of Admission criteria used in counsellors' training programmes.

Sruvastava and Aggarwal (1999) studied the existing pattern of secondary pre-service teacher education in the country, analysed its various components, developed an improved model and prepared guidelines to restructure the internship programme. Mohanasundaram (2000) prepared suggestions about the introduction of communication interaction, multi-media packages, educational telecast and web-based learning activities to make teacher education programmes more effective. Singh (1997) compared the correlation between the scores of non-verbal creative thinking and the behaviour ratios of science student teachers trained through micro-teaching technique and traditional technique.

Patil and Deshmukh (1993) studied the relationship between Aptitude in teaching and teaching efficiency of B.Ed., pupil teachers. Swain (1996) studied differential factors in academic success of science and humanities teacher trainees of B.Ed course. Joshi (1994) studied the reactions of B.Ed trainees towards some innovations in teacher education programmes like orientation, flexibility, planning of learning, distribution of content according to their capacity, peer teaching, self study, discussions, relationships, attitude etc.

Gafoor (1996) made a critical study of the functioning and work efficiency of DIETs, assessing the material, human resources and the efficacy of various training programmes of DIETs. Rao (1997) made a study of the Adilabad agency experiment in activity method, which made an intervention to provide access to primary schools and provide quality education. Pushpamadham (1998) made an experiment to discover the teacher potential through participatory research, as part of capacity building programme for primary school teachers.

Subrahmanyam (1998) made an assessment of the impact of Academic staff orientation programmes of the ASCs (Academic Staff Colleges) on the university and college teachers. Ogunkola (2000) investigated the perception of high school teacherws towards in-service training programmes in Nigeria. Reddy and Srinivas (1997) attempted to study the sources of teacher stress, the nature of its association with teacher effectiveness and to find out the efficacy of behavioural programme to manage stress and improve effectiveness in primary male teachers in the age range 30-40 years.

Discussion and Suggestions

The discussion and suggestions given by Mehrotra (2006) after reviewing the research in Teacher Education are as follows:

Although, it may appear that the studies have covered all aspects-context, pre-stage, process, product of teacher education—very vital areas have not even been touched. Three studies regarding Admissions have undertaken a good assessment of the policies and procedures at present and provide role guidance for future actions. While admission of the right persons to teacher education courses for the teaching profession is very important, it is surprising that not much research has been done in designing appropriate selection procedures. While admission tests are now widely held at state / university/institutional level, it is surprising that not many researches have taken proper care of the validity of the procedure – of the three studies only one concerns the mainstream B.Ed course, while the second is about a correspondence course and the third about counsellor programmes. Indepth studies are needed in the area so that only persons with aptitude towards teaching are selected for teacher education courses.

The researches find it convenient to study several psycho-social, educational and other characteristics of Pre-service Teacher Educations. Also, effect of some practices in their courses has been investigated. Yet, no comprehensive picture emerges. Their attitude;

commitment towards the teaching profession or their study habits during the programme have not been studied.

Effectiveness of the teacher-education programmes needs to be deeply analysed. The outcome of the programmes has been studied on the basis of only 'perceptions' which are generally not seriously responded to. Rigorous systematic studies about the curriculum, the courses, the practices, and the work culture in the institutions should be the concern of research.

The studies in In-service education are mostly in primary education and pertain to the functioning of DIETs, the DPEP programmes and Teacher Empowerment. A few have made deep penetrating studies, but most only touch the issue quite superficially. Even the concept of teacher empowerment has not had adequate clarity.

Distance education should have been studied more thoroughly by the Distance Education institutions themselves. A beginning seems to have been made in studying the In-service programmes in higher education conducted by the Academic Staff Colleges (ASCS). Their functioning and effect should be studied in greater detail. They conduct orientation programmes/Refresher courses for which university teacher attend simply because they are mandatory for promotions.

A survey of the studies under Teacher Education does not present a satisfactory scenario. Teacher education institutions are the live laboratories, which provide plenty of bases in which teacher educators and researchers in the Departments of Education should be interested. The structure of teacher education programmes continues unchanged while the nature of schools, the teachers and the teaching gets changed with civilisational, cultural and technological changes in society. The researchers should provide the fundamental grounds based on their research for effecting the needed changes in teacher education programmes.

Most of the studies under reference were undertaken for the Ph.D. Degree research has its constraints. It is time bound, deals with isolated themes, seldom taking a holistic view. The dominant motive is its evaluation and acquiring the Degree and not necessarily generation of knowledge.

Individual research is found to cover only limited points of any phenomenon. The national organisations, *e.g.*, NCERT, NCTE, UGC should commission and fund national level, holistic comprehensive themes for research. They may be designed centrally and be conducted by involving, if need be, various individuals/ institutions. The trends show some practical steps taken by these organizations to initiate comprehensive research.

High quality research will be promoted by creation of a research culture in our university departments of education, institutions of teacher education and the national institutions. The academics need be encouraged by providing them with time and funds as needed and by flexibility in workload and work assignments.

Teachers, teaching and teacher education are so closely linked that isolated studies in either, without the other two, do not give us much. Teacher education programmes and institutions initiate the teachers into the profession of teaching. The isolation of teacher—education from schools does not promote either. The teachers quickly forgetting what they learnt during their teacher education, is not a healthy happening. This makes a teacher education programme only a formality of a required certification.

Close knit, broad but deep studies, wherein the teacher as a professional, teaching as a profession and teacher education as a professional course effectively perform their respective but related roles need to be considered, designed and executed by individual researcher and institutional agencies.

Measures should be identified for the results of Research being taken seriously by policy makers and administrators. The results of research should be such as would influence or promote action directly or indirectly. Documentation of the research, making them widely and easily available and the use of research accumulated during the last fifty years would profit teacher education, teaching and teachers. It may be that much research has been highly pedantic, limited in scope, tentative and Jargon dominated. Yet, there is enough already which can be put to use. Relevant research findings need to be applied to improve programmes and practices. This would give confidence to researchers.

The researchers need to take into account the dysfunctional nature of some educational research. The researchers need to identify crucial problems. For all educational research and more so that dealing with teachers, teaching and teacher education, the schools and the teacher education institutions should be taken as living laboratories. Most research should be conducted in real situations. Teachers and teaching may be surveyed, observed and analysed in these laboratories, where a vast variety of specimens and subjects for experiments are available and are awaiting observation and experimentation.

REFERENCES

1. *Kothari Education Commission* (1964-66): It is also known as. "*Indian Education Commission*", with Kothari as its Chairman, Report, p. 46.
2. MANCHALA, C. (2005): "*Influence of Certain Psycho-sociological Factors on Scholastic Achievement of B.Ed. Students*"; unplished Ph.D. Thesis, Department of Education, S.V.University, Tirupati.
3. MANCHALA, C. (2007): "*Achievement of B.Ed., Students*". A Text Book; Discovery Publishing House, New Delhi-110002; 2007 pp. 3-12.
4. Mathews, V.S: From '*An Evaluative Study of Primary School Teacher Education Programme in Andhra Pradesh*" by K.Chandra Sekhar (2000) unpublished Ph.D. thesis, Dept. of Education, S.V.University, Tirupati, India, p. 2.
5. Mehrotra, R.N. (2006): "*Teacher and Teaching*" – *A Trend Report in Sixth Survey of Educational Research* (1993-2000) vo. 1, pp.13-53; published by NCERT, Sri Aurobindo Marg, New Delhi-110016; May 2006.
6. *Mudaliar Commission* (1952-53): It is also known as '*Secondary Education Commission*' headed by Mudaliar.
7. *Secondary Education Commission* (1952-53): It is also known as '*Mudaliar Commission*' headed by Mudaliar.

CHAPTER 23

Role of Commercial Banks and Education in the Development of Weaker Sections in India

– *Dr. Naraginti Amareswaran*
– *N. Koteeswarai*
– *Dr. B. Ramchandra Reddy*

Introduction

Now we are living in the Scientific, Technological and Modern world. A lot of changes are occurring in the day to day life of human beings. India is a developing country. Majority of peoples occupation is agriculture. The Planning Commission made a survey for finding out the number of persons below poverty line and estimated that 18.96% of the total peoples live below poverty line as of the year 1993-94. As per 2001 census the literacy rate of Scheduled Castes and Scheduled Tribes was 54.69% and 47.10% respectively. It is necessary to take care about poor and illiteracy. Banks have an eminent role in the development of weaker sections in the society.

History of Banks in India

Banking in India originated in the first decade of 18th century with The General Bank of India coming into existence in 1786. This was followed by Bank of Hindustan. Both these banks are now defunct. The oldest bank in existence in India is the State Bank of India being established as "The Bank of Bengal" in Calcutta in June 1806. A couple of decades later, foreign banks like Credit Lyonnais started their Calcutta operations in the 1850s. At that point of time, Calcutta was the most active trading port, mainly due to the trade of the British Empire, and due to which banking activity took roots there and prospered. The first fully Indian owned bank was the Allahabad Bank, which was established in 1865.

By the 1900s, the market expanded with the establishment of banks such as Punjab National Bank, in 1895 in Lahore and Bank of India, in 1906, in Mumbai—both of which were founded under private ownership. The Reserve Bank of India formally took on the responsibility of regulating the Indian banking sector from 1935. After India's independence in 1947, the Reserve Bank was nationalised and given broader powers.

Current Situation of Banks

Currently (2008), banking in India is generally fairly mature in terms of supply, product range and reach-even though reach in rural India still remains a challenge for the private sector and foreign banks. In terms of quality of assets and capital adequacy, Indian banks are considered to have clean, strong and transparent balance sheets relative to other banks in comparable economies in its region. The Reserve Bank of India is an autonomous body, with minimal pressure from the government. The stated policy of the Bank on the Indian Rupee is to manage volatility but without any fixed exchange rate-and this has mostly been true.

With the growth in the Indian economy expected to be strong for quite some time-especially in its services sector-the demand for banking services, especially retail banking, mortgages and investment services are expected to be strong.

In March 2006, the Reserve Bank of India allowed Warburg Pincus to increase its stake in Kotak Mahindra Bank (a private sector bank) to 10%. This is the first time an investor has been allowed to hold more than 5% in a private sector bank since the RBI announced norms in 2005 that any stake exceeding 5% in the private sector banks would need to be vetted by them.

Currently, India has 88 scheduled commercial banks (SCBs)—28 public sector banks (that is with the Government of India holding a stake), 29 private banks (these do not have government stake; they may be publicly listed and traded on stock exchanges) and 31 foreign banks. They have a combined network of over 53,000 branches and 17,000 ATMs. According to a report by ICRA Limited, a rating agency, the public sector banks hold over 75 per cent of total assets of the banking industry, with the private and foreign banks holding 18.2% and 6.5% respectively.

LIST OF BANKS IN INDIA

Public Sector Banks

SBI group:

State Bank of India, with its seven associate banks commands the largest banking resources in India. SBI and its associate banks are:

- State Bank of India
- State Bank of Bikaner & Jaipur
- State Bank of Hyderabad
- State Bank of Indore
- State Bank of Mysore
- State Bank of Patiala
- State Bank of Saurashtra
- State Bank of Travancore

After the amalgamation of New Bank of India with Punjab National Bank, currently there are 19 nationalised banks in India:

- Allahabad bank
- Andhra Bank
- Bank of Baroda
- Bank of India
- Bank of Maharashtra
- Canara Bank
- Central Bank of India
- Corporation Bank
- Dena Bank
- Indian Bank
- Indian Overseas Bank
- Oriental Bank of Commerce

- Punjab & Sind Bank
- Punjab National Bank
- Syndicate Bank
- Union Bank of India
- United Bank of India
- UCO Bank
- Vijaya Bank

Private Sector Banks

- Axis Bank (formerly UTI Bank)
- Bank of Rajasthan
- Bharat Overseas Bank
- Catholic Syrian Bank
- Centurion Bank of Punjab (Merged with HDFC bank)
- City Union Bank
- Development Credit Bank
- Dhanalakshmi Bank
- Federal Bank
- Kumfu Blade Bank
- Ganesh Bank of Kurundwad
- HDFC Bank
- ICICI Bank
- IDBI Bank
- IndusInd Bank
- ING Vysya Bank
- Jammu & Kashmir Bank
- Karnataka Bank Limited.
- Karur Vysya Bank
- Kotak Mahindra Bank
- Lakshmi Vilas Bank

- Lord Krishna Bank (now Centurion Bank of Punjab)
- Nainital Bank
- Ratnakar Bank
- Rupee Bank
- Saraswat Bank
- SBI Commercial and International Bank
- South Indian Bank
- Tamilnad Mercantile Bank Ltd.
- Thane Janata Sahakari Bank
- Bassein Catholic Bank
- United Western Bank(now IDBI Bank)
- YES Bank
- IDBI Bank

Foreign Banks

- ABN AMRO Bank N.V.
- Abu Dhabi Commercial Bank Ltd
- American Express Bank
- Antwerp Diamond Bank
- Arab Bangladesh Bank
- Bank International Indonesia
- Bank of America
- Bank of Bahrain & Kuwait
- Bank of Ceylon
- Bank of Nova Scotia
- Bank of Tokyo Mitsubishi UFJ
- Barclays Bank
- BNP Paribas
- Calyon Bank
- ChinaTrust Commercial Bank

- Cho Hung Bank
- Citibank
- DBS Bank
- Deutsche Bank
- HSBC (Hongkong & Shanghai Banking Corporation)
- JPMorgan Chase Bank
- Krung Thai Bank
- Mashreq Bank
- Mizuho Corporate Bank
- Oman International Bank
- Société Générale
- Standard Chartered Bank
- State Bank of Mauritius
- Scotia
- Taib Bank

Regional Banks

- Adhiyaman Grama Bank
- Alaknanda Gramin Bank
- Aligarh Gramin Bank
- Avadh Gramin Bank
- Balasore Gramya Bank
- Ballia Kshetriya Gramin Bank
- Banaskantha Mehsana Gramin Bank
- Bareilly Kshetriya Gramin Bank
- Bijapur Grameena Bank
- Bilaspur-Raipur Kshetriya Gramin Bank
- Bolangir Anchalik Gramya Bank
- Bundelkhand Kshetriya Gramin Bank
- BundiChittorgarh KshetriyaGraminBank

- Cauvery Grameena Bank
- Chaitanya Grameena Bank
- Chambal Kshetriya Gramin Bank
- Champaran Kshetriya Gramin Bank
- Chhatrasal Gramin Bank
- ChhindwaraSeoniKshetriyaGraminBank
- Chitradurga Gramin Bank
- Cuttack Gramya Bank
- Damoh Panna Sagar Kshetriya Gramin Bank
- Devipatan Kshetriya Gramin Bank
- Dhenkanal Gramya Bank
- Dungarpur Banswara Kshetriya Gramin Bank
- Ellaquai Dehati Bank
- Farrukhabad Gramin Bank
- Gaur Gramin Bank
- Gurgaon Gramin Bank
- Hadoti Kshetriya Gramin Bank
- Himachal Gramin Bank
- Hissar-Sirsa Kshetriya Gramin Bank
- Indore Ujjain Kshetriya Gramin Bank
- Jaipur Nagaur Aanchalik Gramin Bank
- Jamnagar Rajkot Gramin Bank
- Jamuna Gramin Bank
- Jhabua-Dhar Kshetriya Gramin Bank
- Kakathiya Grameena Bank
- Kalpatharu Grameena Bank
- Kamraz Rural Bank
- Kanpur Kshetriya Gramin Bank
- Kapurthala Ferozpur Kshetriya Gramin Bank

- Kashi Gramin Bank
- Kisan Gramin Bank, Budaun
- Kolar Gramin Bank
- Krishna Grameena Bank
- Kshetriya Gramin Bank, Hoshangabad
- Kutch Grameen Bank
- Malaprabha Grameena Bank
- Mandla Balaghat Kshetriya Gramin Bank
- Manjira Grameena Bank
- Marwar Ganganagar Bikaner Gramin Bank (Previously : Marwar Gramin Bank)
- Mewar Aanchalik Gramin Bank
- Nagarjuna Grameena Bank
- Netravati Grameena Bank
- Nimar Kshetriya Gramin Bank
- North Malabar Gramin Bank
- Panchmahal Vadodara Gramin Bank
- Pandyan Grama Bank
- Pinakini Grameena Bank
- Pragjyotish Gaonlia Bank
- Prathama Bank
- Raigarh Kshetriya Gramin Bank
- Rani Lakshmi Bai Kshetriya Gramin Bank
- Ratlam Mandsaur Kshetriya Gramin Bank
- Rayalaseema Grameena Bank
- Rewa-Sidhi Gramin Bank
- Sahyadri Gramin Bank
- Samyut Kshetriya Gramin Bank
- Sangameshwara Grameena Bank

- Shahjahanpur Kshetriya Gramin Bank
- Shivpuri Guna Kshetriya Gramin Bank
- South Malabar Gramin Bank
- Sree Anantha Grameena Bank
- Sri Saraswati Grameena Bank
- Sri Visakha Grameena Bank
- Surat Bharuch Gramin Bank
- Thar Aanchalik Gramin Bank
- Tripura Gramin Bank
- Tungabhadra Gramin Bank
- Vidur Gramin Bank

Weaker Sections in India

In a fresh twist to the controversy over the proportion of OBCs in India's population, a government survey released 1st September 2007 indicated that backward castes formed about 41% of the populace.

A survey by the National Sample Survey Organisation (NSSO) put the OBC population in the country at 40.94%, the SC population at 19.59%, ST population at 8.63% and the rest at 30.80%.

According to the survey, 91.4% of STs, 79.8% of SCs and 78.0% of OBCs were in rural areas. Conversely, 8.6% of STs, 20.2% of SCs and 22% of OBCs were in urban areas, while 37.7% of 'others' lived in India's towns and cities.

The booming economic growth seems to be reflecting in the expenditure of urban India, which is spending nearly double the amount on an average compared to the rural areas. The per capita monthly expenditure of people living in urban areas was Rs. 1,052.36 a month as against Rs 558.78 of those in rural areas.

With minor exceptions, the general level of spending of SCs and STs was lower than OBCs and the others, while that of OBCs in turn was lower than that of the others. According to the NSSO survey, the all India average spending by rural STs was the lowest at Rs. 426.19, followed by rural SCs at Rs. 474.72, OBCs Rs. 556.72 and others Rs. 685.31. In urban India, STs spent Rs. 857.46, SCs 758.38, OBCs Rs. 870.93 and others Rs. 1,306.10 in a month on an average.

The survey highlights the fact that in rural India, 64.3% of the population continues to be dependent on agriculture as a major source of livelihood, either through self-employment in agriculture (39.4%) or as agricultural labour (24.9%). In this sector, the population dependent on self-employment (agriculture and non-agriculture) was reported to be 49.0% for ST, 36.6% for SC, 60.7% for OBC and 66.4% for others and that dependent on rural (agricultural or non-agricultural) labour was 56.4% for SC, 45.2% for ST, 30.7% for OBC and 21.8% for others.

In urban India, the proportion of population located in regular wage/salary earning households was almost the same (42.0% to 42.9%) for all social groups except OBCs (34.3%). Dependence on self-employment was more prevalent among OBCs (46.4%) as well as the residual class (45.3%) than the SCs (30.9%) and STs (27.4%).

In economically backward states like Bihar, Rajasthan, Madhya Pradesh and Orissa, SCs and STs were spending between Rs 344 to Rs. 527. However, in the educationally advanced state of Kerala, SCs were spending over Rs 750 a month, much higher than the national average.

Literacy of SC/ST

- As per 2001 census the literacy rate of Scheduled Castes and Scheduled Tribes was 54.69% and 47.10% respectively.
- Literacy rate of SC females compared to general population was much lower in the states of Bihar (15.58%), Jharkhand (22.55%), Uttar Pradesh (30.50%) and Rajasthan (33.87%).
- Literacy rate of ST females is extremely low in Bihar (15.54%).
- As per 2001 census the literacy rate was lowest for SCs in Bihar (28.47%) and highest in Mizoram (89.20%) and for STs, it was lowest in Bihar (28.17%) and highest in Mizoram (89.34%).
- Literacy rate of STs was more than the SCs in the states of Jharkhand, Meghalaya, Mizoram and Sikkim.

- In general the SCs were ahead of the STs in literacy. But in urban areas the STs are ahead of SCs.
- The percentage of learners of SCs and STs under literacy Campaigns are 23% and 12% respectively.
- The share of expendicture in implementation of literacy campaigns between the centre and states in tribal areas is 4:1 instead 2:1 in other areas.

Economy of India

The economy of India, when measured in USD exchange-rate terms, is the twelfth largest in the world, with a GDP of US $1.25 trillion (2008). It is the third largest in terms of purchasing power parity. India is the second fastest growing major economy in the world, with a GDP growth rate of 9.4% for the fiscal year 2006–2007. However, India's huge population has a per capita income of $4,542 at PPP and $1,089 in nominal terms (revised 2007 estimate).The World Bank classifies India as a low-income economy.

India's economy is diverse, encompassing agriculture, handicrafts, textile, manufacturing, and a multitude of services. Although two-thirds of the Indian workforces still earn their livelihood directly or indirectly through agriculture, services are a growing sector and play an increasingly important role of India's economy. The advent of the digital age, and the large number of young and educated populace fluent in English, is gradually transforming India as an important 'back office' destination for global outsourcing of customer services and technical support. India is a major exporter of highly-skilled workers in software and financial services, and software engineering. Other sectors like manufacturing, pharmaceuticals, biotechnology, nanotechnology, telecommunication, shipbuilding, aviation and tourism are showing strong potentials with higher growth rates.

India followed a socialist-inspired approach for most of its independent history, with strict government control over private sector participation, foreign trade, and foreign direct investment. However, since the early 1990s, India has gradually opened up its markets through economic reforms by reducing government controls on foreign trade and investment. The privatisation of publicly owned industries and the opening up of certain sectors to private and foreign interests has proceeded slowly amid political debate.

India faces a fast-growing population and the challenge of reducing economic and social inequality. Poverty remains a serious problem, although it has declined significantly since independence. Official surveys estimated that in the year 2004-2005, 27% of Indians were poor.

SC/ST Role in Indian Economy

While the United Progressive Alliance government wants to spread the spectacular gains made by India Inc in the last few years to scheduled castes and scheduled tribes, there are no reliable data on their participation in business, either as employees or as employers. The government, industry and civil society groups agree they have no data, which they admit are the building blocks for any action for inclusive growth.

They, however, agree on one thing — that the participation of scheduled castes and scheduled tribes in business is low, zero in large enterprises, and slightly more in small enterprises. The representation in states like Jharkhand, where their population is high, could be slightly higher.

According to Economic Census, 1998, enterprise distribution under the social group of 'Owner' is 7.7 per cent for scheduled castes, 4 per cent for scheduled tribes and 33.1 per cent for other backward castes. Not only is the data almost a decade old, it is hotly contested by social activists.

"We completely disagree with these numbers. Dalits are being denied ownership in all fields. Even in kirana stores, their proportion is absolutely nil," said Paul Diwakar, convenor, National Campaign for Dalit Human Rights.

Rosemary Vishwanath, a Bangalore-based consultant who works on issues confronting the socially weaker sections, said, "I do not understand what they mean by an entrepreneur. I don't know whether we can term a roadside cobbler an entrepreneur." Ashok Bharati, convenor, National Conference of Dalit Organisations, said, "Their entrepreneurship is almost negligible."

Milind Kamble of Pune-based 125-member Dalit Indian Chamber of Commerce and Industry, said, "If the proportion of scheduled castes and scheduled tribes in business was so high, what was the need for us to protest the economic imbalance all this while?"

However, Diwakar conceded there had been an improvement in the last three decades. "Some pockets of South India have seen a positive change, with Dalits entering fields like tourist services and prawn culture," he said.

There are other indications too. The Confederation of Indian Industry has been running an entrepreneurship development programme for young people from the economically weaker sections for several years.

"We now realise that most of them belong to scheduled castes and scheduled tribes. Several of them have done well and employ a large number of people," said a functionary of the industry association.

The situation is not so good when it comes to estimating the number of scheduled caste and scheduled tribe employees in the private sector. While members of the Federation of Indian Chambers of Commerce and Industry are averse to doing such a count, only 96 of CII's over 7,000 members have given such figures.

"The spread of such employees is between 5 per cent and 82 per cent. There are no trends in the data, except that their participation is more in areas where their population proportion is higher," said a CII functionary.

Role of Commercial Banks and Educational Institutions in Development of Weaker Sections

The 'Profitability Productivity syndrome' in the banking sector has recently turned out to be a topic of hot and perplexing debate. In the academic circle, however, most of the studies confine themselves to the narrow interpretation of the profitability and productivity. Role of Commercial Banks' Lending to Priority Sector is not related to only service but also with the profit. These studies prove the deterioration in profitability and productivity of Indian Commercial Banks, but more often then not, fail to interlink and analyse some crucial aspects of the problem. There are two distinct characteristics of post nationalization banking development in India. First, since nationalization commercial banks have made great and rapid strides in several spheres such as branch expansion, resource mobilisation and credit deployment etc. Consequently, the total number of offices, deposits and advances has stepped up considerably. What is important in the success story of commercial banks is that it involves several structural changes in favour of rural and priority sector. The nationalization 14 + 6 major commercial banks in 1969 and 1980 altered the ownership pattern in favour of public sector and provided wide ranging powers to the Government to influence the banking policy and orientation. At the time of nationalisation the socio-economic objectives were explicitly laid down and the banks were asked to contribute to the maximum possible extent towards economic and social development of the country. It was realised that the traditional banking ethics were not compatible with the needs of economic development and that balanced development was not possible without strengthening the hold of commercial banks in the backward and neglected areas.

New policy measures suitable to the rural lot were introduced and a massive thrust into the rural area thus started. Since then, the commercial banks have traversed a long way revealing a process of transformation from a position of petty dealers of debts to the rank of pioneers of economic development. Secondly, amidst the spectacular progress, however attractive it is, there are some discomforting features accompanied in advertently in the process of banking development. These features have helped in building up' strains and stresses' in the system thereby leading the banks gradually towards a difficult situation. The repercussions of these features can be seen in term of deterioration in profitability productivity and overall efficiency of commercial banks.

Role of Banks

- Bank staff may help the poor borrowers in filling up the forms and completing other formalities so that they are able to get credit facility within a stipulated period from the date of receipt of applications.
- In order to encourage SC/ST borrowers to take advantage of credit facilities, greater awareness among them about various

schemes formulated by banks will have to be created. As a majority of the eligible borrowers would be illiterate persons, publicity through brochures, other literature, etc. will be of limited utility. The more desirable method would be for the field staff of banks to contact such borrowers and explain to them the salient features of the schemes as also the advantages that will accrue. Banks should advise their branches to organise meetings more frequently exclusively for SC/ST beneficiaries to understand their credit needs and to incorporate the same in the credit plan.

- Bank should keep Application Register/ Deposit Register, Complaint Register in desired order and maintain relevant documents and pass book in local language too, besides in Hindi and English.
- Circulars issued by RBI/NABARD should be circulated among the staff for compliance.
- Banks should not insist on deposits while considering loan applications under Government sponsored poverty alleviation schemes/self-employment programmes from borrowers belonging to SCs /STs.It should also be ensured that applicable subsidy is not held back while releasing the loan component till the full repayment of bank dues. Non release of subsidy upfront amounts to under-financing and hampers asset creation/ income generation.
- A National SC/ST Finance and Development Corporation have been set up under the administrative control of Ministry of Welfare. Banks should advise their branches/controlling offices to render all the necessary institutional support to enable the institution to achieve the desired objectives.
- Advances sanctioned to State sponsored organizations of SC/ ST, for the specific purpose of purchase and supply of inputs to and/or the marketing of outputs of the beneficiaries *viz.* artisans, village and cottage industries of these organizations, should be treated as priority sector advances, subject to the condition that the relative advances are exclusively for the purpose of purchase and supply of inputs to and/or marketing of the outputs of beneficiaries of these organisations.

RESERVATIONS FOR SC/ST BENEFICIARIES UNDER MAJOR CENTRALLY SPONSORED SCHEMES

Swarnjayanti Gram Swarozgar Yojana (SGSY)

Under Swarnjayanti Gram Swarozgar Yojana (SGSY) Scheme, which is a major poverty alleviation scheme in rural / semi urban areas, not less than 50 per cent of the families assisted should belong to SCs/STs.

Prime Minister's Rozgar Yojana

The Prime Minister's Rozgar Yojana (PMRY) has been designed to provide credit to educated unemployed youth for setting up of the self-employment ventures in industries, services and business sectors. A reservation of 22.5 per cent has been provided for SCs/STs in the scheme.

Swarna Jayanti Sahari Rozgar Yojana

Under Swarna Jayanti Shahari Rozgar Yojana (SJSRY), which is a poverty alleviation scheme in urban areas, advances should be extended to SCs/STs to the extent of their strength in the local population.

Differential Rate of Interest Scheme

Under the DRI scheme, banks provide finance up to Rs. 6,500/- at a concessional rate of interest of 4% p.a to the weaker sections of the community for engaging in productive and gainful activities. In order to ensure that persons belonging to SCs/STs also derive adequate benefit under the Differential Rate of Interest (DRI) scheme, banks have been advised to grant to eligible borrowers belonging to SCs/STs such advances to the extent of not less than 2/5th (40 per cent) of total DRI advances.

Scheme for Liberation and Rehabilitation of Scavengers

The National Scheme for Liberation and Rehabilitation of Scavengers is for liberating the scavengers and their dependents from the existing hereditary and obnoxious occupation of manually removing night soil and filth and to provide them with alternate dignified occupation. The scheme covers primarily all scavengers belonging to the scheduled caste community. Scavengers belonging to other communities are also eligible for assistance.

Relaxations for SC/ST Beneficiaries under Major Centrally Sponsored Schemes

Under SGSY scheme, beneficiaries belonging to SC/ST are entitled to subsidy of 50% of the project cost with a maximum ceiling of Rs. 10,000/- as against the subsidy of 30% of project cost with a maximum ceiling of Rs. 7,500/- in case of beneficiaries under general category.

There is 10-year relaxation for the beneficiaries belonging to SCs/STs in the upper age limit to be eligible under PMRY (age limit for general category is 18-35).

Under the DRI scheme, the eligibility criteria that size of land holding should not exceed 1 acre of irrigated land and 2.5 acres of unirrigated land is not applicable to SCs/STs. Moreover, members of SCs/STs satisfying the income criteria of Rs. 7, 200/- under the scheme can also avail of housing loan upto Rs. 5, 000/- per beneficiary at a concessional rate of interest of 4% over and above the loan of Rs. 6,500/- available under the scheme.

The main aim of banks is to get profit. They give first priority for profit, then service. The majority of weaker section people are suffering because of banks rules. The banks services are available for only higher (economically) class people in the weaker section. Because of illiteracy the majority of weaker section people are not getting benefits from the governments and from the banks. The corruption is also high in our society when compared to developed countries in the world.

Educational Institutions

Education is the solution for all type of problems in the society. It is necessary to increase number of residential schools and colleges for SC's and ST's. They have no idea about banks. They don't know how to get loan from the banks? It is banks duty to find and give loan to the suitable poor weaker person in the society.

Allotment of Funds for SC/ST Students in the Budget 2008-09

- Navodaya Vidyalayas to be opened in 20 districts with special focus on regions having SC/ST concentration. Allocation of Rs 130 crore for this purpose.
- Rs.750 crore more to be given for merit scholarship to students up to 10th and 12th class.
- Rs. 85 crore sanctioned for scholarships to students pursuing science education.
- Twenty per cent hike in education budget this year from Rs. 28,674 crore to Rs. 34,400 crore.
- Rs. 75 crore sanctioned for Rajiv Gandhi National Fellowship Programme for SC/ST students pursuing M.Phil.
- SC, ST and minority students to continue to get special attention.
- Rs. 230 crore will be extended as additional equity to developmental organizations looking after the welfare of SC.

National Commission for SC/ST

With a view to provide safeguards against the exploitation of SCs and STs and to promote and protect their social, educational, economic and cultural interest, special provisions were made in the constitution. Due to their social disability and economic backwardness, they were grossly handicapped in getting reasonable share in elected offices, Govt. jobs and educational institution and, therefore it was considered necessary to follow a policy of reservation in favour to ensure their equitable participation in governance. For effective implementation of various safeguards provided in the Constitution for the SCs and STs and various other protective legislations, the Constitution provided for appointment of a Special Officer under Article 338 of the Constitution. The Special Officer who was designated as Commissioner for SC/STs was assigned the duty to investigate all matters relating to the safeguards provided for SCs/STs various statutes and to report to the President upon the working of these safeguards. In order to facilitate effective functioning of the office of the Commissioner for SC/STs 17 regional offices of the Commissioner were set up in different part of the country.

Conclusion

We are living in the Modern and Technological world. We developed in all the fields. But, the position of weaker sections in the society is not good. The poor becoming very poor and the rich becoming very rich. The economic inequalities are very much in between poor and rich in the society. The majority people occupation is agriculture. We are seeing suicide attempts of farmers daily in the newspapers. It shows the economic position and problems and farmers in the society. Banks have a prominent role in the development of farmers and other people in the society. The main aim of banks is profit oriented. It is necessary to change the attitude of banks towards weaker sections. Education is a solution for all type of problems. Through education it is possible to change the economic position and inequalities in the society. It is government duty to take necessary steps for the development of weaker section in the society.

REFERENCE

1. Budget 2008-09 - Highlights — India Development Gateway.
2. Census of India, 2001.
3. National Literacy Mission— Literacy Scenario in India— Literacy Rates for Total Population, Schedule Caste Population and Schedule Tribe Population by Sex.
4. Reserve Bank of India Report—2007-08.
5. The Evaluation of State Bank of India (Volume III).
6. Times of India, 1st Septembr 2007.

CHAPTER 24

Role of Higher Educational Institutions in Promotion of Rural Human Resources

– *Dr. Naraginti Amareswaran*
– *Dr. C. Manchala*

Introduction

The development of any nation depends mainly on the standards of its educational institutions. Education is the most powerful and effective instrument for inducing radical changes in the behaviour of students. Education is the process through which an individual is developed into individuality and a person into a personality. Education should be individualized and personalized to the utmost and should constitute preparation for self-learning.

First Higher Educational Institution

Education has been around for as long as man has been, though its structure and perception has varied over centuries and civilisations. The beginning of historically-documented higher education began with the Nanjing University founded in 258 AD in China which is generally believed to be the oldest higher education institution in the world, later becoming the first modern Chinese university in the early 1920s.

During the Vedic and Upanishadic period, India had some of the prominent institutions of higher education, which attracted scholars from distant places located in different parts of the world to come to India in pursuit of knowledge. The ancient universities of Takshashila and Nalanda, which survived till the end of the fifth and twelfth Century AD respectively, imparted knowledge in different areas according to the requirements of the contemporary society.

In the knowledge economy, the objectives of a society changes from fulfilling the basic needs of all round development to empowerment. The education system instead of going by text-book teaching will be promoted by reactive, interactive self learning, both formal and informal, with focus on values, merit and quality. The workers instead of being skilled or semi-skilled will be knowledgeable, self-empowered and flexibly skilled. Finally, the economy will be knowledge driven and not industry driven.

All fields of human activity, including education, have been influenced by the process of globalisation clubbed with unexpected advancements in information and communication technology. Within the various sectors of education, higher academic and technical education has been affected the most. It is now increasingly realised that knowledge is universal and its creation and dissemination cannot be confined within national boundaries. The world is now like a global village, and continuous international interaction has become an essential component of human survival. The globalisation of economy has led to internationalization of higher education, not merely for economic benefits, but also for increased social interaction and promotion of international understanding.

The main aim of primary educational institutions is to develop four skills. Whish are listening, speaking, reading and writing.

Importance of Education

Education means the gradual process of acquiring knowledge. Education is a preparation for life. Swami Vivekananda, the great thinker and reformer of India had remarked: "We want that education by which character is formed, strength of mind is increased, intellect is expanded and by which one can stand on one's own feet. Education is the manifestation of the perfection already in man."

The great Nobel Laureate and writer Rabindra Nath Tagore was one of the earliest educators to think in terms of the global education village, and his educational model has a unique sensitivity and aptness for education within multi-racial, multi-lingual and multi-cultural situations.

Development through Educational Institutions

Independent India has witnessed an upsurge in the growth of higher education. Yet from an international perspective, we are relatively slow, despite being steady in registering advancements in learning. Today India has the second largest education system in the world, next only to the USA. Yet, the total number of students represents hardly six percent of the relevant age group, i.e. 18-23 years, which is much below the average of developed countries which is about 47 per cent. The gap is glaring. Hence the phenomenal challenge. The journey from being 'Good' to being 'Great' appears to be long and arduous.

India is a developing country. 70% of people are living in the villages. The rural area literacy percentage is very low when compared to urban area literacy rate. The main occupation of Indians is cultivation. The duty of higher educational institutions is to introduce courses which help to improve the rural people socio-economic status in the society. Through education it is possible to change the world. Because of globalisation now world become a village. We get any type of information with in the seconds. Educational institutions have prominent role in the development of rural people in the society.

The development of India depends mainly on the development of villages. But today the state and central governments are not taking good steps to develop villages. The economic positions of farmers are not good. The suicide attempts of farmers are increasing. The unemployment percentage is also increasing. By introducing new agricultural and self-employment courses in the vocational institutions it is possible overall development of rural areas.

The first citizen of India today, Dr. A P J Abdul Kalam, while envisioning India of 2020, recently observed - "Spirit of Inquiry, creativity, entrepreneurial and moral leadership are the capabilities central to nation building in a democracy. Educators should develop in our children these capacities and make them autonomous learners who are self-directed and self-controlled."

Earlier all over the world, education, especially higher education, was available only to a privileged few. In the context of a knowledge society and the goals of sustainable development, higher education needs to percolate to the masses, not only just in terms of quantity, but also quality. In the last few years, this shift has been slowly taking place. Still, glaring deficiencies remain in the access to higher education, overall development of the student, sensitivity to human needs and equality in our society.

Also come into play, concerns in higher education that come with globalization and rapidity of change like fast rate of obsolescence of knowledge, quality, competitiveness of education services, networking of institutions and innovations and new practices in delivery. Combined with this are the concerns for sustainable development of the world.

Conclusion

The higher educational institutions have a prominent role in the development of rural areas. Through education it is easy to motivate people in the society. Education gives knowledge, wealth and health. Education is a part in our daily life. Through education it is possible to learn new things. The higher educational institutions duty is to give training for adults in the society to proper utilization of sources in the nature. India has a large number of human resources in the world after China. It is necessary to establish some higher educational institutions in our country. It is also educational institution duty to motivate people to use advanced technology in the field of agriculture and self-employment fields like poultry and architecture etc.

CHAPTER 25

Role of Information Technology in Teacher Education

—Dr. Naraginti Amareswaran
—Dr. B. Ramachandra Reddy

Education is the learning of human souls to what is best, and making what is best out of them? —***John Ruskin***

Now we are living in the modern world. A lot of change is occurring in every day. With the help of science and technology we have developed in all the fields. With the help of technology now it is easy to know any type of information with in seconds throughout the world.

Radio, Television, Phone, Mobile, Computer and Internet have changed the human life. Through education we can learn any thing easily with the help of these instruments. According to Mahatma Gandhi, the father of Indian Nation, by giving good education to each and every one we can remove poverty and develop good character.

India is a developing country. Now we have very much demand in the IT filed. The development of IT is a wonder. Now lacks of student are entering in to the IT filed. Our central and state governments are also giving more importance for Information Technology.

There is a separate department for Information Technology under the Ministry of Communication and Information Technology.

Definition of Information Technology

Information Technology (IT): The science and activity of using computers and other electronic equipment to store and send information.

Information Technology is also defined as :

"The technology involved with the transmission and storage of information, especially the development, installation, implementation, and management of computer systems within companies, universities" and other organisations".

Goals and Objectives

1. To provide in-service training to teachers and teacher educators on computers and IT.
2. To incorporate all the IT facilities into teacher education model.
3. To extend Internet, e-mail facilities to all teachers and students in teacher education.
4. To provide network how to operate computers and Internet to all the student teachers.
5. To provide network to teacher education centres all over India.
6. To extend distance mode of teacher education online and also include a live interactive practical teaching.
7. To restructure teacher education curriculum.
8. To incorporate use of IT in special education.
9. To use IT in teacher education research.
10. To create a virtual teacher education centre.
11. To incorporate good hidden curriculum strategies to restore the humanistic tendencies required for a teacher.
12. Ensure the protection and security of data.
13. Minimise duplication of effort, services and resources.
14. Eliminate inefficient and costly redundancies.
15. Define what services, if any, should be restructured or eliminated.
16. Eliminate non-compatible standards and architectures.
17. Identify obstacles for departments wanting to move computing operations to the Division of Information Technology.

18. Recommend a strategy for evaluating the university-wide impacts of major information technology purchases including analysis of total cost of ownership.
19. Evaluate the complexity and risks of managing a complex distributed computing environment, including system security, exposure to data loss and virus protection.
20. Identify issues and trends in technology that may affect the university's technology infrastructure and long-term architecture.
21. Recommend the most effective balance of central and distributed technology services, staffing and resources. Detail any logical alternatives. Recommendations will include background, advice and alternatives that address the following:
    - Create a cost efficient blend of centralisation and decentralisation of information technology resources—properly aligning the university's information technology infrastructure to best meet the needs of its teaching, research and outreach missions.
    - Create a coherent campus-wide information technology computing architecture and a solid foundation for the university's information technology infrastructure.
    - Develop a long-term organisational process and structure to ensure the best utilisation of the university's information technology resources for the future.
    - Estimate the costs of infrastructure and support, including personnel and training, in the current distributed environment and to estimate the same costs for the alternatives proposed.

Need of Information Technology in Teacher Education

It is well known fact that IT and Cyber age have brought a revolutionary transformation and drifted the whole life style of people. No area left untouched with it. We have arrived at global village concept with all virtual realities on our desktops. But is it the teacher education, which has remained untouched in this direction.

We have a lot of educational institutions in the filed of Information Technology like 'Indian Institute of Information Technology (IIIT), 'International Institute of Information Technology, 'Tata Institute of Information Technolgoy' and 'Deerubai Ambani Institute of Information Technology'. There are so many Information Technology departments in the universities at both state and central level. The effect of Information Technology in our daily life is very much. It is very necessary to take Information Technology help for teacher education. There is a separate subject for trainee teacher 'Educational Technology'. With the help of Information Technology it is possible to give quality and effective education for trainee teachers.

A nation's development potential depends upon its ability to continuously educate its population and its ability to create armies of skilled manpower. In particular, use of Information Technology (IT) in acquiring knowledge and skill has become an essential element in education and training. These IT elements in the educational process have magical effects.

Higher education without the support of IT makes the lives of learner and teachers equally difficult. A nation's intellectual strength depends on IT support. The use of computing and communication technology to enhance the efficacy of transaction and productivity is the driving force in this new era of social and economic transformation in the new society called Information Society.

A strong IT infrastructure can give an institution a competitive advantage for the best students and faculty and an advantage in competition for absorbing external research grants to execute studies, research etc. in a short time and with great resolution. The quality of an institution's environment for digital information storage and retrieval has, for any disciplines, become more important than the institution's conventional, library resources in print media.

Virtually every economic sector that is labour intensive has managed to improve productivity through the use of technology except education. Faculty/student ratios in higher education have changed significantly in more than 50 years. The most advanced technology in common use in the classroom today in our country is the overhead projector, and it took nearly three decades to migrate from the national level training institute to the classroom. Institutions like UGC, IGNOU, and CIET have begun to transact curriculum on DD 1 but the ETV programmes are mostly of enrichment type and not as per the demand of the students. It is unlikely that IT will have a major impact on teaching and learning if the current paradigm for instruction changes.

Generally majority trainee teachers have no knowledge about usage of technology. Because their lower classes curriculum is separate. It is necessary to change curriculum at school level and implement Information Technology at school level also. 'Today's children are tomorrow's citizens', so it is necessary to take care about school curriculum. It is government duty to provide Information Technology labs for all type of Educational Institutions in the country.

Uses of Information Technology

Now we are using Information Technology in all the fields like education agriculture, banking, transport, medicine, research and manufacturing and in social service mode.

Specific Uses of Information Technology

- Animation for simulation of urban environments and video for assembling and disseminating results of the analysis and design work.
- Graphic Information System (GIS) for the study of housing and development patterns.
- Computer Aided Design (CAD) for geometric modeling: Digital image archival systems for compiling data about the built environment.

ROLE OF INFORMATION TECHNOLOGY IN TEACHER EDUCATION

In-service Training

There is a need to provide in-service training to all the teachers and teacher educators with updated computer operation skills and provide with IT know how. To utilize the facilities to access updated information and solutions to their problems in their areas of specialisation, it can be provide on-line.

Teacher Education Training Programmes through IT Facilities

A virtual teacher education centre can be created. All the necessary skills and training can be provided in different modes on the network. It should incorporate all the available facilities like, tele-education, teleconferencing, floppy diskettes and CD-ROMs in teacher education. Networks like ERNET, INTERNET and futuristic concept of bringing satellite channels directly to homes by DTS (Direct to Home) service and expert talks through virtual classrooms can also be made available.

Distance Mode of Education

The present practice of TV and other media in distance mode of education can be substituted by multimedia systems which have an extra advantage of intractability through GUI (Graphics User Interface) which controls the response of information transfer process according to the learners pace. It helps in using screen as an instructor for self-learning.

IT in special Education

IT is providing solutions for the education of physically challenged people as well. As reported by BBC web-site (web-site at BBC news, science), the Germans have developed a technology and associated software for which people, where computer will sense the signals from the head of a paralyzed person through two attached electrodes, and thereby, allow him to surf the net like a normal person. These facilities will transform the lives of the physically challenged and IT can be used even for diagnosing.

Research and Internet

Internet facilities should be made available to research students, teacher educators. All the departments should have internet connectivity. It helps in accessing information about the ongoing research in their respective fields and it also avoids overlapping.

Restructuring Curricula of Teacher Education

1. Teacher education curriculum needs drastic changes by incorporating all facilities available through IT. Primarily IT

can be used to keep on par with the existing knowledge structure. It can be thoroughly incorporated into methodologies of teacher education.

2. There should not be exclusive theoretical orientation in curriculum. It shall have more practically demonstrable skill and strategies in the curriculum.
3. All possible attempts should be made to train teachers apart from virtual classrooms, to incorporate the necessary live interactive experiences to understand the significance of physical interaction with the child in the classroom.
4. Humanistic and affective hidden curriculum and an effective training to acquire all traits and qualities required in teacher to handle human society should also be included in the curriculum.

Conclusion

Information Technology has a prominent role in the filed of teacher education. With the help of information technology it is easy to know any type of information with in seconds through out the world. The advanced knowledge of information technology is much helpful for research in all the fields of education. With the help of Information Technology it is easy to educate trainee teachers. By knowing the usage of technology they have a change to share their opinions with other teacher through out the world. Information Technology motivates the teacher to learn lot of things in their subject area.

Now we are happy that our State and Central Governments have taking good steps to introduce online education in the educational institutions. There are separate subjects in D.Ed., and B.Ed., like Computer Education and Educational Technology. Now teachers are using computers and Internet in the educational institutions. But the percentage is very less. It is more important to give equal importance to theory and practical in the computer education and educational technology subjects. It is the duty of the Government to provide Computer and Educational technology labs for each and every teacher education institution in the country.

Now NCTE, CIET, NIEPA, NCERT, SCERT and other educational departments have recognized the advantages of Information Technology in the field of education. They motivate the students to use IT. They are conducting national seminars, workshops, and conferences about Information Technology. Teachers must be given excellent training in setting, grading papers and preparing assignment, etc. These can be used in teacher training network. Excellent stimulated models can be made available to access on network.

REFERENCES

1. *Promotion of Quality of Teacher Education for 21st Century*, Dr. N. Ramanath Kishan, Editor, Ashoka Krishna Offset Printers, Warangal.
2. http://www.ciet.nic.in/
3. http://www.aponline.gov.in/

CHAPTER 26

Role of NCTE, NCERT, CIET, SCERT for the Cause of Teacher Education

–Dr. B. Ramschandra Reddy
–Dr. C. Manchala
–Dr. Naraginti Amareswaran

According to Sri *Sarvapalli Radha Krishnan*, Teacher is a national builder. Education is a powerful instrument of national development. Education is a solution of all types of problems in the society. Through education we get knowledge, good habits, character, morals and values. We have thousands of years of tradition and culture. In Vedas the teacher was called 'Guru'. According to Indians teacher is third god. We give more respect to teacher after mother and father in the society.

Teacher is a national builder. It is necessary to give importance to teacher education. Today's children are tomorrow's citizens. By taking good steps in the framing of teacher education curriculum, we can give good quality and value based education to the teachers.

National Council for Teacher Education, National Council of Educational Research and Training, Central Institute of Educational Technology, State Council of Educational Research and Training etc. are the institutions for the strengthening the teacher education in India.

National Council for Teacher Education (NCTE)

The National Council for Teacher Education, in its previous status since 1973, was an advisory body for the Central and State Governments on all matters pertaining to teacher education, with its Secretariat in the Department of Teacher Education of the National Council of Educational Research and Training (NCERT). Despite its commendable work in the academic fields, it could not perform essential regulatory functions, to ensure maintenance of standards in teacher education and preventing proliferation of substandard teacher education institutions. The National Policy on Education (NPE), 1986 and the Programme of Action thereunder, envisaged a National Council for Teacher Education with statutory status and necessary resources as a first step for overhauling the system of teacher education. The National Council for Teacher Education as a statutory body came into existence in pursuance of the National Council for Teacher Education Act, 1993 (No. 73 of 1993) on the 17th August,1995.

Objective of NCTE

The main objective of the NCTE is to achieve planned and coordinated development of the teacher education system throughout the country, the regulation and proper maintenance of Norms and Standards in the teacher education system and for matters connected therewith. The mandate given to the NCTE is very broad and covers the whole gamut of teacher education programmes including research and training of persons for equipping them to teach at pre-primary, primary, secondary and senior secondary stages in schools, and non-formal education, part-time education, adult education and distance (correspondence) education courses.

Organisational Structure of NCTE

NCTE has its headquarter at New Delhi and four Regional Committees at Banglore, Bhopal, Bhubaneshwar and Jaipur to look after its statutory responsibilities. In order to enable the NCTE to perform the assigned functions including planned and co-ordinated development and initiating innovations in teacher education, the NCTE in Delhi as well as its four Reginal Committees have administrative and academic wings to deal respectively with finance, establishment and legal matters and with research, policy planning, monitoring, curriculum, innovations, co-ordination, library and documentation, in-service programmes. The NCTE Headquarters is headed by the Chairperson, while each Regional Committee is headed by a Regional Director.

All teacher education colleges are under the control of NCTE. There are 24 Government D.Ed. colleges, 324 B.Ed., Government, aided and un-aided colleges, 17 Telugu pandit training colleges, 5 UGDPEd colleges, 7 B.P.Ed. Colleges, 5 Urdu pandit training colleges and 20 M.Ed., colleges under the control of NCTE in Andhra Pradesh. Nearly 50 thousands of trainee teachers are studying in all the above colleges. It is the duty of NCTE to provide quality education in all the above colleges. It is the duty of NCTE to frame curriculum for teacher education.

The Parliament appreciated the role of quality teacher education in providing quality teachers for quality school education and passed an Act in 1993 for setting up of the National Council for Teacher Education (NCTE) as a statutory body. The broad mandate given to the NCTE is to achieve planned and co-ordinated development of the teacher education system throughout the country, the regulation and proper maintenance of norms and standards in the teacher education system and for matters connected therewith.

The NCTE has been conducting orientation programmes on education in human values for teacher educators and repackaging electronically the contributions of the experts and those of the participants. The outcomes of its programmes are distributed to each of its recognised institutions on multimedia CD-ROMs and through the World Wide Web of the Internet. Full texts of publications on value education in easily downloadable form have been made available on the NCTE web site (http://www.ncte-in.org). Titles related to value education available from the NCTE web site are: Education for Character Development; Education for Tomorrow; Report of the Working Group to Review Teachers' Training Programme; Role and Responsibility of Teachers in Building up Modern India; Gandhi on Education; Sri Aurobindo on Education; and Tilak on Education. The titles of the NCTE CD-ROMs on value education are New Education for New India—Integral Education of Sri Aurobindo, Jeevan Vigyan and Teachers as Transformers. A CD-ROM based on the workshop that was organised by the NCTE jointly with the Chinmaya World Centre will be released shortly. Recently, in December 2001 two workshops on value orientation in teacher education for teacher educators of the Southern States were organised by the RIMSE (Ramakrishna Institute for Moral and Spiritual Education).

It may be appreciated that the role of the NCTE in bringing any curricular change in teacher education programme, even providing facilitation in integration of education in human values in it, at best, is that of a catalytic agent. What NCTE is trying is to make available a basketful of resource materials on education in human values to teacher education institutions.

National Counsel of Educational Research and Training (NCERT)

The National Council of Educational Research and Training (NCERT) is an apex resource organisation set up by the Government of India, with headquarters at New Delhi, to assist and advise the Central and State Governments on academic matters related to school education. NCERT doing so many researches to improve the quality of teacher education. The objective of NCERT is to assist and advise the Ministry of Education and Social Welfare in the implementation of its policies and major programmes in the field of education, particularly school education. The NCERT provides academic and technical support for improvement of school education through its various constituents, which are:

- National Institute of Education, New Delhi
- Central Institute of Education Technology, New Delhi
- Pandit Sunderlal Sharma Central Institute of Vocational Education, Bhopal
- Regional Institute of Education, Ajmer
- Regional Institute of Education, Bhopal
- Regional Institute of Education, Bhubaneswar
- Regional Institute of Education, Mysore.
- North Eastern-Regional Institute of Education, Shillong

Priorities

Among the top priorities of NCERT are:

- Implementation of National Curriculum framework
- Universalisation of Elementary Education (UEE)
- Vocational education
- Education of groups with special needs
- Early childhood education
- Evaluation and examination reform information technology (IT) education
- Value Education
- Educational Technology
- Development of exemplary textbooks/workbooks/teacher's guide/supplementary reading materials
- Production of the girl child
- Identification and nurturing of talent
- Guidance and counselling
- Improvement in teacher education
- International relations

By conducting national seminars, workshops and conferences NCERT gives valuable recommendations to teacher education. Now we are living in the technological world.

Programmes and Activities

The NCERT undertakes the following programmes and activities.

Research

Being an apex national body for research in school education, the NCERT performs the important functions of conducting and supporting research and offering training in educational research methodology. The different Departments of the National Institute of Education (NIE), Regional Institutes of Education (RIEs), Central Institute of Educational Technology (CIET) and Pandit Sunderlal

Sharma Central Institute of Vocational Education (PSSCIVE) undertake programmes of research related to different aspects of school education, including teacher education.

Besides conducting in-house research, the NCERT supports research programmes of other institutions/organizations by providing financial assistance and academic guidance. Assistance is given to scholars for publication of their Ph.D. theses. Research fellowships are offered to encourage studies in school education to create a research base for developmental, training and extension programmes and to create a pool of competent research workers. It also organises courses for educational research workers. The NCERT also organises educational research in the country. It has computer facilities for storing, processing and retrieval of data. It collaborates with international agencies in inter-country research projects.

Development

Developmental activities in school education constitute an important function of the NCERT. The major developmental activities include development and renewal of curricula and instructional materials for various levels of school education and making them relevant to changing needs of children and society. The innovative developmental activities include development of curricula and instructional materials in school education in the area of pre-school education, formal and non-formal education, vocationalisation of education and teacher education. Developmental activities are also undertaken in the domains of educational technology, population education, and education of the disabled and other special groups.

Training

Another important dimension of NCERT's activities is the pre-service and in-service training of teachers at various levels; pre-primary, elementary, secondary and higher secondary, and also in such areas as vocational education, educational technology, guidance and counseling, and special education. The pre-service teacher education programmes at the Regional Institutes of Education (RIEs) incorporate innovative features such as integration of content and methodology of teaching, long-term internship of teacher trainees in the actual classroom setting, and participation of students in community work. The RIEs also undertake the training of key personnel of the states and of state level institutions and training of teacher educators and in-service teachers.

Extension

The NCERT has comprehensive extension programmes in which various Departments of the NIE, RIEs, CIET, PSSCIVE and the offices of the Field Advisers in the states are engaged in various ways. It works in close collaboration with various agencies and institutions in the states and also works extensively with Extension Service Departments and Centres in teacher training colleges and schools with the purpose of providing assistance to various categories of personnel, including teachers, teacher educators, educational administrators, question-paper setters, textbook writers, etc. Conferences, seminars, workshops and competitions are organised *as* regular on-going programmes as a part of the extension activities. Several programmes are organised in rural and backward areas in order to reach out to the functionaries in these areas where special problems exist and where special efforts are needed. Special programmes are organised for the education of the disadvantaged sections of the society. The extension programmes cover all States and Union Territories of the country.

Publication and Dissemination

The NCERT publishes textbooks for different school subjects for Classes I to XII. It also brings out workbooks, teachers guides, supplementary readers, research reports, etc. In addition, it publishes instructional materials for the use of teacher educators, teacher trainees and in-service teachers. These instructional materials, produced through research and developmental work, serve as models to various agencies in States and Union Territories. These are made available to state level agencies for adoption and/or adaptation. The textbooks are published in English, Hindi and Urdu.

For dissemination of educational information, or the NCERT publishes six journals: *The Primary Teacher* is published both in English and Hindi and aims at giving meaningful and relevant educational inputs to primary school teachers for direct use in the classroom; *School Science* serves as an open forum for discussion on various aspects of science education; *Journal of Indian Education* provides a forum for encouraging original and critical thinking in education through discussion on current educational issues; *Indian Educational Review* contains research articles and provides a forum for researchers in education; and *Bharatiya Adhunik Shiksha,* published in Hindi, provides a forum for encouraging critical thinking in education on contemporary issues and for dissemination of educational problems and practices. Besides these, a house journal called *NCERT Newsletter* is also published in English and Hindi. The title of the Hindi version of the newsletter is *Shaikshik Darpan.*

Exchange Programmes

The NCERT interacts with international organisations such as UNESCO, UNICEF, UNDP (United Nations Development Progammes), NFPA (National Federation of Paralegal Associations) and the World Bank to study specific educational problems and to arrange training programmes for personnel from developing countries. It is one of the Associated Centres of APEID (Asia-Pacific Programme of Educational Innovation for Development). It also acts as the Secretariat of the National Development Group (NDG) for Educational Innovations. The NCERT has been offering training facilities, usually through attachment programmes and participation in workshops, to educational workers of other countries. The NCERT also acts as a major agency for implementing the Bilateral Cultural Exchange Programmes entered into by the Government of India with the governments of other countries in the fields of school education and teacher education by sending delegations to study specific educational problems relevant to Indian requirements and by arranging training and study visits for scholars from other countries. Educational materials are exchanged with other countries. On request, the faculty members are deputed to participate in international conferences, seminars, workshops, symposia, etc.

Central Institute of Educational Technology (CIET)—India

Central Institute of Educational Technology (CIET) is a constituent unit of the National Council of Educational Research and Training (NCERT), an autonomous organisation under the Ministry of Human Resources Development, Government of India. Established in 1984 with the merger of the Centre of Educational Technology and Department of Teaching Aids. Its chief aim is to promote Educational Technology especially mass media singly or in combinations (multimedia packages) to extend educational opportunities and improve quality of educational processes at the school level.

As a premier institute of Educational Technology at the apex level, major functions of the CIET are:

- To design, develop, try out and disseminate alternative learning systems to achieve the national goal of universalisation of primary education
- To address various educational problems at micro and macro levels. The broad areas of activities of the CIET are as given below:
- To design and produce media software materials *viz.*, television/ radio (for both broadcast as well as non-broadcast use) film, graphics and other programmes for strengthening the transaction of curricular and co-curricular activities at the school level.
- To create competencies in development and use of educational software materials mentioned above through training in areas such as script development, media production, media communication, media research, technical operations, setting up studios, repair and maintenance of equipment.
- To train the faculty of Institutes of Advanced Study in Education/Colleges of Teacher Education and District Institutes of Education and Training in the use of Educational Technology in their teacher education programmes.
- To undertake research evaluation and monitoring of the systems, programmes and materials with a view to improving the materials and increasing their effectiveness.

- To document and disseminate information, materials and media programmes for better utilization and to function as a clearing house / agency in the field of Educational Technology.
- To advise and coordinate the academic and technical programmes and activities of the SIET set up by the MHRD in six states of India.
- To ensure a continuous progress in the quality of production, various evaluation studies are carried out on a regular basis. Some of the important research programmes undertaken during the year 1997-98 are:

  — Monitoring and evaluation of Training

  — Analysis of viewer's mail

  — Field-testing of media programmes

  — Review of research with implications for media production

  — A need assessment for media programmes for the middle schools.

Sate Counsel of Educational Research and Training

The State Council of Educational Research and Training (SCERT) Andhra Pradesh was established on 27-07-1967, amalgamating the following institutions:

- The State Institute of Education
- The State Bureau of Education and Vocational Guidance
- The State Science Education Unit, and
- The State Evaluation Unit

Objectives

- To organise in—service training for teacher educators and to teachers of Primary, Upper Primary and Secondary Schools.
- To Act as a clearing house for ideas and information to keep the teacher educators and teachers abreast of the latest developments in the field of Education

- To provide academic guidance to the schools through extension services.
- To undertake studies, investigations and surveys relating to educational matters on the appraisal of educational programmes.
- To Undertake and co – ordinate action research projects on instructional practices, Educational problems etc.
- To undertake publication of books, periodicals and other literature necessary for furtherance of knowledge for teachers.
- To undertake evaluation and research studies to find out the impact of educational programmes in the state.

Functions

Based on its objectives as the academic wing of the Department of School Education. The following are the functions of SCERT:

- Preparation of curricula, syllabi, instructional material for Primary, Upper Primary, Secondary and alternative systems of education.
- Department of evaluation procedures and material which are helpful to the practicing teachers.
- Bridging gaps between the methods and techniques advocated in training and the actual classroom practices.
- Dissemination of knowledge to improved methods and techniques to be followed by educational institutions.
- Co-ordination with national and international organisations in academic programmes.
- Organisation of orientation programmes for the professional growth of teachers, teacher—education, supervisor's etc.
- Publication of journals, periodicals, books etc. ,
- Resource support to implement the academic policies lay down by the Government.

SERVICES

Constituent Units

SCERT has some constituent units spread over the entire state. They are:

- Institutes or Advances Study in Education (IASEs) Colleges of Teacher Education. (CTEs)
- District institutes of Education and Training (DIETs) / Teacher Training institutes (T. T. I. s)
- Extension Service Departments.
- Science Teacher's Centres.

Professional Growth

For the professional growth of teachers, SCERT takes up in-service training courses for Primary, Upper—Primary, Secondary teachers and teacher—educators, besides providing sources of material like hand books, manuals and other publications.

SCERT also organises seminars workshops, conferences involving teachers, teacher—educators, supervisors and administrators.

Research and Evaluation

SCERT undertakes action research, studies, experimental research and evaluation of the programmes implemented by it. It also promotes research and evaluation studies by teacher educators and action research by the practicing teachers.

Co-ordinate Efforts

SCERT co-ordinates various academic programmes of IASE's CTE's. DIETs. TTIs and the Extention Services Departments functioning in IASE, CTEs and DIETs.

Future Vision of the Department

National Policy of Education 1986 and Programme of action lay a lot of stress on the qualitative improvement of education. The Govt. of

India has made the State Councils of Education Research and Training as nodal agencies to look into the task of qualitative improvement of Elementary Education at Elementary and Secondary Education levels. Teacher Education Institution like DIETs, IASEs, CTEs etc., co-ordinate and implement UNICEF projects like UGC, EFA (Education For All) and other projects like MLL (Minimum Level of Learning), Distance Education. The institution's major responsibility is to ensure quality in teacher education.

SCERT organises seminars, workshops, conferences with the help of NCERT, NCTE AND NIEPA to give quality education for teachers.

Conclusion

We know teacher is a national builder. He has a power to change the world. It is necessary to take care about teacher education. NCTE, NCERT, CIET and SCERT have to play prominent role in the development of quality in teacher education. NCTE has major role in framing of teacher education curriculum and establishment of teacher education institutions. We are living in the modern world. It is necessary to use technology. It is necessary to provide computer and technology labs and other type of labs.

REFERENCES:

1. http://www.aponline.gov.in/
2. http://www.ciet.nic.in/
3. http://www.ncert.nic.in/
4. http://www.ncte-in.org/

CHAPTER

27

Role of Teachers in Building Modern India

– Dr. Naraginti Amareswaran

Introduction

Education means an all round drawing out of the best in child and man—body, mind and spirit. ***—Mahatma Gandhi***

The development of any nation depends mainly on the standards of its educational institutions. Education is the most powerful and effective instrument for inducing radical changes in the behaviour of students. Education is a powerful instrument of national development—social, economic and cultural. The teacher occupies pivotal position in the system of education. Teaching has been one of the oldest and most respected professions in the world.

According to Indians, Teacher is the third god. Today we are living in the technological world. India developed in the fields of Science and Technology. It is possible to know each and everything with in seconds through out the world. Today's children are tomorrow's citizens. It is necessary to give quality and value-based education to each and every student in the society. Then only all children will become good citizens in the future.

About India

India is a developing country. We have thousands of years of tradition and culture. 'Unity in diversity' is the greatness of Indian culture. According to the latest World Developing Report of World Bank, Indian Economy is the fourth largest economy in the world. The population of India is 1,129,866,154 (July 2007 est.). The literacy of

India is 61% (73% male and 48% female literacy) according to 2000 report. Adult literacy rate is 61.3% for the age group 15 years and above. Youth literacy rate is 76.4% (2000-2004) for the age group 15-24 years. There are 268.42 million illiterates in India (2000). The unemployment rate in India is 10.1% out of the total population (2004). The Planning Commission made a survey for finding out the number of persons below poverty line and estimated that 18.96% of the total peoples live below poverty line as of the year 1993-94.

Indian Education System and Teacher

"*No system of education, no syllabus, no methodology, no text book can rise above the level of its teachers. If a country wants to have quality education it must have quality teachers*" ***—V.S. Mathews***

"*Of all the different factors which influence the quality of education and its contribution to national development; the quality, competence and character of teachers are undoubtedly the most significant....*" ***—Kothari Education Commission (1964-66)***

Mahatma Gandhi in his debate with British Parliamentarian Philip Hartog in 1931 is said to have described the indigenous Indian education system as 'The Beautiful Tree'. And the root of this beautiful tree of Indian education was the nourishing relationship between the teacher and the student. The acharya or the guru was not merely an instrument for transmission of knowledge, he /she was an all-pervasive influence on the life and character of the student. The guru was a father, mother, friend, counsellor, motivator, role model and spiritual guide, all rolled into one.

Teacher plays an important role in the field of education. Today's education is child-centred. But the child centred education cannot be successful without the teacher. The teacher is the maker of the future of the child. The children of today are the citizens and leaders of tomorrow. It means that the teacher is the maker of the leaders or rulers of the nation.

Like a master architect, the teacher has a very thorough knowledge of all the details essential to his work. He knows the real nature of the objectives of his work and the ends to be attained. Besides an understanding of the nature of the outcomes desired, he understands the nature of the different kinds of learning experiences necessary to attain them. He also knows how to organise and direct such learning experiences. Further, to do this satisfactorily he knows how to use effectively the best teaching techniques and devices available. He guides learning and gives suggestions and directions to the students in order to make them able to attain the desired knowledge. In any system of education, teacher has a pivotal role to play. The responsibility of making the education work successful lies with the teacher. He is undoubtedly the key point in all educational programmes and the quality of education depends on the quality of teachers.

The teacher today is required to be able to cope up with the aspirations of rising generations of youth and the changing needs of the society and has to play a multi-dimensional role.

Teaching has always been considered to be essential for preservation and development of all intellectual life. Among other agencies, teachers are considered to be the major transmitters of accumulated knowledge and experience of human race from one generation to the next. The very foundation of the social order rests on citizens who are taught and trained in the classroom with or without walls. Teachers thus, determine to a great extent the character and destination of a nation.

Values and Teacher

Now we are living in modern and technological world. A lot of changes are occurring in the day to day life of human beings because of Science and Technology. Because of westernisation a lot of changes are occurring in the tradition and culture of the today's people. Teacher has a pivotal role to preserve all these things and he is the first person to preserve all these things.

Values are the guiding principles, decisive in day to day behaviours as also in critical life situations. Values are a set of principles or standards of behaviour. Values are regarded desirable, important and held in high esteem by a particular society in which a person lives. Thus values give meaning and strength to a person with character by occupying a central place in his life. Values reflect one's personal attitudes and judgments, decisions and choices, behaviour and relationships, dreams and vision. They influence our thoughts, feelings and actions. They guide us to do the right things.

Value education means inculcating in the children a sense of humanism, a deep concern for the well being of others and the nation. This can be accomplished only when we instill in the children a deep feeling of commitment to values that would build this country and bring back to the people pride in work that brings order, security and assured progress.

Through value education, we like to develop the social, moral, aesthetic and spiritual sides of a person which are often undermined in formal education. Value education teaches us to preserve whatever is good and worthwhile in what we have inherited from our culture. It helps us to respect the attitude and behaviour of those who differ from us. Value education does not mean value imposition or indoctrination.

Values are the guiding principles of life which are conductive to all round development. They give direction and firmness to life and bring joy, satisfaction and peace of life. Values are like the rails that keep a train on the track and help it move smoothly, quickly and with direction. They bring qualities to life.

Role of Teacher in Building Modern India

The role of the modern teacher is not confined to teaching alone. He/she is expected to participate in the development programmes of the community life. The question arises as to how this could be integrated with the teacher education programmes. Mudaliar Commission (1952-53) Report stated rightly, "we are convinced that the most important factor in the contemplated education reconstruction is the teacher—his personal qualities, his educational qualifications, his professional training and the place that he occupies in the school as well as in the community". On similar lines Kothari Commission (1964-66) stated that, "Nothing is more important than securing a sufficient supply of high quality recruits to the teaching profession, providing them with the best possible professional preparation and creating satisfactory conditions of work in which they can be fully effective".

The importance of the teachers in the Educational Programme of a country is too great. The greatness of a country does not depend on lofty buildings, gigantic projects and large armies, but on the quality of its citizens. If a nation has young men of sterling character and unimpeachable patriotism, she is found to make rapid progress in all fields. Young men are entrusted to the care of the teacher and it is therefore the sacred duty of the teacher to impart the right type of knowledge and make them good citizens. It is the teacher who impresses his children with his personality.

The teacher, a national integrator as he is, is the backbone of society, particularly so in the remote villages. He stands as an outstanding figure among the illiterate and semi-literate families. He is their friend, philosopher and guide. The teacher actively shares the responsibility of reconstructing a social order, with all the cherished values and traditional beliefs, which are being eroded by the surge of new ideals and practices. He acts as a social reformer and counsellor to the community.

Conclusion

According to *Swami Vivekananda* "We want that education by which character is formed, strength of mind is increased, and the intellect is expanded, and by which one can stand on one's own feet.

(*a*) Technology based 'Teacher Education' is necessary for trainee teachers in India.

(*b*) Give more importance for Teachers after Doctors.

(*c*) Education is the solution for all types of problems. So, it is necessary to educate all types of persons in the society.

(*d*) Advanced Technology and Lab facility is necessary for all types of teachers.

REFERENCES

1. *Kothari Education Commission* (1964-66): It is also known as. "*Indian Education Commission*", with Kothari as its Chairman, Report, p. 46.
2. Mathews, V.S: From '*An Evaluative Study of Primary School Teacher Education Programme in Andhra Pradesh*" by K.Chandra Sekhar (2000) unpublished Ph.D. thesis, Dept. of Education, S.V.University, Tirupati, India, p. 2.

3. Mehrotra, R.N. (2006): "*Teacher and Teaching"—A Trend Report in Sixth Survey of Educational Research* (1993-2000) vol. 1. pp.13-53; published by NCERT, Sri Aurobindo Marg, New Delhi-110016; May 2006.
4. Mudaliar Commission 91952-53): It is also known as '*Secondary Education Commission*' headed by Mudaliar.
5. Saxena N.R., Mishra B.K., Mohanthy R.K. '*Teacher Education', Surya* Publications, Near Govt. Inter College, Meerut, First Edition, 1998.
6. *Secondary Education Commission* (1952-53): It is also known as '*Mudaliar Commission*' headed by Mudaliar.
7. *Value Education in India*, Usha Rai Negi, Editor, Published by Association of Indian Universities, AIU House, 16 Kotla Marg, New Delhi – 110 002, 2000.
8. *Value Education*, Dr. Venkataiah, Editor, APH Publishing Corporation, 5, Ansari Road, Daryaganj, New Delhi – 110 002, First Edition, 1998.

CHAPTER 28

Some Reflections on Public Transportation for Disabled Persons in Academic Institution

—Dr. B. Ramachandra Reddy
—Dr. Naraginti Amareswaran
—Dr. C. Manchala

Introduction

- Look first at my strengths and not at my weaknesses.
- Great pleasure in life is doing what people say you cannot do.
- Open your arms to change, but don't let go of your values.
- The most pathetic person in the world is someone who has sight but has no vision.
- The tragedy of life is what dies inside a man while he lives.
- I am always doing that which I cannot do, in order that I may learn how to do it.

The Universe is so beautiful. Human being is the greatest animal in the animal kingdom. Because of Education and Science and Technology he became a greatest and strongest animal in the world. All persons in the world are good at the time of birth. But, they will become different types of criminals because of society. Men and Women are parts in the society. If the society takes care about each and every person in the community then there will be no place for cruel, theft, corruption, non-violence, harassment and inequality. We want that type of society. We want such people which have full kindness, co-operation, co-ordination, helping nature and sensitiveness.

Disabled Persons

The Disability Discrimination Act (DDA) of United Kingdom defines a disabled person as someone who has a physical or mental impairment that has a substantial and long-term adverse effect on his or her ability to carry out normal day-to-day activities.

The Constitution of India ensures equality, freedom, justice and dignity of all individuals and implicitly mandates an inclusive society for all including persons with disabilities. In the recent years, there have been vast and positive changes in the perception of the society towards persons with disabilities. It has been realised that a majority of persons with disabilities can lead a better quality of life if they have equal opportunities and effective access to rehabilitation measures.

Facts and Figures

The World Health Organisation estimates that there are 600 million disabled people worldwide, about 10% of the world population. It is also estimated that about 80% of all disabled people worldwide live in developing countries.

According to the Census 2001, there are 2.19 crore persons with disabilities in India who constitute 2.13 per cent of the total population. This includes persons with visual, hearing, speech, locomotors and mental disabilities. 75 per cent of persons with disabilities live in rural areas, 49 per cent of disabled population is literate and only 34 per cent are employed. The earlier emphasis on medical rehabilitation has now been replaced by an emphasis on social rehabilitation. There has been an increasing recognition of abilities of persons with disabilities and emphasis on mainstreaming them in the society based on their capabilities.

More and more, disability is seen as a social issue which is not only based on medical reasons. The organisation "Disabled Peoples' International" defines disability as the interaction between the person with impairment and environmental and attitudinal barriers he or she may face. Therefore the reasons for disability are always complex and can only be understood within the context of societies and cultures.

Types of Disability

According to Government of India, there are five types of disabilities in our society.

- Mental Retardation
- Visual Disability
- Speech Disability
- Hearing Disability
- Locomotors Disabilities

Causes of Disability

According to WHO there are so many causes for disability. The main causes are given bellow:

Causes of Disability	In millions
Non-contagious somatic illnesses	100
Injuries/wounds	78
Malnutrition	100
Functional psychiatric disorders	40
Chronic alcoholism and drug abuse	100
Congenital diseases	100
Contagious diseases	56

Programmes and Policies for the Development of Disabled Persons

The Government of India has enacted three legislations for persons with disabilities *viz*.

(*i*) Persons with Disability (Equal Opportunities, Protection of Rights and Full Participation) Act, 1995, which provides for education, employment, creation of barrier free environment, social security, etc.

(*ii*) National Trust for Welfare of Persons with Autism, Cerebral Palsy, Mental Retardation and Multiple Disability Act, 1999 has provisions for legal guardianship of the four categories and creation of enabling environment for as much independent living as possible.

(*iii*) Rehabilitation Council of India Act, 1992 deals with the development of manpower for providing rehabilitation services.

In addition to the legal framework, extensive infrastructure has been developed. The following seven national institutes are working for development of manpower in different areas, namely:

- Institute for the Physically Handicapped, New Delhi.
- National Institute of Visually Handicapped, Dehradun
- National Institute for Orthopaedically Handicapped, Kolkata
- National Institute for Mentally Handicapped, Secunderabad.
- National Institute for Hearing Handicapped, Mumbai
- National Institute of Rehabilitation Training and Research, Cuttack.
- National Institute for Empowerment of Persons with Multiple Disabilities, Chennai.

There are five Composite Rehabilitation Centres, four Regional Rehabilitation Centres and 120 District Disability Rehabilitation Centres (DDRCs) providing various kinds of rehabilitation services to persons with disabilities. There are also several national institutions under the Ministry of Health and Family Welfare working in the field of rehabilitation, like National Institute of Mental Health and Neuro Sciences, Bangalore; All India Institute of Physical Medicine and Rehabilitation, Mumbai; All India Institute of Speech and Hearing, Mysore; Central Institute of Psychiatry, Ranchi, etc. In addition, certain State Government institutions also provide rehabilitation services. Besides, 250 private institutions conduct training courses for rehabilitation professionals.

National Handicapped and Finance Development Corporation (NHFDC) has been providing loans on concessional terms for undertaking self-employment ventures by the persons with disabilities through State Channelising Agencies.

Panchayati Raj Institutions at village level, intermediary level and district level have been entrusted with the welfare of persons with disabilities.

India is a signatory to the Declaration on the Full Participation and Equality of People with Disabilities in the Asia Pacific Region. India is also a signatory to the Biwako Millennium Framework for action towards an inclusive, barrier free and rights based society. India is currently participating in the negotiations on the UN Convention on Protection and promotion of the Rights and Dignity of Persons with Disabilities.

National Policy Statement

The National Policy recognises that Persons with Disabilities are valuable human resource for the country and seeks to create an environment that provides those equal opportunities, protection of their rights and full participation in society. The focus of the policy shall be on the following:

Prevention of Disabilities

Since disability, in a large number of cases, is preventable, there will be strong emphasis on prevention of disabilities. Programme for prevention of diseases, which result in disability and the creation of awareness regarding measures to be taken for prevention of disabilities during the period of pregnancy and thereafter will be intensified and their coverage expanded.

Rehabilitation Measures

Rehabilitation measures can be classified into three distinct groups: (*i*) physical rehabilitation, which includes early detection and intervention, counseling and medical interventions and provision of aids and appliances. It will also include the development of rehabilitation professionals; (*ii*) Educational rehabilitation including vocational education; and (*iii*) economic rehabilitation for a dignified life in society.

Education and Disabled Persons

Persons with disabilities have a right to lead a life of dignity and self-respect, this is not a favour given to them. This can be possible only if they get adequate opportunities to pursue their education and thereafter, get gainful employment and status in society. The goal of inclusive and universal education is being pursued under the Sarva Shiksha Abhiyan.

Our Hon'ble President ***Smt. Pratibha Devisingh Patil*** gave a great lecture at the presentation of the national awards for the empowerment of persons with disabilities and release of a postal stamp on the occasion of 'International Day of the Disabled People' (3rd December). She gave much importance for education. Her own words...... Society and social attitudes play an important role in determining the participation of disabled people in social and economic life, often even within their own families. In fact, families of the disabled have a leading role in being a source of strength and encouragement. In cases, when the family neglects the disabled person on account of either poverty or lack of resources or sometimes apathy, the disabled person is confronted with a difficult situation. Education and awareness can correct negative perceptions. NGOs can play an important part in making society and families aware of the needs of the disabled and to make them face the world with confidence. I would urge NGOs to undertake projects for disabled people, particularly in rural areas and urban slums.

According to ***Swami Vivekanada*** "We want that education by which character is formed, strength of mind is increased, and the intellect is expanded and by which one can stand on one's own feet". If we give this type of education for disabled persons, they live happily. Education is the solution for all types of problems in the society. Through education it is possible to change any type of person in the society. Education changes the life style of the disabled persons.

Persons with Disability (Equal Opportunities, Protection of Rights and Full Participation) Act, 1995, which provides for education, employment, creation of barrier free environment, social security, etc.

Education for Persons with Disabilities

Education is the most effective vehicle of social and economic empowerment. In keeping with the spirit of the Article 21A of the Constitution guaranteeing education as a fundamental right and Section 26 of the Persons with Disabilities Act, 1995, free and compulsory education has to be provided to all children with disabilities up to the minimum age of 18 years. According to the Census, 2001, 51 per cent persons with disabilities are illiterate. This is a very large percentage. There is a need for mainstreaming of the persons with disabilities in the general education system through inclusive education.

Sarva Shiksha Abhiyan (SSA) launched by the Government has the goal of eight years of elementary schooling for all children including children with disabilities in the age group of 6-14 years by 2010. Children with disabilities in the age group of 15-18 years are provided free education under Integrated Education for Disabled Children (IEDC) Scheme.

Under SSA, a continuum of educational options, learning aids and tools, mobility assistance, support services etc. are being made available to students with disabilities. This includes education through an open learning system and open schools, alternative schooling, distance education, special schools, wherever necessary home based education, itinerant teacher model, remedial teaching, part time classes, Community Based Rehabilitation (CBR) and vocational education.

IEDC Scheme implemented through the State Governments, Autonomous Bodies and Voluntary Organisations provides hundred percent financial assistance for various facilities like special teachers, books and stationery, uniform, transport, readers allowance for the visually handicapped, hostel allowance, equipment cost, removal/ modification of architectural barriers, financial assistance for purchase/production of instructional material, training of general teachers and equipment for resource rooms.

There will be concerted effort on the part of the Government to improve identification of children with disabilities through regular surveys, their enrollment in appropriate schools and their continuation till they successfully complete their education. The Government will endeavour to provide right kind of learning material and books to the children with disabilities, suitably trained and sensitised teachers and schools which are accessible and disabled friendly.

Government of India is providing scholarships to students with disabilities for pursuing studies at post school level. Government will continue to support the scholarships and expand its coverage.

Facilities for technical and vocational education designed to inculcate and bolster skill development suited to various types of productive activities by adaptation of the existing institutes or accelerated setting up of institutes in un-served/underserved areas will be encouraged. NGOs will also be encouraged to provide vocational training.

Persons with disabilities will be provided access to the Universities, technical institutions and other institutions of higher learning to pursue higher and professional courses.

International Day of Disabled People

"Nothing about us without us" is the motto of 2007 year's International Day of the Disabled People. Proclaimed by the General Assembly in October 1992, this day aims to raise awareness on disabled people's rights at national and international levels.

On the 3rd December 1982, the UN General Assembly decided on the World Programme of Action for Disabled People. The United Nations committed itself and its members to promote the full participation of disabled people in social life and development as well as prevention and rehabilitation measures.

Disabled people are not yet fully considered within international development issues. They are still excluded from society in many countries of the world. Even where effective disability legislation is in place, the implementation lacks ideas and is hindered by negative attitudes towards disabled people.

The United Nations (UN) has set up an international human rights convention on the rights of disabled people.

Public Transportation for Disabled People

Every individual including people with disabilities have an equal right to travel and use public transportation with dignity and independence. It should be regarded as a fundamental right of all citizens, since travel is usually a daily necessity for education, employment, medical attention, entertainment etc. Transport is important in facilitating human communication and face-to-face meetings. It plays a significant role in economic development of the nation.

People with diverse disabilities (sensory or physical) and reduced mobility (people with health problems for example respiratory, cardio-vascular, joint problems or temporary ailments; senior citizens; pregnant women; families with young children and people with heavy luggage, etc.,) constitute sizeable number of the population.

Since majority of this segment belong to lower and middle-income group, it is beyond their economic capacity to use private taxis/three-wheeled auto rickshaws or purchase their own vehicle and are, therefore, dependent on public transport.

Existing transportation system, *i.e.*, vehicles, terminals, and operations are either full of obstacles or impossible to use. It induces fatigue, restricts educational and employment opportunities, causing frustration. It hinders right to freedom of movement, equal participation and access to health and other social services.

Move Towards Accessible Transportation

The Persons with Disability (Equal Opportunities, Protection of Rights and Full Participation) Act 1995, states non-discrimination in built environment and transportation in Delhi has set the lead in accessible transportation. The best example is Delhi Metro Rail Corporation (DMRC), a joint venture of Government of India and Government of National Capital Territory of Delhi.

Access Provisions for Public Transport

Transport facilities and means of transport include land, water and air transport systems.

(*a*) Road transport : Public buses are common man's transport but it is not fully used by people with reduced mobility and people with disabilities.

(*i*) Regulations should specify that new vehicles bought by public and private transport companies be accessible for people with disabilities. Studies indicate that buying a bus with lifts adds only 5 per cent to its cost.

(*ii*) Access regulations should specify modifications required for public buses, which are already in use.

(*iii*) A minimum of four seats in all buses should be designated for persons with disabilities. Those seats should be near entrance/ exit doors.

(*iv*) Adequate space for one wheelchair should be provided in all buses.

(*v*) Parallel transport services for persons with disabilities who cannot use mainline systems are recommended.

(*vi*) Access regulations should be adapted to meet the needs of rural communities.

Note: Concessions are provided for persons with physical impairments and visually handicaps. Student concessions are provided to all children. Mostly each state has its own policy.

(*b*) Rail transport (including local trains, under and over ground trains and inter-city trains)

(*i*) Access regulations should stipulate that new rail transport facilities must be accessible for persons with disabilities.

(*ii*) All mainline train stations must be modified to become accessible.

(*iii*) One car per existing train should be modified to incorporate access features.

(*iv*) A minimum of two seats per car should be designated for persons with disabilities. Those seats should be near entrance/ exit doors.

(*v*) A minimum of one accessible toilet should be available near the above-mentioned seats.

Note: Railways allow disabled persons to travel at concession fares up to 75% in the first and second classes. Escorts accompanying blind, orthopaedically and mentally handicapped persons are also eligible to 75% concession in the basic fare.

(*c*) Sea and river transport (including ferries, as well as domestic and international passenger ships)

(*i*) Access regulations should stipulate that new sea/river transportation must be barrier-free.

(*ii*) A minimum of one deck in ferries and domestic and international passenger ships should be modified to incorporate access features.

(*iii*) Ramps, passageways, gangways, safety equipment and at least two berths or cabins must be modified to incorporate access features.

(*d*) Air transport (including domestic and international passenger aircrafts)

(*i*) Access regulations should stipulate that new air transport facilities must be barrier-free.

(*ii*) A minimum of two seats near the entrance/exit doors in all domestic passenger aircraft should be available for persons with disabilities.

(*iii*) A minimum of one accessible toilet should be near the above-mentioned seats.

Note: The Indian Airlines Corporation allows 50% concessional fare to disabled persons.

Transport Allowance

Disabled persons are entitled to double the normal transport allowance to other similarly placed employees. However, disabled persons who are provided with government transport are not entitled to transport allowance. Transport allowance is allowed at normal rates if the disabled person has been provided with government accommodation.

Conclusion

Today we are living in the Scientific and Techological Modern world. With the help of science and techology the disabled people are also participating and entering into all types of jobs by fulfilling the governement rules. It is necessary to take care about them. The literacy rate of disabled persons is very low. Necessary programmes are important to raise the literacy rate. Education gives strength and power. Give priority and importance for disabled persons in the public transportation. Teachers and NGOs role are very important for the development of disabled persons. Celebrate 'International Day for

Disabled Persons' in a grand manner. Talk lovely with disabled persons. If you like, encourage them but don't discourage. Try to see their strengths but not their weaknesses.

REFERENCES

1. "*Disability India Journal*", Volume III, Issue XXXXV, December 2007.
2. "*National Policy for Persons with Disabilities*", Ministry of Social Justice and Empowerment, Government of India, New Delhi, December, 2006.
3. "*Research Study on Accessibility of Buses and Bus Shelter*", 2006.
4. "*Research Study on Accessibility of Indian Railways*", 2005.
5. http://www.samarthyaindia.com/researchrailways.html.
6. http://www.google.com
7. http://www.yahoosearch.com

CHAPTER 29

Strategies to Create Awareness on Domestic Violence Through Educational Institutions

–Dr. B. Ramachandra Reddy
–Dr. C. Manchala
–Dr. Naraginti Amareswaran

Introduction

"Woman in the companion of man, gifted with equal mental capacities. She has the right to participate in the minutest details in the activities of man; and she has equal right to liberty of freedom and liberty with him."

"There will have to be rigid and iron discipline before we achieve anything great and enduring, and that discipline will not come by mere academic argument and appeal to reason and logic. Discipline is learnt in the school of adversity." **—Mahatma Gandhi**

The development of any nation depends mainly on the standards of its educational institutions. Education is the most powerful and effective instrument for inducing radical changes in the behaviour of students. Education is a powerful instrument of national development—social, economic and cultural. The teacher occupies pivotal position in the system of education. Teaching has been one of the oldest and most respected professions in the world.

Once the first Prime Minister of India, Jawaharlal Nehru said, "you can tell the condition of a nation by looking at the status of its women". This is absolutely true. Woman of any nation is the mirror to its civilisation. If women enjoy good status it shows that the society has reached a level of maturity and sense of responsibility while a decadent image conjures up if the opposite is true. The story of Indian women is as old as the history of Indian civilisation.

Domestic Violence

Across cultures, the family, whether natal or marital, is often associated with love, support, and bonding among members. Though these characteristics are often present, it has become evident through recent research that the home is also frequently the site of violent human relationships. Eight recent studies coordinated by the International Center for Research on Women (ICRW) document the pervasiveness of domestic violence among women in India regardless of age, education level, class, length of marriage, and family living arrangement. For example, in a multi-site study of nearly 10,000 households, 40 per cent of the women reported experiencing at least one form of physical abuse and 26 per cent reported severe physical abuse, including being hit, kicked, or beaten. Fifty per cent of the women experiencing severe physical abuse reported being beaten three or more times in their lifetime and at least once during pregnancy (INCLEN 2000, Visaria 1999)

What is Domestic Violence?

"Non-violence is not a garment to be put on and off at will. Its seat is in the heart, and it must be an inseparable part of our being."

—Mahatma Gandhi

Domestic violence is controlling behaviour and includes all kinds of physical, sexual, economic, psychological and emotional abuse within all kinds of intimate relationships. The perpetrators of domestic violence or abuse are usually men and the victims or survivors are usually women and children that they know. It includes:

- Punching and slapping
- Kicking and hair pulling
- Biting and pinching
- Pushing and shoving
- Being forced to have sex
- Being beaten or cut with other objects
- Disrespect, neglect and emotional blackmail
- Verbal abuse and swearing

- Being prevented from going out or seeing people – being isolated.

Forms of Domestic Violence

The following are the forms of Domestic Violence:

1. Physical Abuse
2. Sexual Abuse
3. Psychological Abuse
4. Emotional Abuse
5. Financial Abuse

Education and Employment of Indian Women

Women constitute almost half of the population in the world. But the hegemonic masculine ideology made them suffer a lot as they were denied equal opportunities in different parts of the world. The rise of feminist ideas has, however, led to the tremendous improvement of women's condition through out the world in recent times. Access to education has been one of the most pressing demands of theses women's rights movements. Women's education in India has also been a major preoccupation of both the government and civil society as educated women can play a very important role in the development of the country.

According to last census held in 2001, the percentage of female literacy in the country is 54.16%. The literacy rate in the country has increased from 18.33% in 1951 to 65.38% as per 2001 census. The female literacy rate has also increased from 8.86% in 1951 to 54.16%. It is noticed that the female literacy rate during the period 1991-2001 increased by 14.87% whereas male literacy rate rose by 11.72%. Hence the female literacy rate actually increased by 3.15% more compared to male literacy rate.

Kumud Sharma of the Centre for Women's Development Studies in New Delhi traced the correlation between education and domestic violence to patriarchal attitudes. "Educated women are aware of their rights," she said. "They are no longer willing to follow commands blindly. When they ask questions, it causes conflicts, which, in turn, leads to violence. In many Indian states, working women are asked to hand over their paycheck to the husband and have no control over their finances. So, if they stop doing so or start asserting their right, there is bound to be friction."

Women Universities in India

The Government of India and State Governments established separate universities for women for the development of women in India.

- **Andhra Pradesh :** Sri Padmavati University, Tirupati
- **Delhi :** Lady Shri Ram College for Women, Lajpat Nagar
- **Maharashtra :** SNDT Women's University, Mumbai
- **Rajasthan :** Banasthali Vidyapith, Banasthali

After living in the shadows, women in India have entered the workplace with a vengeance, snapping up a larger chunk of jobs whereas the employment figures for men have declined. Indian women have outshone their male counterparts with a 3.35 per cent rise in the employment growth rate for the period of seven years from 1998 to 2004 as against a dip of 8 per cent in case of men in the country, an Assocham survey reveals. The chamber's study on 'women employment growth rate and gender budgeting' shows that the total number of women employed in the public and private sector has increased to 49.34 lakh in 2004 from 47.74 lakh in 1998, while the number of men employed has fallen to 215.09 lakh in 2004 from 233.92 lakh in 1998.

"The public sector has been hiring women much more aggressively than the private sector. The number of women employed in the public sector has risen from 27.63 lakh in 1998 to 28.9 lakh in 2004, witnessing a growth of close to 4.6 per cent. The private sector added 0.33 lakh women staff with a growth of 1.64 per cent over 1998, taking the total number to 20.44 lakh," the study said.

STRATEGIES TO CREATE AWARENESS ON DOMESTIC VIOLENCE

Minimising the Dangers of Domestic Violence

A victim does not want to willingly continue living in an abusive relationship. However, until circumstances improve, she may have no choice but to continue living with her abuser. In this situation, there are a few things she can do to try to prevent serious injury to members of her family.

Avoid certain areas : A victim cannot control where her abuser is going to attack her. However, she and her children can take a few precautions. If the abuser confronts her or the children and starts arguing with them, be prepared to be attacked. Avoid being attacked in an area like the kitchen or bathroom. These are small enclosed spaces with only a single entry or exit point. If any member of the family is in either of these places when the abuser confronts her, she should back away slowly and try to exit the room. This should be done discreetly, so as not to trigger the violent instincts of the abuser. A victim must never appear as if she is trying to run away.

Not only are areas like the kitchen and bathroom small, they are also filled with potential weapons. These include knives, razors, plates, etc. Similarly, keep potential weapons out of reach or not easily accessible to your abuser. Objects like heavy bowls, knives, rolling pins, etc. should be kept inside cabinets so that the abuser is less likely to use them.

Keep children informed : Children are living in the same home and are definitely going to be affected by the violence. Explain to them what is happening, in a calm and rational manner. Make sure that they know it is not their fault. Children are very sensitive and often perceive situations as being caused due to their behaviour. Make sure that children do not harbour any guilt over the situation.

Make sure that children do not get involved in any of the violence. If they hear a fight, they should stay out of sight or retreat to their room. At no time should they attempt to interfere. Children will naturally want to try to protect the abused parent. However noble the gesture, it is one of the main reasons why children get hurt. An abuser might turn on the children in a fit of rage and strike them. At the same time, the abused partner may not be in a position to attempt to step in and shield the children. For an abused parent, her first priority should still be to protect her children at all costs.

A victim of domestic violence cannot be blamed for her situation. Although she may not be able to leave her home, there are ways in which she can seek help. The police are duty bound to register a complaint and investigate the situation if a victim approaches them. In addition, there are a number of non-governmental organisations, which provide legal and financial aid to victims of domestic violence.

Safety Plans against Domestic Violence

The National Coalition against Domestic Violence (US) urges women in abusive relationships to create a safety plan. The following plan may help woman in difficult situations:

1. Find a safe place to go in your home if an argument begins. Avoid rooms without an exit and rooms with potential dangers such as a kitchen.
2. Know who to contact in a crisis and establish a code word or sign among trusted family or friends to let them know you need help.
3. Memorise all important phone numbers.
4. Always keep money and change with you.
5. Keep important papers and documents in a place you can easily access if necessary, including: social security cards, birth certificates, marriage licence, checkbook, charge cards, bank statements, health insurance cards, and any records of past abuse including photographs and police reports.

Strategies to Create Awareness on Domestic Violence through Education

According to Swami Vivekananda "We want that education by which character is formed, strength of mind is increased, and the intellect is expanded, and by which one can stand one's own feet". So this type of education is necessary for all type of persons mainly children and women in the society. Education gives strength, power, knowledge, courage and creativity. We can solve any type of problem in the society through education. Today the world is suffering from so many problems like terrorism, poverty, illiteracy and high population. Domestic violence is also a world problem. Because in each and every county domestic violence is happening. The following steps are necessary to create awareness on domestic violence through education.

- Educate all types of women and children in the society.
- Establish some more schools, colleges and universities for girls and women respectively.
- Introduce lessons about domestic violence in the curriculum.
- Conduct awareness programmes about domestic violence every month in the selected area.
- Introduce Value Education in the curriculum.
- Tell the women; domestic violence is crime. You are not alone. A helping hand is always is ready for you.
- Tell the women about 'Women Protection Act'.
- Tell the women about 'Safety Plans against Domestic Violence'.
- Tell the women about Government and Non-Government organisations working against domestic violence.
- Conduct awareness programme for men about gender equality.
- Tell the women about constitutional rights about women.
- Establish some more women police stations for better protection of women.
- Establish separate women special courts.
- Create awareness about domestic violence with the help of print and electronic media.
- Educate all types of parents in the family and create awareness about domestic violence and rights of women.
- Write good articles against domestic violence in the newspaper.
- Create awareness about domestic violence with the help of documentary. Mass media is more effective than others.
- Create awareness about domestic violence through speeches of great persons like cine stars, sports men and women, writers, poets and models in the society. Because they are role models.
- Create awareness about domestic violence through simple advertisements.

- Create awareness about domestic violence with the help of SGHs (Self Help Groups).
- Celebrate 'Women's Day' and 'Mother's Day' in a grand manner to tell the importance and power of women in the society.
- Establish some more research institutes to study about women development in the society. And create awareness about domestic violence through these institutions.

Conclusion

We know mother is the first teacher. Respect of women is respect of God. Domestic violence is cruel and unsocial thing. We can't encourage this thing. Education is the instrument for the development of women in the society. Through education we can solve any type of problem in the society. Education gives strength, power, creativity and courage for the individual. Give preference for women education in the society. Establish some more schools, colleges, universities and research centers for the benefits of women. Create awareness about domestic violence through schools, colleges, universities, research centers, prints media, mass media, electronic media and great persons in the society. Celebrate 'Women's Day' and 'Mother's Day' in a grand manner every year.

REFERENCES

1. *Child and Women Development Report*, (2006), Ministry of Women and Child Development, Government of India, New Delhi.
2. Heilbroner, R. L. (1995) *Visions of the Future: the Distant Past, Yesterday, Today, and Tomorrow* (New York: Oxford University Press).
3. *National Crime Records Bureau*, (2007), Government of India, New Delhi.
4. *National Family Health Survey*, (2006), Government of India, New Delhi.
5. *National Institute of Child Health and Human Development.* (2001). The National Reading Panel: Reports of the Subgroups.
6. *UNESCO Institute for Statistics: Literacy Rates, Youth (15-24) and Adult (15+), by Region and Gender* (September 2006 Assessment).

CHAPTER 30

Values in Teacher Education

–Dr. Naraginti Amareswaran

Education means an all round drawing out of the best in child and man—body, mind and spirit. —***Mahatma Gandhi***

Introduction

The development of any nation depends mainly on the standards of its educational institutions. Education is the most powerful and effective instrument for inducing radical changes in the behaviour of students. Education is a powerful instrument of national development—social, economic and cultural. The teacher occupies pivotal position in the system of education. Teaching has been one of the oldest and most respected professions in the world.

According to Indians, Teacher is the third god. Today we are living in the technological world. India developed in the fields of Science and Technology. It is possible to know each and every-thing with in seconds through out the world. Today's children are tomorrow's citizens. It is necessary to give quality and value-based education to each and every student in the society. Then only all children will become good citizens in the future.

Values

Values are the guiding principles, decisive in day to day behaviours as also in critical life situations. Values are a set of principles or standards of behaviour. Values are regarded desirable, important and held in high esteem by a particular society in which a person lives. Thus values give meaning and strength to a person with character by occupying a central place in his life. Values reflect one's personal attitudes and judgments, decisions and choices, behaviour and relationships, dreams and vision. They influence our thoughts, feelings and actions. They guide us to do the right things.

Values are the guiding principles of life which are conductive to all round development. They give direction and firmness to life and bring joy, satisfaction and peace of life. Values are like the rails that keep a train on the track and help it move smoothly, quickly and with direction. They bring qualities to life.

Value Education

Value education means inculcating in the children a sense of humanism, a deep concern for the well being of others and the nation. This can be accomplished only when we instill in the children a deep feeling of commitment to values that would build this country and bring back to the people pride in work that brings order, security and assured progress.

Through value education, we like to develop the social, moral, aesthetic and spiritual sides of a person which are often undermined in formal education. Value education teaches us to preserve whatever is good and worthwhile in what we have inherited from our culture. It helps us to respect the attitude and behaviour of those who differ from us. Value education does not mean value imposition or indoctrination.

Value education has the capacity to transform a diseased mind into a very young, fresh, healthy, natural and attentive mind. The transformed mind is capable of higher sensitivity and a heightened level of perception this leads to fulfillment of the evolutionary role in man and in life. Values in general, could be classified broadly under five headings—personal, social, moral, spiritual and behavioural.

Education in general and value education in particular occupies a prestigious place in the modern context of the contemporary society. The problem of value education of the young has assumed increasing prominence in educational discussions during recent times. Parents, teachers, administrators and society at large are concerned of about values and value education of children.

"The destiny of India is now being shaped in her class rooms". This is the opening sentence of the Kothari Education Commission report (1964-66). What kind of destiny has been actually shaped during the last sixty years? There are thousands of schools without primary needs. The position of teacher's economic condition is also poor when compared to USA teachers.

Nature of Values

- Values relate to the aims of human life. For the achievement of aims man frames certain notions and these notions are called values.
- Our conduct is motivated by our values.
- Value is the act of cherishing something. A person who values justice will spend a lot of energy in search for it.
- Values are masterminds which give direction to one's strivings. Values represent feelings, wants, interests, attitudes, preferences and opinions about what is right, just fair or desirable.

Classification of Values

There are so many classifications of values. According to Plato's classification, there are three types of values: (1) Truth, (2) Beauty and (3) Goodness.

Gandhi's Classification

In order to create new social order Gandhiji introduced Nai Talim in the year 1937, which is popularly known as Basic Education.

1. Truth
2. Non-violence
3. Freedom
4. Democracy
5. Sarva Dharma Samabhava
6. Equality
7. Self-realisation

8. Purity of ends and means
9. Self-discipline
10. Suddhi

The numbers of values are unlimited. The NCERT listed 83 values. It is unmanageable to deal with so many values in schools. Under the Sathya Sai Organization, these 83 values are classified and grouped under the five well known prime values. These five are: Sathya (Truth), Dharma (righteousness), Prema (Love in its broadest Sense), Shanti (Peace) and Ahimsa (Non-violence in various forms and actions, thoughts, feelings etc).

We have the constitution of India which we are bound to follow: major values embedded there in are (1) Justice, Equality, liberty and Fraternity and (2) Democracy, Secularism, and Social Justice.

Next we have individual and personal values: Cleanliness, Neatness, Punctuality, Regularity, Industriousness, Healthcare, honesty, Self respect, Self reliance etc.

We must add values necessary for Peace and Harmony. These are concern and compassion for others, co-operation, self-sacrifice, national integrity and unity and world/ universal brotherhood. For all values, the approach has to be through a spirit of enquiry, persuit of truth, logical thinking, open mindedness, sharing and a scientific bent of mind.

Characteristics of a Real Teacher

Teacher is a national builder. He has a power to change the society. In the 13th chapter of the "Bhagavad Gita" the characteristics of a real teacher are laid down as follows: absence of pride, free from hypocrisy, non-violence, forgiving nature, straight forwardness, service of the preceptor, purity of mind and body, steadfastness and self-control. Centuries ago in this land of Vedas the teacher devoted all his time for the upliftment of his pupils in all directions—knowledge, morals, values etc. He was called the 'Guru or Acharya'.

According to V.S.Mathews "No system of education, no syllabus, no methodology, no text book can rise above the level of its teachers. If a country wants to have quality education it must have quality teachers". So, it is necessary to give importance for values in the teacher education.

Teacher Education

"Values are to be caught and not taught', is a very old saying. It was perhaps true in days gone by when parents at home and leaders in community in various walks of life were all value-based people. Therefore younger children and growing adolescents could catch values of elderly people and either by imitation or by special efforts developed appropriate values accepted and respected in society. Much water has flowed under the bridge since then and there is a grave deterioration both among parents and community leaders in terms of their being value models for the younger generation. We cannot therefore expect values to be caught from undesirable situations and persons in society. In today's world, therefore values have got to be taught in addition to being caught from selected situations and personalities.

According to V.S.Mathews "No system of education, no syllabus, no methodology, no text book can rise above the level of its teachers. If a country wants to have quality education it must have quality teachers". So, it is necessary to give importance for values in the teacher education.

Let we observe the teacher education system in the state of Andhra Pradesh, India. There are 24 Government D.Ed. colleges for the academic year 2006-07 with 2565 students, 324 B.Ed. colleges with 36009 students, 3B.Ed. institution in distance mode with 1500 students, 17 Telugu Pandit colleges with 1700 students, 10 Urdu Pandit Colleges with 480 students, 35 Hindi Pandit colleges with 2090 students, 5 D.P.Ed.colleges with 400 students, seven B.P.Ed. colleges with 435 students and 20 M.Ed. colleges with 457 students both in Government and Private sectors.

It is necessary to take care in the framing of teacher education curriculum. Teacher is a national builder. So, it is important to give good quality and value based education to the teacher in teacher education. It is necessary to provide all types of labs and library facilities to improve quality education in teacher education.

Need for Value-based Teacher Education

Today we are in a technological world where things are happening fast. Parents and teachers would like to be getting results fast. India has kept pace in science and technology with forward nations but we have shown slower pace in our value system even when we have a strong heritage of human values. India was quoted by great visionaries and saints as a punya bhumi. Swami Vivekananda reiterated in his powerful words: " *If there is any land on this earth that can lay claim to be the blessed punya bhumi, to be land to which souls on this earth must come to account for karma, the land to which every soul is wending its way Godward must come to attain its lost home, the land where humanity has attained its highest towards gentleness, towards generosity, towards purity, towards calmness, above all, the land of introspection and of spirituality—It is India.*" Thus value education has been elucidated by swamiji. From such a state, we are in the pythonic grip of deepening value crisis. How unfortunate it is!!!

How can we overcome this? When can we become capable of training the young citizens to be the carriers of the noble human resources? What value, value has changed to? Present scenario and surroundings looms large with terroristic acts, violence, negative thoughts, anti-social acts, many an immoral qualities are all seen every where and the world looks a big booming , buzzing confusion. . Such is the case in all fields, braving such conditions the wise men of our country has been trying to put forth issues like a national system of education and a national policy of education which should focus and bridge the gaps that are widening.

The NPE (*1986) and subsequently the POA's have been emphasising the faith in *vidya dadati vinayam, vinayat yati patratam, patratwat dhanamapnoti, dhanat dharmam tataha sukham*—it is learning and knowledge that gives capability to earn, and earning the ability to do dharma for a noble cause and this results in gaining peace. The analysts and educationists of our country have consciously changed the curriculum and prioritised universalisation of primary education, the girl child education, and inculcating value-based education in their recent policy recommendations like –the Eshwarbhai Patel's; Ramamurthy Commission; Prof .Yashpal's Commission and the present focus on the same issues through the national curriculum framework. All these Commissions, reports and recommendations have one thing in common and that is, changing curriculum at different levels for capacity building among teachers. Further, recent studies and analysis of evaluation of achievements at different levels have clearly shown the quality concerns and that teacher factor and his / her performance is poor but his responsibilities are more and there is need to train teachers in several of the new techniques and bring him to the frontline in this task of building a national system of education with a focus on value education. Thus educating the whole child and developing values assumed importance in recent years.

Implementation Process

The following points may be considered for implementing the value education in in-service and pre-service teacher training programmes and at different stage of educational institutions.

In-service Teacher Training

As a first step, three training camps may be arranged for teachers: (1) coaching camp; (2) evaluation camps; and (3) refresher courses. A minimum of two teachers from each school must be covered by this programme. The above programmes for the teachers should be in such a way that it kindles the vast potentialities lying dormant in a teacher resulting in the teacher developing his/her own ways of imparting VE. These courses should enable the teacher to have his perspective in all the activities of school *viz.* classes on subjects, sports and games, cultural activities, youth festivals and all other extra-curricular activities. *In other words, moral education will not get confined to one moral class only.*

A teacher's manual of guidelines may be prepared, based on the values listed above, containing portions from the existing textbooks that deal with values, to help them give a special thrust to values while teaching the students.

Progammes

- Conduct periodically essay writing, elocution, story telling, poems recital, quiz on value-based subjects.
- Teach life stories of eminent characters in the epics and history, poems that would spur national favour and devotion, patriotic songs, environmental hygiene etc.
- Motivate children to write short notes on value-based topics from the school library books. This will also encourage the development of reading habit.
- Organise special programmes on value-based subjects on every January 26, August 15 and October 2, and give awards to all the participants in the form of leaflets/pamphlets/books containing value-oriented articles and stories.
- Conduct a class exclusively for moral instruction, based on Gandhian lines, in every school once a week to focus the student's attention on the observance of a proper code of conduct and good behaviour at home, in school, in public places, and while moving about in the society.
- Begin the classes every day with a universal peace prayer.
- Display every day, messages and sayings of Mahastmas and great thinkers related to values at a prominent place in the schools under the caption 'Thought for the Day'. Such sayings may be read out and explained in the morning school assembly.
- Invite distinguished persons to talk to the students and parents on the need for importance of leading a value-based life.
- Organise occasionally common gatherings of students of government, aided and unaided schools to bridge the gap in the level of their awareness and absorption capacity.
- Institute recognition and bravery awards for those students whose assimilation of values outshines that of their fellow-students.
- Observe once a year a Parents' Day; to enable the children to express their abiding love, reverence and gratitude for all that their parents have been doing for them.
- Celebrate Teachers' Day in the true spirit to enable children to remember with great reverence and abiding gratitude what their teachers have done for them.

- Arrange debates, speeches and skits on the life and teachings of outstanding national leaders, who can be considered as role models for the young generation.

Outdoor Camps

- Conduct periodical outdoor camps for selected children from a group of schools. This is an easy way to enable the children to understand the gifts of nature and to study the infallible laws of nature.
- In this context, it may be most appropriate to arrange for at least one outdoor self-contained campsite in each of the approximately 50 districts in the country. This site may also provide facilities for nature cure, organic farming and yoga as it is felt that there is growing importance given to this in many countries and therefore, students may be trained in this at an early age itself. Such a facility would basis in the outdoor camps that may be conducted every weekend in each district.

Conclusion

According to Sarvapalli Radhakrishnan teacher is a national builder. He has a power to change the society. It is government duty to provide quality education for prospective and in-service teachers. Teacher is a backbone for national development. Through education we can change the world. Teacher is a good resource to develop values in the society. Without teacher the education have no meaning. Value-oriented education is necessary for today's situation.

REFERENCES

1. *Achievement of B.Ed. Students*, Dr. C. Manchala, Discovery Publishing House, New Delhi-110002.
2. http://www.ncte-in.org.
3. *Value Education in India*, Usha Rai Negi, Editor, Published by Association of Indian Universities, AIU House, 16 Kotla Marg, New Delhi-110 002, 2000.
4. *Value Education*, Dr. Venkataiah, Editor, APH Publishing Corporation, 5, Ansari Road, Daryaganj, New Delhi-110 002, First Edition, 1998.

Index

A

Adult education, 14-21
- awareness generation, 20
- concept and chronology of adult education in India, 17-18
- increasing effectiveness of development programmes, 19
- mobilisation and co-ordination of the resources, 20
- motivation of the learners, 21
- new estimates, 15-16
- poverty scenario in India, 14-15
- promotion of employment, 19
- provisions, 16-17
- role of adult education in poverty alleviation, 19
- strengthening of communication channels, 20

All India Council for Mass Education and Development (AICMED), 139

Amareswaran, Naraginti, 1, 14, 22, 28, 39, 46, 53, 65, 74, 84, 92, 100, 110, 119, 131, 138, 154, 166, 173, 183, 193200, 211, 230, 234, 242, 255, 261, 273

Ambedkar, Baba Saheb, 71

Andhra Mahila Sabha (AMS), 139

Ashramam, 28

Assessment and accreditation of schools, 22-27

Ayurveda, 191

B

Baba, Sathya Sai, 100

Bal Bhavan Society of India, 61

Bal Mitra Kendras, 61

Bank of Bengal, 211

Bank of Hindustan, 211

Beattie, Bill, 173

Beevi, Justice M Fatima, 82

Bezant, Annie, 82

Bhagavad Gita, 103, 175

Bihar Education Project, 60

Brahma (creator), 175

Buddhism, 2

C

Camara, Dom Helder, 110

Central Advisory Board of Education (CABE), 61

Central Institute of Educational Technology, 242

CIET, 241

Citrus auran tifolia, 87

Commissions and Committees, 30

Computer Aided Design (CAD), 238

Constitution of India, 262

Curricular changes in teacher education, 28-38
- curriculum content and transaction, 33
- definitions of curriculum, from

Oliva (1997), 31-32
education of the gifted and talented, 35
flexibility of the curriculum, 32-33
guidelines/suggestions, 36-37
implications for pre-service teacher education, 34
implications for pre-service teacher education, 34-35
in-service education of teachers, 35-36
NCTE, 33
scenario of teacher education, 30-31
teacher education, 29-30

D

Dancus carota, 88
Delhi Metro Rail Corporation (DMRC), 269
Democracy, 103
DIET, 208
Disability Act, 1995, 266
Disability Discrimination Act (DDA), 261
District Primary Education (DPED), 60
Drought Prone Area Programme (DPAP), 16
Dyslectic, 40
Dyslexia, 40

E

Economic Development, 20
Educating children with learning difficulty dyslexia, 39-45
are boys affected by dyslexia, 41
can dyslexia be cured, 41
causes of dyslexia, 40
classroom adjustments, 44
classroom assistants, 44
direct instruction, 43-44
does dyslexia affect a child self-esteem, 41-42
dyslexia, 40
how can a parent help their dyslexic child, 42-43
how many people are affected by dyslexia, 41
interventions include, 43
introduction, 39
limited career prospects, 42
mastery model, 43
special education, 44
special equipment, 44
symptoms of dyslexia, 40-41
treatment and intervention, 43
what age does it become a problem, 41
what level of intelligence does it affect, 41
Education Commission (1964-66), 30
Education for All, 21
Educational school psychology in the pursuit of human well-being, 46-52
introduction, 46
definition of education, 46
importance of education, 47
educational psychology, 47-48
uses of educational psychology, 48
for finding individual differences and disabilities, 48-49
social, moral and cognitive development, 49-50

F

Female education in India, 53-64
action needed to improve female education, 63-64
community participation in education, 60-62

community participation, 59-60
drop-out rates of female students, 57
enrolment of female students, 54-56
female literacy in India, 54
introduction, 53-54
participation, 59
percentage of girls enrolment to total enrolment, 56-57
strategies for participation, 62-63
why female education is important, 57-59

Food For All, 21

Forms of domestic violence and development of women through education, 65-73
introduction, 65
what is domestic violence, 66
forms of domestic violence, 66-68
emotional abuse, 67
financial abuse, 67-68
physical abuse, 66-67
psychological abuse, 67
sexual abuse, 67
crime against women in India, 68
main problems of Indian women, 68-69
lack of education, 68
malnutrition, 68
mistreatment, 68-69
overwork, 68
poor health, 68
powerlessness, 69
unskilled, 68
government role to minimise domestic violence, 69-70
development of women through education, 70
female literacy in India, 70
factors responsible for poor female literacy rate, 70
main strategies adopted by the government for increasing female literacy in the country include, 70-72

Fuller, Thomas, 183

G

Gandhi, Indira, 82

Gandhi, M.K., 1, 14, 39, 74, 92, 138, 255, 282

GATT, 113

Government Development Departments, 20

Government of India, 18

Guru or *Acharya*, 28, 175

H

High Yield Variety Programme (HYVP), 16

Higher education, 22

Hindola, 60

Hoffer, Eric, 173

I

Impact of education on domestic violence and development of women through education, 74-83
child violence, 77-78
children living with domestic violence may, 78
crime against women in India, 76
development of women through education, 79
female literacy in India, 80
First Woman of India, 81-82
introduction, 74-75
modern Indian women, 81

recent figures from the international labour organisation show that, 79
vision of national commission for women, 81
what is domestic violence, 75
women universities in India, 80-81
women violence in different states of India, 75-76
Impact of education on ethno-medicine and healthcare practices among the tribal people of India, 84-91
diseases due to wrath of the supernatural, 89
ethno-medicine and healthcare practices among sonowalkacharis in Assam, 87-89
herbal history and tradition in Indian context, 85
introduction, 84
present position of tribes, 90
saving the plant is saving the life, 90
tribes and ethno-medicine, 85-86
tribes in India, 84-85
Impact of globalisation on teacher education, 92-99
development through educational institutions, 95-96
globalisation, 92-94
impact of globalisation on teacher education, 97
importance of education, 94-95
introduction, 92
negative impact of globalisation on teacher education, 98
positive impact of globalisation on teacher education, 97-98
role of teacher in building modern India, 96-97
Importance of values in teacher education, 100-109
characteristics of a real teacher, 103-104
classification of values, 102
gandhi classification, 102-103
implementation process, 106
in-service teacher training, 106-107
introduction, 100
nature of values, 102
need for value based teacher education, 105-106
outdoor camps, 108
programmes, 107-108
teacher education, 104-105
value education, 101-102
values, 101
Inculcation of ethics through education and globalisation effects on ethics, 110-118
introduction, 110
ethics, 110-111
why ethics, 111
ethics and economics, 112
economists have ethical values, 112
what is unethical, 112
ethics and globalisation, 113-114
positive aspects of globalisation, 114
negative aspects of globalisation, 114-116
centre for globalisation, 116
inculcation ethics though education, 116-117
Gandhi values, 117

Inculcation of human values through education, 119-130
- classification of values, 120
- importance of values, 120
- inculcation of values through education, 120-121
- introduction, 119-120
- love, 125-126
- non-violence, 127
- peace, 122-123
- right conduct, 121
- truth, 124
- values related to
  - love, 126-127
  - non-violence, 128-129
  - peace, 123-124
  - right conduct, 121-122
  - truth, 125

Inculcation of organisational ethics in management students through education, 131-137
- introduction, 131-132
- organisational ethics, 132
- importance of organisational ethics, 133
- inculcation of organsiaitonal ethics in management students through education, 134-135
- organisational ethics programmes are recommended by, 135
- excellent ethics programmes contain the following characteristics in one form or another, 135
- through organisational ethics education it is easy to give answers to the following questions, 135-136
- stages of moral development, 136

India National Crime Records Bureau, 69

Indian Adult Education Association (IAEA), 139

Indian Adult Education, 18

Indian Institutes of Technology, 4

Individual Interest Promotion Programmes, 21

International Women day, 83

J

Jefferson, Thomas, 110

K

Kalam, A P J Abdul, 95

Koteeswari, 173

Koteeswari, N., 154, 211

Kothari Commission (1964-66), 30, 96

Kothari Education Commission (1964-66), 202

Krishnan, Sarvapalli Radha, 242

L

Life Improvement Programmes in Continuing Education Centres, 20

Londen, William, 183

M

Mahila Samakhya Project, 60

Manchala, C., 65, 74, 110, 119, 131, 166, 193, 230, 242, 261, 273

Marx, Karl, 59

Mathews, V.S., 201, 256

Minimum Needs Programme (MNP), 16

Ministry of Education, 3

Ministry of Human Resource Development, 4

Montessori, Maria, 39

Mudaliar Commission (1952-53), 96

Muslims, 2

N

Nalanda, 2
National assessment and accreditation Council (NAAC) in 1994, 22
National Commission for Women (NCW), 69
National Commission for Women Act, 1990, 69
National Council for Teacher Education (NCTE), 31
National Council of Educational Research and Training, 242
National Council of Teacher Education (NCTE), 35
National Education Policy (1986), 35
National Family Health Survey-III, 75
National Literacy Mission, 18, 70
National Policy on Education (NPE) 1986, 22, 53
National Sample Survey Organisation (NSSO), 219
NCERT, 241
NCTE, 241
Nehru, Jawaharlal, 70, 74
NGO Prayas, 78
NGOs, 20, 61, 266
NIEPA, 241
NSPCC (National Society for the Prevention of Cruelty to Children), 78

O

Ocimum sanctum, 89

P

Pandit, Vijay Lakshmi, 82
Patil, Pratibha Devisingh, 266
People Republic of China, 3
Phule, Mahatma Jyotiba, 71
Pioneering institutions in adult education, 138-153
  activities, 140-141
  aims and objectives, 139-140
  andhra Mahila Sabha, Hyderabad, 141-143
  Indian adult education association, new delhi, 143-147
  introduction, 138-139
  literacy house, lucknow, 147-149
  RDT, Anatapur, 149-150
  seva mandir, 150-151
Planning Commission of India, 14, 131
Poverty, education and health in India, 154-165
  education, 158-160
  health, 156-157
  introduction, 154
  major issues, 160-162
  poverty and its reduction in India, 154-155
  poverty, health, education and development, 162-164
  programmes launched to reduce poverty, 156
Poverty, illiteracy and alcoholism in India and solutions through education, 166-172
  alcoholism in India, 171-172
  illiteracy in India, 169-170
  introduction, 166
  official response to the alcohol problem, 172
  poverty in India, 166-167
  rural poverty in India, 167
  steps to minimize
    alcohol use through education, 172
    illiteracy rate in India, 170-171

poverty ratio through education, 168-169
urban poverty in India, 167-168
Preservation of Indian values and culture through education, 173-182
concept of culture, 177-179
concept of value, 175-177
introduction, 173-174
man and education, 174-175
preservation value and culture through education, 179-181
Preservation of medicinal plants by tribes through education in India, 183-192
by farmers through education in India, 186-187
by tribes through adult education in India, 185-186
herbal history in Indian context, 184
introduction, 183
medicinal plants in India, 183-184
saving the plant is saving the life, 191
tribes in India, 184-185
uses of medicinal plants, 187-191
Privatization of professional education, 193-199
higher and professional education in India, 193-194
importance of education, 193
introduction, 193
present status of teacher education, 198
privatisation experience, 194-197
privatisation of teacher education, 197
Programme of Action (POA) 1992, 22
Punica granatum, 88

R

Radhika, K., 53, 92
Rajiv Gandhi National Fellowship Programme, 228
Ramalingaswami, Vulimiri, 65
Rand, Ayn, 173
Rani, K. Sudha, 14, 138, 154
Reddy, B. Ramachandra, 65, 74, 22, 110, 193, 200, 211, 234, 242, 261, 273
Reddy, C. B. Ramachandra, 119, 131
Reddy, Ramachandra, 166
Research in teacher education, 200-210
concept of teacher education, 203-204
discussion, 207
importance of teacher, 200-201
introduction, 200
need and significance of teacher education, 204-205
place of teacher in any education system, 201-203
review of research in teacher education, 205
some of the studies are mentioned hereunder, 206-207
Reserve Bank of India, 212
Role of commercial banks and education in the development of weaker sections in India, 211-229
current situation of banks, 212-213
economy of India, 221-222
history of banks in India, 211-212
introduction, 211
list of banks in India, 213-219
literacy of SC/ST, 220-221
reservations for SC/ST beneficiaries under major

centrally sponsored schemes, 226-229
role of banks, 224-225
role of commercial banks and educational institutions in development of weaker sections, 223-224
SC/ST role in Indian economy, 222-223
weaker sections in India, 219-220
Role of higher educational institutions in promotion of rural human resources, 230-233
introduction, 230
first higher educational institution, 230-231
importance of education, 231
development through educational institutions, 232-233
Role of information technology in teacher education, 234-241
definition of information technology, 234-235
distance mode of education, 239
goals and objectives, 235-236
in-service training, 238
IT in special education, 239
need of information technology in teacher education, 237-238
research and internet, 239
restructuring curricula of teacher education, 239-240
specific uses of information technology, 238
teacher education training programmes through IT facilities, 239
uses of information technology, 238
Role of NCTE, NCERT, CIET, SCERT for the cause of teacher education, 242-254
Central Institute of Educational Technology, 250-251
constituent units, 253
development, 247
exchange programmes, 249
extension, 248
functions, 252
National Council for Teacher Education, 242-243
National Counsel of Educational Research and Training, 245
objective of NCTE, 243
objectives, 251-252
organisational structure of NCTE, 243-245
priorities, 246
professional growth, 253-254
programmes and activities, 246
publication and dissemination, 248-249
research, 246-247
services, 253
state counsel of educational research and training, 251
training, 247-248
Role of teachers in building modern India, 255-260
about India, 255-256
Indian education system and teacher, 256-257
introduction, 255
role of teacher in building modern India, 258-259
values and teacher, 257-258
Roy, Raja Ram Mohan, 71
Ruskin, John, 46, 234

S

Sa Vidya Ya Vimuktaye, 175
Sarva Shiksha Abhiyan (Education for all) , 4, 53
Sarvepalli Radhakrishnan Commission (1948), 30
SC/ST, 72
SCERT, 241
Schedule Castes and Tribes, 61, 226
Science For All, 21
Secondary Education Commission (1953), 30
Secularism, 103
Shaw, Bernard, 183
Shiksha Karmi and Lok-Jambish Project in Rajasthan, 60
Shiva (transformer), 175
Singh, Manmohan, 11
Some reflections on public transportation for disabled persons in academic institution, 261-272
- access provisions for public transport, 269-271
- causes of disability, 263
- disabled persons, 261-262
- education and disabled persons, 265-266
- education for persons with disabilities, 266-268
- facts and figures, 262
- international day of disabled people, 268
- introduction, 261
- move towards accessible transportation, 269
- national policy statement, 265
- prevention of disabilities, 265
- programmes and policies for the development of disabled persons, 263-265
- public transportation for disabled people, 268-269
- rehabilitation measures, 265
- transport allowance, 271
- types of disability, 262-263

Stalin, Joseph, 46
Strategies to create awareness on domestic violence through educational institutions, 273-280
- domestic violence, 274
- education and employment of Indian women, 275-276
- forms of domestic violence, 275
- introduction, 273
- minimizing the dangers of domestic violence, 276-278
- safety plans against domestic violence, 278
- strategies to create awareness on domestic violence through education, 278-280
- strategies to create awareness on domestic violence, 276
- what is domestic violence, 274-275
- women universities in India, 276

Study of education in India and Asia-pacific, 1-13
- education around the world, 11
- educational institutions, 4-5
- history of education n India, 1-2
- importance of education, 1
- introduction, 1
- literacy facts and figures in asia and pacific, 5-10
- main points related to education in the present year budget of India, 11
- public education expenditure, 10-11

stages of education, 2-4
Swarnajayanti Gram Swarojagar Yojana (SGSY), 16

T

Tagore, Rabindranath, 72
Takshashila, 2
Teacher Education Curriculum Framework in 1978, 31
Teacher Education Curriculum, 38
The Asian Engima, 65
Training of Rural Youth for Self-Employment (TRYSEM), 16
Tribal Area Development Programme (TADP), 16
TRYSEM, 156

U

Udan Khatolas, 60
UGC, 22
UNESCO, 74
UNICEF, 77
United Nations Development Programme, 5
United States of America, 11
Unity in Diversity, 255
Universal Declaration of Human Rights, 74
Universalisation of Elementary Education (UEE), 53
Universities, 20
Uttar Pradesh Basic Education Programme, 60

V

Values in teacher education, 281-289
 characteristics of a real teacher, 284-285
 classification of values, 283
 Gandhi classification, 283-284
 implementation process, 287
 in-service teacher training, 287
 introduction, 281
 nature of values, 283
 need for value-based teacher education, 286-287
 outdoor camps, 289
 programmes, 288-289
 teacher education, 285
 value education, 282-283
 values, 281-282
Vathi, R.B. Sathya, 14
Vedas, 28
Vidyasagar, Iswar Chandra, 71
Vikramshila, 2
Vishnu (preserver), 175
Vishnu Samhita, 191
Vivekananda, Swami, 38, 72, 259
Vyasa, Veda, 28

W

Women and Child development, 71
World Bank, 15
World Health Organisation (WHO), 86
WTO, 113

Y

Youth Club(s), 20, 63